The Mildmay Family and the Marwell Estate 1744 - 1859:

Transcripts of Various Documents Prepared for a Sale of Estate in 1859

Wayne Piotr Cronin-Wojdat

The Mildmay Family and the Marwell Estate 1744 – 1859: Transcripts of Various Documents Prepared for a Sale of Estate in 1859

Wayne Cronin-Wojdat

Published 2012, Copyright 2012 ©

All rights reserved. No part of this publication may be reproduced or transmitted in any form or by any means, electronic, mechanical, including photocopying, recording or by any information storage retrieval system without permission from the author.

The right of Wayne Cronin-Wojdat to be identified as the author of this work has been asserted by him in accordance with the Copyright, Designs and Patents Act 1988.

Contact details for the author: Historical Gems, 25 Claypit Lane, Gresford, Wrexham, LL12 8PB, United Kingdom

www.historicalgems.co.uk

Contents

Introduction

Abstract Number One: Mildmay Estates, General Abstract of Title to the Manor of Marwell in the County of Southampton

General Abstract of Title to the Manor of Marwell in the County of Southampton 27th & 28th November 1789

Michaelmas Term 30th George 3rd Southampton

Abstract Number Two: Mildmay Estates, Abstract of the Title of the Several Persons Claiming under an Indenture of Settlement of the 28th November 1789 to the Manor of Marwell in the County of Southampton

Abstract of the Title of the Several Persons claiming under an Indenture of Settlement of the 28th November 1789 (set out in Abstract No.1) to the Manor of Marwell in the County of Southampton

11th November 1808

As to share to which Jane Dorothea St John Mildmay (afterwards Lady Methuen) became entitled of the above Estates

7th July 1810

Trinity Term 50 George 3rd Southampton

28th & 30th July 1810

As to the accruing shares vested in Frederick Henry Paul Lord Methuen as heir in law to his mother the Lady Methuen

20th July 1850

1st June 1854

3rd March 1855

3rd July 1857

As to the share to which the said Maria St John Mildmay (afterwards Lady Bolingbroke) became entitled of the above Estates

11th May 1812

Easter Term 52 George 3rd Southampton

2nd & 3rd June 1812

11th August 1841

As to the accrued shares vested in the said Henry Mildmay Viscount Bolingbroke in lieu in tail of his mother the Lady Bolingbroke

6th March 1858

As to the share to which Judith Anne St John Mildmay (afterwards Lady Radnor) became entitled of the above Estates

20th May 1814

Easter Term 54 George 3rd Southampton

23rd & 24th May 1814

22nd & 23rd August 1825

24th & 25th August 1825

December 1857 (Number 1)

December 1857 (Number 2)

December 1857 (Number 3)

As to the share to which the said George William St John Mildmay became entitled of the above Estates

26th & 27th April 1832

Easter Term 2 William 4th Southampton

23rd & 24th November 1832

4th December 1849

30th August 1830

1st December 1832

14th December 1832

23rd November 1840

9th August 1845

14th February 1851

22nd June 1858

As to the accruing shares vested in Herbert Alexander St John Mildmay Esquire as heir in tail to his father the late George William St John Mildmay

23rd July 1857

As to the share to which Humphrey St John Mildmay & Edward St John Mildmay respectively became entitled of the above Estates

4th November 1824

Michaelmas Term 5th George 4th

As to the share to which Humphrey St John Mildmay became entitled of the above Estates

2nd July 1850

9th August 1853

As to the share to which Edward St John Mildmay became entitled of the above Estates

11th June 1818

20th & 21st December 1826

1 William 4 1830

20th March 1832

The schedule to which the foregoing Indenture refers. Twyford and Owslebury Estate, Hampshire. The Manors of Twyford and Marwell

5th July 1856

1856

As to the interest of Mrs Marianne Jane Barnett formally Miss Mary Anne Jane Mildmay one of the daughters of the said Edward St John Mildmay in her father's share

16th April 1847

As to the interest of Mrs Jane Catherine Vernon formally Miss Jane Catherine St John Mildmay another of the daughters of the said Edward St John Mildmay in her fathers share

18th April 1849

As to the interest of Arthur George St John Mildmay the son of the said Edward St John Mildmay in his fathers share

10th August 1849

As to the share to which the Reverend Carew Anthony St John Mildmay became entitled in the above estates

15th & 16th November 1830

Michaelmas Term 1st William 4th

11th & 13th December 1830

7th July 1848

Abstract Number Three: Abstract Relating to the Charges upon the Estates in the County of Southampton Comprised in a Settlement of 28th November 1789

29th September 1815

23rd May 1821

3rd December 1823

18th September 1824

6th July 1831

7th July 1831

14th December 1842

15th September 1847 (Number One)

15th September 1847 (Number Two)

30th June 1848

9th February 1849

26th May 1858

23rd June 1858

Requisitions, Observations etc on Title to Manor Of Marwell, County of Southampton and Answers

Abstract Two

Lady Methuen's Share

Lady Bolingbroke's Share

Lady Radnor's Share

George William St John Mildmay's Share

Humphrey St John. Mildmay and Edward St John Mildmay Shares

Share of the Reverand Carew Anthony St John Mildmay

Abstract Number Three

Mildmay Title, Manor of Marwell, Answers to Purchasers Requisitions and Replies thereto

Lady Methuen's Share

Lady Bolingbrokes Share

Lady Radnor's Share

George William St John Mildmay's Share

Humphrey St John Mildmay and Edward St Mildmay Shares

Share of the Reverend Carew Anthony St John Mildmay

Abstract Number Three

Mildmay Title, Manor of Marwell: Replies to Answers to Purchasers Requisitions & Further Answers

Lady Methuen's Share

Lady Bolingbroke's Share

Lady Radnor's Share

George William St John Mildmay's Share

Humphrey St John Mildmay and Edward St John Mildmay's Shares

The Revd Carew Anthony St John Mildmay's Share

Mildmay Title, Manor of Marwell, Third Set of Requisitions and Answers

Introduction

The contents of this book are transcripts of a large set of handwritten documents that are currently in private ownership, and for that reason, are not accessible to researchers. This book has been produced so these fascinating documents are available to researchers, both now, and in the future.

By reading the documents in detail it is possible to ascertain that the documents have been created in preparation for a sale of the Mildmay estate of Marwell, in the parishes of Owslebury and Twyford, in the County of Hampshire, at the end of 1858, and the beginning of 1859. Although the documents were prepared in 1859, they obviously recite documents relating to the estate from a much earlier time. The earliest document recited in the document is from 1744.

The documents are handwritten in ink on paper sheets that approximately measure 33cm by 40cm. The documents are divided into 7 folios that are bound together in the upper left hand corner with ribbon. Two of the folios relate to the title of the estate at Marwell; one folio relates to charges on the estate; and the remaining four folios are sets of requisitions and answers that have passed between the vendors and purchasers solicitors in late 1858, and early 1859. Together the documents provide an insight into the finances of the Mildmay family, and their associates, who themselves are from notable families from that time.

The original documents contain a large number of abbreviations, most likely to save the author time and paper. Additionally, the documents contain some variations in the spelling of names and places, and also spelling mistakes. In the tradition of transcribing, these variations and spelling mistakes have not been altered or changed, so that the text remains faithful to that of the original documents.

The requisition and requisition answers make reference to page numbers in the three abstracts. To allow the reader to follow the requisitions and answers to them, the original page number of the abstract is included in the abstract, for example, *{Page 1}*, indicates page 1 of the original document.

Abstract Number One: Mildmay Estates, General Abstract of Title to the Manor of Marwell in the County of Southampton

{Front Cover}

No.1

Mildmay Estates

General Abstract of Title to the Manor of Marwell in the County of Southampton

Bradley Castleford

{Page 1}

General Abstract of Title to the Manor of Marwell in the County of Southampton

27th & 28th November 1789

Ind'res of Lease & Release the Rel'e between the Revd Sir Peter Rivers Gay of the City of Winchester on the coy of Southampton Bart James Rivers of the same place Esq & the Revd Thomas Salmon of St. Johns College Cambridge of the 1st Part Jane Mildmay of Shawford House in the Parish of Twyford in the s^d co'y of Southampton W^o & relict of Carew Mildmay late of Shawford afs^d Esq of the 2nd part Sir H^y Paulet St John Mildmay of Dogmersfield on the s^d County of Southampton Bar't & Dame Jane his wife late Jane Mildmay sp^r eldest Dau^r & Devisee named in the last will & testament of the s^d Carew Mildmay & also one of his coheiresses at Law of the 3rd part Ann Mildmay & Letitia Mildmay both of Shawford House afs^d sp'^{rs} the 2 younger dau'rs & the other coheiresses at Law of the s^d Carew Mildmay of the 4th part Edwd Bray of Great Russell Street Bloomsbury in the County of Midd'x Gent^n of the 5th part the Revd William St John of Dogmersfield afs^d & Jno Pollen of andover in the coy of Southampton Esq of the 6th part & Henry Peters of Hendon in the County of Midd'x & Wm Bragg of the Temple London Esq of the 7th Part

  Reciting that by Ind'res of Lease & Release of the 11th & 12th Feby 1761 being the settlem^t made previous to the marr'e of the s^d Carew Mildmay dec'ed with the s^d Jane Mildmay (party the'to) divers mess's farms lands tenem^{ts} & heres part of the est^{es} of the s^d Carew Mildmay in the parishes of Twyford & Owslebury in the s^d Co'y of Southampton were ch'ged with a yearly Rent charge of £350 by way of jointure to the s^d Jane Mildmay (party the'to) during her life in bar of dower with powers of distress & entry and were also limited for a term of 99 years to trustees for securing the same Rent Charge & were also charged with the sum of £4500 secured by a sum of 1000 years therein limited to trustees for portions of the dau'r or dau'rs of the s^d then intended marr'e on such failure of issue as therein ment^d And subject to said jointure rent charge & portions & powers remedies & terms of years for securing the same & the limit'ons therein contained to the issue male of the said marr'e the s^d prem's were limited to the use of the said Carew Mildmay his heirs & assigns for ever

And reciting that there was no issue male of the s^d marr'e but 3 dau'rs to wit the s^d Dame Jane St John Mildmay Ann Mildmay and *{page 2}* Letitia Mildmay parties the'to & no other child wherefore the Dame Jane St John Mildmay Ann Mildmay & Letitia Mildmay became & were then intitled to the s^d £4500 in equal proportions that is to say £1500 each

And reciting that the s^d Carew Mildmay by his will bearing date the 27th of June 1768 & attested in such manner as the law required to pass real estates Reciting that by the will of his Great Grandfather Henry Mildmay Esq then long since dec'ed he was become seized in & entitled to the Manors of Twyford & Marwell & to several lands & her'es in the parish of Twyford & Owslebury in the County of Southampton afs^d & that the s^d Manors of Twyford & Marwell with the he'es afs^d were (in case his late Mother Letitia died without issue male) entailed by s^d Henry Mildmay on several persons And that his late father Humphrey Mildmay jointly with him & the s^d Letitia his mother in Easter or Trinity Term 1774 had suffered a Common Recovery of the s^d Freehold estates whereby those est^s were settled on him s^d Carew Mildmay & his heirs for ever The s^d Carew Mildmay gave and devised his said Manors of Twyford & Marwell & the lands tenem^ts & heredits to them severally belonging & within the parishes of Twyford and Owslebury afs^d unto the s^d Sir Peter Rivers Gay (by the name & Description of the Revd Sir Peter Rivers Baronet) Sir Wm Mildmay Bar't (since dec'ed) the s^d James Rivers & Geo Pescod Esqre Upon Trust to permit his wife the s^d Jane Mildmay (party thereto) to take & receive out of the rents & profits of the afs^d Manors & her'es & cert'n copyhold estates therein ment^d the yearly sum of £120 during her life over & above what she would be entitled to under the jointure in case she survived him nevertheless it was his will that his s^d wife should bestow & apply the s^d £120 annually on the education of his 3 daughters Jane Ann & Letitia over and above the int^t of £4500 ment^d in his marr'e settlement with his said wife as a provision for his said daughters and in case his s^d wife should be inclined to reside after his de'ce at his house at Shawford then he directed she should hold & enjoy the same with the gardens & all the grounds then occupied by him rent free so long a time as she should reside at Shawford House and from & immed^y after the de'ce of him s^d Carew Mildmay & his s^d wife Jane He gave & devised all his afs^d Manors & heredits in the co'y of Southampton unto his eldest dau'r Jane Mildmay afw'ds the s^d Dame Jane St John Mildmay & to the heirs male of her *{page 3}* body lawfully begotten with rem^rs over & in case his s^d Eldest daughter Jane should live to be posses^d of all his est^es & should have issue male lawfully begotten on her body that then his s^d est'e should be charged with the sum of £6000 to each of her sisters the s^d Ann & Letitia Mildmay and of his s^d will s^d Carew Mildmay did appoint his wife the said Jane Mildmay sole ext'rio as in by his s^d will duly proved by s^d test'ors w^o Jane Mildmay in the Registry of the Lord Archbishop of Canterbury

And reciting Ind'res of Lease & Release bearing date respl'y the 20th & 21st of June 1786 made previous to & in contempl'on of the marr'e then intended & since solemnized between Sir Henry Paulet St John Mildmay & s^d Dame Jane then his wife wh'by on cons'on of s^d intended marr'e of the settlement the'by made by s^d Sir Henry Paulet St John Mildway It was agreed & decl^d the s^d Sir H^y Paulet St John Mildmay for himself his heirs ex's & adm'ors and s^d Dame Jane then Jane Mildmay sp^r for herself her heirs ex's & adm'ors did covenant & agree with s^d William St John & John Polten their heirs ex's & adm'ors that in case said marr'e sho^d take effect they so soon as they or either of them should be seized of a suff^t estate in law of s^d Manors of Twyford & Marwell & the hereditaments the'to bel^g to enable them to suffer an effectual recovery the'of or by any means to bar the estates tail & rem^rs the'in or as soon as the persons entitled in rem^r & all other necessary parties would join to enable them to suffer an effectual recovery th'of or by any means to bar the est^s tail & the rem^rs & the reversions in the said manor & estates wo^d by such good & sufficient assur'ces as the counsel of the s^d W^m St John & John Pollen their heirs ex's or adm'ors should advise convey & assure & settle the s^d manors of Twyford & Marwell & the lands & here's th'unto belong^g subject to the several incumb'ces th'on & part'arly to the legacies of £6000 a piece given by the s^d Carew Mildmay to the s^d Ann & Letitia Mildmay & to securing the same as absolute vested provisions for them at their resp'ive ages or days of marr'e instead of depending on the contingencies expressed in the s^d will To the use of the s^d H^y Paulet St Jno Mildmay for life sans waste rem^r to trees to be named & their heirs during his life to preserve contingent remainders rem^r To the use of s^d Jane then the wife of s^d Sir Henry Paulet Saint John Mildmay for her life sans waste Rem^r to tr'ees for her life to preserve *{page 4}* contingent Remainders Remainder To the use of all & every the you'r son & sons daur' & daug'rs of the then intended marr'e (except such son & sons as were th'by excluded upon the conting^s th'in & in the now abst^g Ind're ment^d) as tenants in common in tail general with cross remainders between them & if but one such younger son or daughter (except as before excepted) then To the use of such only younger son or daughter in like tail general remainder To the use of the first or second son of the then intended marr'e or of all & every or any of the son or sons daughter or dau'rs of s^d Dame Jane by any future husband for such est^e or estates as she the said Dame Jane should direct or appoint and for want of such appointm't To the use of the heirs of the body of the said Dame Jane – Remainder – To the use of s^d Ann Mildmay in tail general Remainder To the use of said Letitia Mildmay in tail general – Remainder To the use of s^d Dame Jane her heirs and assigns for ever And in which then intended settlement were to be contained such provisos powers and agreements as were the'in par'larly mentioned & were in the now abst^g indenture after contained –

After reciting that said Ann and Letitia Mildmay had attained their ages of 21 years

And reciting that said Sir William Mildmay died in or about the month of august 1771 leaving said Sir Peter Rivers Gay James Rivers & Geo Pescod him surviving whereby the est^e limited by the said will became vested in them

And reciting that a Commission of Lunacy dated 30th July 1784 had been taken against s^d Geo Pescod & the custody of him granted to Charles Knott of the City of Winchester Gent^n and that such Commission of Lunacy & Grant then remained in full force

And rec't^g that by an Order of the Court of Chancery dated the 30th June then last made in a cause in which said Jane Mildmay Sir Henry Paulet St John Mildmay & Dame Jane his wife Ann and Letitia Mildmay were Plt^s S^d Sir Peter Rivers Gay James Rivers & Geo Pescod by S^d Charles Knott and the s^d Chas Knott were Defend^{ts} It was ordered that said Geo^e Pescod should be discharged from his s^d trust under s^d will that it should be referred to Mr Ord one of the Masters of the Court to appoint a tr'ee in his room and that the s^d Geo^e Pescod should pursuant to the act 4th Geo 2nd therein ment^d release and convey all his estate and {page 5} int in the est in question so as to vest same in such new trustee & s^d Sir Peter Rivers Gay and James Rivers

And reciting a Report of s^d Mr Ord dated the 28th of July then last whereby he app^{td} s^d Thomas Salmon to be such new tr'ee which Report was confirmed by an Order of the Court dated 30th July then last

And reciting that by Ind'res of Lease and Rel'e bearing date the 25th &26th days of Novr then inst't the rel'e made bet^n said Sir Peter Rivers Gay James Rivers & Geo^e Pescod of first part & Jane Mildmay Widow Sir H^y Paulet St John Mildmay and Dame Jane his wife Anne Mildmay and Letitia Mildmay of the second part said Edward Bray of the third part and Thomas Salmon of fourth part Reciting the s^d will of the s^d Carew Mildmay & the s^d Decree & Master's Report the s^d Sir Peter Rivers Gay James Rivers & Geo^e Pescod in obedience to s^d Order & to preserve the trusts of the s^d will and in cons'on of 10/ and at the request of s^d Jane Mildmay Sir Henry Paulet St John Mildmay and Dame Jane his wife Ann Mildmay and Letitia Mildmay Did bargain sell release & confirm to s^d Edwd Bray and his heirs The s^d freehold Manors & he'res devised by s^d will to s^d trustees To hold the same to s^d Edwd Bray his his & assigns To the use of s^d Sir Peter Rivers Gay James Rivers & Thomas Salmon their heirs & assigns for and during the estate and interest and upon and subject to the trusts and for the end intents and purposes for & upon which the same were devised to or become vested in the s^d Sir Peter Rivers Gay Sir William Mildmay James Rivers and Geo^e Pescod by virtue of the will of s^d Carew Mildmay

And reciting that s^d Sir Henry Paulet St John Mildmay & Dame Jane his wife were desirous of suffering a Recovery of the said Manors & prem's comprised in the s^d will and of settling the same To the uses and for the pp'ses mentioned expressed and agreed upon by the s^d ind're of 21st June 1786

And reciting that the s^d Dame Jane Mildmay Ann Mildmay & Letitia Mildmay were desirous that s^d Recovery and settlement should be perfected in order to secure to s^d Ann and Letitia Mildmay the portions of £6000 each as absolute and vested instead of the uncertain eventual portions of £6000 each provided for them by their said father's will on the contingency therein expressed and over & above the s^d portions of £1500 each to which they were entitled under their s^d father's marr'e settlement & in cons'on of the portions so intended to be secured that they as well as the s^d Jane Mildmay had agreed absolutely to relinquish all title to all or any implicative {page 6} resulting or other trust of or in the s^d Manors hereditaments & premises or any of them other than & except the Ann'y of £120 provided for the S^d Jane Mildmay and except the right of occupying Shawford House but subject to the jointure of £350 limited to the s^d Jane Mildmay by her s^d Marr'e Settlement and the portions of £1500 a piece which the s^d Dame Jane St John Mildmay Ann Mildmay and Letitia Mildmay were entitled under the s^d settlement & that to that end the s^d Jane Mildmay Ann Mildmay and Letitia Mildmay had all agreed to join in a direction to the s^d Sir Peter Rivers Gay James Rivers & T Salmon to form in a proper conveyance for making a tenant for the precipe for suffering a Recovery and accomplishing a Settlement of the s^d freehold manors heredits subject as afs^d To the uses upon the trusts and for the ends intents & purposes & in manner th'inafter limited expressed & declared being the same as agreed upon by the s^d Ind're of the 21st June 1786

It is witnessed that for docking & barring all estates tail remainders and reversions in s^d freehold Manors lands tenements & hereditaments devised by the said will of the said Carew Mildmay & in performance of the agreement in s^d Indre of the 21st June 1786 and for settling the same to the uses intents & purposes thinaf expressed and in cons'on of 10/ to s^d Sir Peter Rivers Gay James Rivers & Thomas Salmon & to the s^d Sir Henry Paulet St John Mildmay and Dame Jane his wife Jane, Ann & Letitia Mildmay paid by s^d Edwd Bray the receipt They the s^d Sir P. R. Gay James Rivers and Thomas Salmon (at the request and by the dir'on of s^d Sir Henry Paulet St John Mildmay & Dame Jane his wife Jane Mildmay Ann Mildmay & Letitia Mildmay) did bargain sell alien rel'e & confirm and s^d Sir Henry Paulet St John Mildmay & Dame Jane his wife Ann Mildmay and Letitia Mildmay according to their several estates Did grant bargain sell alien rel'e ratify & confirm (but without prejudice to the jointure rent charge of £350 to said Jane Mildmay and to the portions of £1500 each to s^d Dame Jane Mildmay Ann Mildmay and Letitia Mildmay) unto the said Edwd Bray & his heirs in his actual posson (inter alia)

All those the Manors of Twyford & Marwell o'wise Old Marwell in the said County of Southampton and also all and singular Mess'es House Cottages Edifices Buildings Mills Crofts Curtilages Dovehouses Orchards Gardens Lands Tenements Meadows Leagures Pastures Closes Feedings Commons Common *{Page 7}* of Pasture and Turbary Heaths Moors [illegible] Marshes Waters Waste Grounds ways watercourses Ponds Pools Rivers Fishings Wears Woods Underwoods Trees Coppices & the soil & ground of the same Rents reversions services Courts Baron Courts Leet views of Frankpledge and all that thereto belongs perquisites & profits of Courts Leet escheats [illegible] Fines Amerciaments Forfeitures Ways Estrays Goods and Chattels of Felons Outlaws & Fugitives Goods of Felons Convict Parks Chases Warrens Advowsons Free Chappels & all other Royalties Liberties Franchises Casualties Privileges rights free customs pre-eminences Jurisdictions Profits Commodities advantages Emoluments Heredits & appu'ts whats'e to the s^d Manors Lordships Mess'es Lands Tenements Heres & Premises theinbefore ment^d & thereby granted & released or expressed or intended so to be or any of them belonging or in anywise appertaining accepted reputed taken known & occupied or enjoyed with the same or any of them or any part thereof

And the rev'on

And all the Estate (except the s^d jointure of £350 and the said 3 parties of £1500 each)

To hold to & to the use of the said Edward Bray his heirs and assigns for the purpose of his being tenant to the proper precipe for suffering a Recovery in which said W^m St John & John Pollen were to be demandants & s^d Edwd Bray Tenant who was to vouch to warrants the s^d Sir Henry Paulet St John Mildmay and Dame Jane his wife who were to vouch over the common vouchee

Decl'on that said recovery should enure in the first place to confirm the jointure Rent Charge of £350 to the said Jane Mildmay & also to corroborate the term by the s^d Settlement limited in use to trustees for securing portions for the daughters of the s^d Carew Mildmay by the s^d Jane his wife so far as respected the portions of £1500 each & as to the s^d thinbef released prem's to the said Rent Charge of £350 to said Jane Mildmay and the powers and remedies and trusts for securing *{Page 8}* and recovering the same & to the said portions of £1500 each to the said Dame Jane St John Mildmay Ann Mildmay and Letitia Mildmay and the term and interest trust for raising & paying the same and int^t as afs^d in the lands respl'y charged th'with

To the use of the said Henry Peters and William Bragg their ex'ors adm'ors & assigns for 1000 years from the day next before the day of the date of the said Indenture without impeachment of waste upon the trusts th'inar declared with remainder subject to the said term and the trust thereof

To the use of the said Sir Henry Paulet St John Mildmay & his assigns for his life sans waste

Rem^{rs}

To the use of s^d W^m St John and John Pollen & their heirs during the life of said Sir Henry Paulet St John Mildmay upon trust to preserve contingent remainders

Remainder

To the use of the s^d Dame Jane St John Mildmay & her assigns for her life sans waste …Rem^r

To the use of s^d W^m St John & J Pollen & their heirs during the life of the said Dame Jane St John Mildmay upon trust to preserve contingent rem^{rs}

Rem^r

To the use of all and every the younger son and sons and the dau' and daur's of the said Henry Paulet St John Mildmay by s^d Dame Jane (other than an only or other son entitled in poss'on or in rem^r immed'ly on his mother's death to the estates devised to her for life after the decease and failure of the issue of Ann Henry Mildmay by the will of Carew Henry Mildmay late of Haslegrove in the County of Somerset dec'ed by virtue of the limit'ons contained in that will and except such son as should by virtue of the limit'ons contained in the s^d Ind're of the 21st of June 1786 or of the appt^t of s^d Sir Henry Paulet St John Mildmay pursuant to the power therein contained be entitled to the hereditaments thereby released) equally to be divided between or among *{Page 9}* them if more than one as Tenants in Common and not as joint Tenants & of the several and respective heirs of his her or their body or respective bodies and in default of lawful issue of the body or bodies of any such younger son or daughter younger sons or daughters then as to the original part or share parts or shares of such younger son or sons daughter or daughters whose issue should so fail as well as to such other part or share parts or shares as by virtue of the clause now being abst^d sho^d have accrued unto any of them or his her or their issue

To the use of the remain^g or other or others of the said younger son or sons daur or daur's (except as before excepted) equally to be divided between or amongst them if more than one as Tenants in Common & not as joint Tenant and of the sev^l & respective heirs of the body and bodies of such rem^d & other younger son or sons daur or daur's (except as before excepted & in case all such younger son & sons daur & daur's but one (except as before excepted) should happen to die without lawful issue or in case there should be but one such younger son or daur (except as before excepted) then

To the use of such remaining or only younger son or daughter and the heirs of his or her body issuing with divers remainders over

Proviso and Declaration that if any younger son entitled by virtue of the limit'ons th'inbefore contained to any part or share of the prem's thereby granted sho^d either during the lives of s^d Sir Henry Paulet St John Mildmay and Dame Jane or the survivor or within 21 days after the death of such survivor become entitles in poss'on or in remainder immediately expectant only on the decease of s^d Dame Jane to the estates devised by the will of the said Carew Henry Mildmay by virtue of the limitations in his will or should by virtue of the limit'ons in s^d Ind're of 21st June 1786 or of the Appointment of s^d Sir Henry Paulet St John Mildmay become entitled to the hereditaments therein granted then and immed'y th'upon the estate and use which such son should so become *{Page 10}* entitled to in the here's by the now abstracting Ind're granted and rel'ed by virtue of the limitations thereinbefore cont^d should thenceforth cease determine and be void and the s^d hereditaments or so much thereof as such son would orwise have taken th'in should immedi'y go to s^d W^m St John and John Pollen and their heirs should stand seized thof To the use of the p'sons or p'son next in remainder by virtue of the afs^d limit'ons as if such son was dead without issue

Declaration that said term of 1000 years was so limited to s^d Henry Peters and William Bragg their ex'ors and adm'ors upon trust to permit s^d Jane Mildmay w^o to reside at Shawford House & to pay her the s^d yearly sum of £120 for her life over and above the s^d sum of £350 and subject to the s^d right of residence & to the said annuity of £120 and also to the s^d Jointure of £350 as to the lands charged th'with and to the s^d portions of £1500 each as to the lands charged therewith to which s^d Dame Jane St John Mildmay Ann Mildmay & Letitia Mildmay were entitled under their said late fathers settlement and to the trust for raising the same upon further trust they the s^d H J Peters and Wm Bragg or the survivor of them his ex'ors admors or assigns should as soon as conveniently might be by sale or mortgage or other disposition of the premises comprised in the s^d term of 1000 years or by and out of the rents issues & profits of the said premises or by all or any of the s^d ways and means raise levy and pay the 2 several sums of £6000 and £6000 and interest for the same respectively for the portions of the s^d Ann Mildmay and Letitia Mildmay in lieu of the s^d portions of £6000 a piece provided or intended for the'in by their late fathers will in the contingency th'in ment^d that is to say £6000 for the portion of the s^d Ann Mildmay with int^t at £4 per cent to be computed from the day of the de'ce of the s^d Jane Mildmay the mother & £6000 for the portion of the said Letitia Mildmay with interest at the s^d rate of £4 per cent from the s^d [blank space] the said sums to become vested in the said Ann Mildmay and Letitia from the days of their ma'ing their s^d ages and to carry int't as afs^d till the times of payment and it was declared that the said portions and interest were to be paid over and above the said portions of £1500 each to which the said Ann Mildmay & Letitia Mildmay were entitled under their father's settlement but in lieu *{Page 11}* and satisfaction of the port'ns of £6000 a piece provided for them by the s^d will of their s^d father and which said several portions of £6000 and £6000 the s^d Ann Mildmay and Letitia Mildmay did by abstracting indenture resp'ly absolutely release and discharge all & every the Manors mess'es lands tenements and here's devised by the will of the s^d Carew Mildmay of & from the portions of £6000 each & all & every the portion or portions thereby provided or intended for them or either of them on the contingency or contingencies therein ment^d and from all right claim and demand of the s^d Ann Mildmay and Letitia Mildmay their ex'ors or adm'ors or either of them resp'ly for or in respect thof

Proviso for cesser of the s^d term of 1000 years

Declarations that the receipts of the s^d H. Peters & Wm Bragg or the survivor of them his ex'ors or ad's to any purchaser or m'gee of the s^d term or of certain hereditaments th'inbef lastly rel'ed (being the parsonage & tithes of Twyford) upon any purchases or mortgage in pursuance of the said trusts should be a sufficient discharge & that such purchasers or mortgagees should not be answerable for the applic'on of the money in such receipts expressed to be received

Power to appoint new trustees

Several Covenants by the said Sir H. P. St John Mildmay for himself and the said Dame Jane his wife and by s^d Ann Mildmay and Letitia Mildmay for quiet enjoyment free from incumb^{ces} except the s^d jointures of £350 and £120 and the s^d portions of £1500 and except subsisting leases and mortgages – and for further assurance

Executed by all the parties except the parties of the 6th and 7th parts & attested by two witnesses

Michaelmas Term 30th Geo 3rd Southampton

Exemplification of a Recovery wherein the said W^m St John and John Pollen were demandants Edwd Bray Tenant Sir H^y Paulet St John Mildmay Bart & Jane his wife vouchee who vouched the common vouchee of

The Manors of Twyford and Marwell otherwise Old Marwell with the appurtenant & 30 mess'es 3 Dovehouses One water born Mill 80 Gardens 1100 acres of land 240 acres of meadow 240 acres of pasture *{Page 12}* 320 acres of wood 2000 acres of furze & heath 40% rent common of pasture for all manors of cattle [illegible] of frankpledge courts Leet Courts Baron Goods & chattels of felons & felons themselves fugitives waifs estrays deodands customs franchises liberties & privileges with the appurt's in Shawford Twyford and Marwell otherwise Old Marwell and in the parishes of Twyford & Owslebury and also the advowsons of the churches of Twyford and Owslebury

Abstract Number Two: Mildmay Estates, Abstract of the Title of the several persons claiming under an Indenture of Settlement of the 28th November 1789 to the Manor of Marwell in the County of Southampton

{Front Cover}

No.2

Mildmay Estates

1858

Abstract of the Title of the Several Persons Claiming under an Indenture of Settlement of the 28th November 1789 to the Manor of Marwell in the County of Southampton

Bradley Castleford

{Page 1}

Abstract of the Title of the Several Persons claiming under an Indenture of Settlement of the 28th November 1789 (set out in Abstract No.1) to the Manor of Marwell in the County of Southampton

11th November 1808

Sir Henry Paulet St John Mildmay died and was buried at Dogmersfield Hants.

There were 15 children of the marriage between the s^d Sir H^y St John Mildmay & Dame Jane his wife viz

Henry St John Carew St John Mildmay baptised at Dogmersfield 8th June 1787 his eldest son (afterwards Sir H^y St John Carew St John Mildmay) who became entitled in remainder immedly expectant on the decease of the s^d Dame Jane St John Mildmay to the estates devised by the will of Carew Hervey Mildmay & who therefore took no part of the above estates.

Jane Dorothea St John Mildmay baptised at Dogmersfield 20th May 1788. Married Paul Lord Methuen 31st July 1810. There was issue of the marriage 3 Sons, Paul Mildmay Methuen, who died s.p. 16th July 1837. Frederick Henry Paul (now Lord Methuen), St John George Paul Methuen, and two Daughters.

Maria St John Mildmay baptised at Dogmersfield 4th Septr 1790. Married Henry Viscount Bolingbroke 3rd June 1812. There was issue of the marriage two Sons, Henry Mildmay now Lord Bolingbroke, Spencer Mildmay St John who died without leaving issue 20th July 1849 and 4 Daughters.

Judith Ann St John Mildmay baptised at Dogmersfield 4th Septr 1790. Married William Earl of Radnor 24th May 1814 and has issue.

Paulet St John Mildmay baptised at Dogmersfield 21st May 1791 *{Page 2}* (the second son) who became entitled in possession to the heredits settled by the s^d Sir Henry Paulet St John Mildmay by the Ind're of 21st June 1786 & who therefore took no part in the above estates.

George W^m St John Mildmay baptised at Dogmersfield Hants 22nd May 1792. Married April 1832 Mary Widow of John Morritt Esqre. There was issue of the marriage one Daughter Geraldine St John Mildmay & one Son Herbert St John Mildmay. The s^d George W^m St John Mildmay died 14th Feby 1851.

Charles William Paulet St John Mildmay baptised at Dogmersfield 18th Septr 1793 died 16th Jany 1830 s.p.

Humphrey St John Mildmay baptised at Dogmersfield Septr 1794. Married 28th Septr 1823 & died 9th Aug 1853 leaving Humphrey St John Mildmay his eldest son.

John Francis St John Mildmay baptised at Dogmersfield 16th June 1796 died Septr 1823 s.p.

Edward St John Mildmay baptised at Dogmersfield 7th July 1797. Married [blank space] 1818 Marianne C. Sherson. There was issue of the marriage 2 Sons Edwd Whealey St John Mildmay who died an infant Arthur George St John Mildmay & two Daughters Marianne Jane (now the wife of Charles Geo^e Barnett Esqre) and Jane Caroline (now the wife of the Revd E. H. H. Vernon).

Gualher St John Mildmay baptised at Dogmersfield 1st Jany 1799 died 31st July 1835 s.p

Carew Anthony St John Mildmay baptised at Dogmersfield 5th Aug 1800. Married Decr 1830, The Honble Eliz^th C. Waldegrave & has issue.

Augustus Tucker St John Mildmay baptised at Dogmersfield 6th Jany 1803 died Decr 1817 s.p.

{Page 3}

Letitia St John Mildmay baptised at Dogmersfield 31st July 1804 died 18th August 1844 s.p.

Hugh Cornwall St John Mildmay baptised at Dogmersfield 28th June 1805 died 28th Jany s.p.

The S^d Augustus Tucker, John Francis, Chas Wm Paulet, Gualher also called Walter, Cornwall, Letitia St John Mildmay all died without leaving any issue & without having done any act to bar their respective estates tail or the remainders expectant thereon so that the above estates became divisible among the 7 other younger Sons and Daughters and their issue.

6th May 1857 The S^d Dame Jane St John Mildmay died.

The estates are divisible as follows

Original and accrued shares	Tenants in Tail under the Settlement of 1789	Proportions in which now divisible	Persons now having the Legal Title of Estate in Fee of the Freehold Estates or power to convey
1/7th	Lady Methuen	1/13th	The Trustees of Lady Methuen's Settlement
		6/91^ths	Frederick Henry Paul Lord Methuen and his mortgagee
1/7th	Lady Bolingbroke	1/13th	The Trustees of Lady Bolingbroke's Settlement
		6/91^ths	Henry Mildmay

1/7th	Lady Radnor	1/7th	Viscount Bolingbroke The Trustees of Lady Radnor's Settlement
1/7th	Edward St John Mildmay		Edward St John Mildmay for life – remainder to M^rs D'Orville for life, remainder
		1/21st	The Trustees of the Marriage Settlem^t of Mrs Barnett
		1/21st	D^o of Mrs Vernon
		1/21st	D^o of Arthur Geo St John Mildmay
1/7th	Humphrey St John Mildmay	1/7th	Humphrey Francis St John Mildmay
1/7th	Carew Anthony St John Mildmay	1/7th	The Trustees of the Settlement of Mr Carew Mildmay
1/7th	George W^m St John Mildmay	1/10th	The Trustees of the Settlement of Mr Geo. W. St John Mildmay and their mortgagee
		3/70th	Herbert Alexandra St John Mildmay

{Page 4}

As to share to which Jane Dorothea St John Mildmay (afterwards Lady Methuen) became entitled of the above estates

7th July 1810

By Ind're of Bargain & Sale made bet^n Dame Jane St John Mildmay & Jane St John Mildmay of the 1st part Edward Bray of the 2nd part & Wm Bray of the 3rd part.

It is witn'ed that for docking & barring all estates tail & all rem^rs & rev'ons expectant in the undivided share th'inaf^r described & for conveying and assuring same to the uses th'inaf^r declared & in cons'on of 10^s/ to s^d Dame Jane & Jane Dorothea St John Mildmay paid by s^d Edwd Bray s^d Dame Jane & Jane Dorothea St John Mildmay (accord^g to their resp'ive rights & interests Did grant bargain sell & confirm unto the s^d Edwd Bray his heirs & ass^s

All that one undiv^d 13th part or share (the whole into 13 equal parts or shares to be divided) of and in All those the Manors & by the decript^n in the settlem^t of 1789. And also of & in All other the manors mess'es lands tenem^ts & heredits in the s^d Parishes of Twyford & Owslebury or elsewhere in the s^d County of Southampton if any such there were ment^d & comprised in the s^d Settlement of 1789.

And of & in all houses

And the Reversions

And all the estate

To hold unto & to the use of the s^d Edwd Bray his heirs & assigns

To the intent that he might become Tenant of the Freehold thereof in order that a Common Recovery with double vouchers might be suffered thereof in which the s^d Wm Bray should be Demandant s^d Edwd Bray Tenant who should vouch for warranty the s^d Dame Jane & Jane Dorothea St John Mildmay who should vouch over the Common Vouchee

And it was thereby directed that the s^d Recovery when suffered should enure (subject to the sums of money then charged on the s^d manors heredits to which the s^d Dame Jane St John Mildmay was then entitled in her own right or as executrix of the s^d Sir Henry *{Page 5}* Paulet St John Mildmay.

To the use of s^d Dame Jane St John Mildmay & her assigns for her life sans waste with such powers of leasing as she had by the s^d abstracted Ind're of 28th Novr 1789 with ……Rem^r.

To the use of s^d Wm Bray & his heirs during the life of s^d Dame Jane St John Mildmay.

Upon Trust to preserve the uses th'inaf^r limited from being defeated…..Rem^r.

To the use of the s^d Dame Jane St John Mildmay her heirs & ass^s for ever.

Executed by s^d Dame Jane & Jane Dorothea St John Mildmay & Edwd Bray & attested.

Inrolled in Chancery 17th July 1810

Trinity Term 50 George 3rd Southampton

A Recovery was suffered wherein s^d ~~Edwd~~ William Bray was Demandant s^d Edwd Bray tenant & s^d Dame Jane & Jane Dorothea St John Mildmay were vouchees of

One thirteenth part of

The Manors of Twyford and Marwell otherwise Old Marwell with the appurt's and 1/13th of 30 mess'es 3 dovehouses 1 water corn mill 80 gardens 1,500 acres of land 300 acres of meadow 300 acres of pasture 400 acres of wood 2000 acres of furze and heath and 40^s/ rent common of pasture with the appurt's in Shawford Twyford & Marwell o'rwise Old Marwell & in the Parishes of Twyford & Owslebury & also the Advowsons of the Churches of Twyford & Owslebury

28th & 30th July 1810

By Ind'res of Lease & Release the latter made bet^n Dame Jane St John Mildmay Widow & Jane Dorothea St John Mildmay Spinster of the 1st part Paul Methuen of Corsham House in the County of Wilts Esqre of the 2nd part & The Hon. Bartholomew Bouverie of Edward Street Portman Square in the Parish of Marylebone in the Co^y of Midd'x The Honble George Irby af^twards Geo Lord Boston of Brickwell House in the Co^y of Bucks Sir H^y St John Carew St John Mildmay of Shawford House in the Co^y of Southampton Bart & John Clerk of Bugle Hall in the s^d Co^y *{Page 6}* of Southampton Esqre of the 3rd part.

After recit^g an Ind're of 15th Octr 1803 relating to a Leasehold tenement called Drakes in Netherham.

And recit^g s^d Ind're of Bargain & Sale of 7th July then instant & the Common Recovery suffered in Southampton pursuant to the same.

And recit^g certain Ind'res of Lease & Release of the 6th & 7th July then instant relating to certain Leasehold prem'es in the County of Southampton known as the Parsonage of Twyford.

And recit^g that a Marriage was intended between s^d Paul Methuen & Jane Dorothea St John Mildmay.

And recit^g that in contempl'on of the s^d Marr'e & of the Settlem^t of even date made by Paul Cobb Methuen Esqre & the s^d Paul Methuen it was agreed amongst other things that the afores^d freehold & leasehold p'pty of the s^d Jane Dorothea St John Mildmay & also such freehold & leasehold property (if any) as she the s^d Jane Dorothea St John Mildmay might be seized or possessed of in the Co^y of Somerset should be settled as th'inaf^r mentioned

The first witnessing part relates to s^d le'hold prem'es at Somerset.

And it was fur^r witnessed that for the cons'on before ment^d & in fur^r purs'ce of s^d Agreem^t on the part of s^d Jane Dorothea St John Mildmay & for the other cons'ons th'in ment^d She the s^d Jane Dorothea St John Mildmay with the consent of Paul Methuen testified Did grant barg^n sell alien release & confirm unto s^d B. Bouverie Geo Irby Sir Henry St John Carew St John Mildmay & John Clerk (in their actual posson) & to their heirs (inter alia)

All that the rev'on or rem^r in the simple expect' upon & to take effect immed'ly after the decease of s^d Dame Jane St John Mildmay. Of and in

All that one undivided 13th part or share the whole into 13 equal parts or shares to be divided of and in All those the Manors by the description in the settlem' of 28th Novr 1789 And also of and in All other the mess'es lands tenem^{ts} in the s^d Parishes of Twyford & Owslebury or elsewhere in s^d Co^y of Southampton if any to an undiv^d 13th part wh'of s^d Jane Dorothea *{Page 7}* St John Mildmay was entitled in reversion or rem^r as afs^d under or by virtue of s^d abst^d Ind'res of Lease & Rel'e of the 27th & 28th days of Novr 1789.

And also under or by virtue of the thereinbefore rec^d Ind're of bargain & sale & the recovery suffered in pursuance thereof.

And the Rev'on

And all the estate

To have & to hold the s^d rev'on in fee simple of & in the undivided parts or shares of the s^d manors with the appurt's unto & to the use of the s^d B. Bouverie Geo Irby Sir Henry St John Carew St John Mildmay & John Clerk their heirs & ass^s for ever.

Upon the trusts th'inafter declared.

And it was thereby declared & agreed that the heredit's compr^d in s^d recited Ind're of 15th Octr 1803 th'inbefore assigned & s^d undivided parts or shares & heredit's granted & rel'ed as afores^d were so resp'ly assigned & granted & released.

Upon trust for the s^d Jane Dorothea St John Mildmay her ex'ors adm'ors & ass^s until the s^d marr'e & from & after the solemnis'on thereof.

Upon trust as to the heredit's comprised in s^d Ind're of the 15th Octr 1803 And also as to such heredit's th'rby assigned & granted & released as were situate or arising in the Co^y of Somerset And as to the undivided parts or shares wh'of the rev'ons or rem^rs were th'inbefore granted & rel'ed when & so soon as the same should come into poss'on or sooner if s^d Dame Jane St John Mildmay would consent to join in the sale with the consent approb'on of s^d Paul Methuen & Jane Dorothea St John Mildmay during their joint lives & after the de'ce of either of them then with the consent of sur'vor (test^d) & after the decease of such sur'vor then of the proper auth^y of them the same tr'ees or of the sur'vors or sur'vor of them or the h'rs ex'ors adm'ors or ass^s of such sur'vor to make sale & absolutely dispose of the same heredit's *{Page 8}* comprised in s^d Ind're of 15th Octr 1803 & s^d undivided parts or shares & other heredit's thereby assigned & granted & rel'ed either by Public Auction or Private Sale & either tog^r or in lots or parcels in such manner as they the s^d B. Bouverie George Irby Sir Henry St John Carew St John Mildmay & John Clerk or the sur'vors or sur'vor of them or the h'rs ex'ors or adm'ors of such sur'vor with such consent or of such auth^y as afs^d should think proper unto any p'sons willing to become purch^rs for the most money that could be got for the same if sold by auction & if sold by Private Contract then for such price or prices as by them or him with such consent or such auth^y as afs^d sho^d be thought fit or reasonable & on paym^t of the purchase moneys for which the heredit's or any part thereof sho^d be so sold sho^d convey ass^n & assure the s^d heredit's or such of them as sho^d be so sold unto the purch^rs th'of their h'rs ex'ors adm'ors & ass^s accord^g to the resp'ive natures & qualities th'of or as they lawfully sho^d direct app^t And for the p'pses afs^d it sho^d be lawful for the s^d tr'ees & the sur'vor or sur'vors of them & the h'rs ex'ors adm'ors & ass^s of such sur'vor with such consent & authority as afs^d to enter into sign & execute in their his or her names or name any Contract or Contracts for sale of the s^d heredit's or any part th'of to any p'sons willing to become purch^rs & to receive any sums of money on the execution of such cont^ts by way of deposit mo^y or any part th'of to return to the p'sons paying the same with int^t if it sho^d be thought advisible.

Declaration that the rec^t or rec^ts of the s^d Bartholomew Bouverie George Irby Sir Henry St John Carew St John Mildmay & John Clerk & the sur'vor or sur'vors of them or the heirs ex'ors adm'ors or ass^s of such sur'vor sho^d be a good & suff^t discharge to the p'sons or p'son paying such purchase mo^y & deposit as afs^d for so much money as sho^d be expressed on such rec^t or rec^ts resp'ly & such p'son or persons sho^d not be answerable after any rec^t or rec^ts so given for *{Page 9}* the misapplic'on or nonapplic'on or in anywise concerned to see to the applic'on of the money for which such receipts should be so given.

Declaration that the money to arise from such sale or sales should be laid out & invested by them s^d tr'ees with the consent of s^d Paul Methuen & Jane Dorothea St John Mildmay or of the sur'vor of them & in case of their deaths of the proper authority of s^d Tr'ees or Tr'ee for the time being in their or his names or name in or upon governm^t or other public stocks funds or sect^s or upon real sect^s at int^t with power with such consent as afs^d to sell dispose of alter vary & change the same & those which should be substituted in lieu thereof or any of them for others of the like nature.

And upon fur^r trust that they the s^d tr'ees for the time being sho^d stand poss'ed of the same stocks funds & sect^s as sho^d be purchased with or be produced from monies aris^g by sale of s^d undiv^d 13th parts or shares th'rby granted & rel'ed

Upon trust for s^d Dame Jane St John Mildmay & her ass^s dur^g her life & after her decease as to the same stocks funds & securities & as to all other the s^d stocks funds & securities th'inbef: directed to be purchased from & after the resp'ive purchases th'of & sho^d stand poss'ed of a sum of £942.0.7 Bank 3 per cent Ann^y standing in the names of s^d trustees.

Upon trust to pay the dividends & int' or permit same to be rec'ed by s^d Paul Methuen & his assigns during his life Rem^r

Upon trust for s^d Jane Dor^y Mildmay & her ass^s dur^g her life Rem^r

Upon trust to be paid to or divided between all & every the child & child^n of s^d intended marr'e (except an eldest or only Son) at such ages days or times in such parts shares & proportions & under & subject to such limit'ons over (such limit'ons to be for the benefit of some or one of the same child^n except as afs^d) & in such manner as the s^d Paul Methuen & Jane Dorothea St John Mildmay dur^g their joint lives sho^d by writ^g with or with' power of revoc'on & new appt' att^d by two witn^s or the sur'vor of them by deed att^d as afs^d or by will

Powers of partition of the Manors & whereof such shares as afs^d were th'inbef expressed to be granted & released.

Power of appointing new trustees

{Page 10}

Proviso for indemnity of s^d trustees

Covenant from s^d Jane Dorothea St John Mildmay that she had good right to grant & release. – for quiet enjoym^t free from incumbr's except as appeared by now abst^g Ind're & except Leases & Est^s for years then in being & for further assurance.

Executed by all parties except Geo Irby & attested.

The s^d Paul Methuen was aft'wds created Baron Methuen on the 13th July 1838 & died on the 14th Sepr 1849.

Jane Dorothea Lady Methuen died on the 14th March 1846.

The Honble Geo Irby became Lord Boston on the death of his father in March 1825 & survived his 3 co-he'es & died on the [blank space] without hav^g made any devise of est^s vested in him upon trust & leav^g the present Lord Boston his heir at law.

Sir Henry St John Carew St John Mildmay died on the 27th January 1848.

The Honble Bartholomew Bouverie died 31st May 1835.

John Clerk died 31st October 1842.

As to the accruing shares vested in Frederick Henry Paul Lord Methuen as heir in Law to his Mother the Lady Methuen

20th July 1850

By Ind'res of this date made bet^n The Right Honble Fred^k H^y Paul Methuen Baron of Corsham Court in the Co^y of Wilts of the one part & Gabriel Goldney of Chippenham in the s^d Co^y of Wilts Gent^n of the o^r part.

Recit^g the Ind're of the 21st June 1786 the abst^d Lease & Release of the 27th & 28th days of Novr 1789 & the Common Recovery suffered in pursuance thereof.

And recit^g that the s^d Sir H^y Paul St John Mildmay departed *{Page 11}* this life sev^l years since & there was issue of him & the s^d Dame Jane St John Mildmay his wife 11 Sons & 4 Daughters therein named their only children.

And recit^g that in the events which happened 13 only out of the s^d children of the s^d Sir H^y Paulet St John Mildmay & Dame Jane St John Mildmay his wife became seized of or entitled to the s^d settled estates & heredit's as tenants in common in tail general with such cross rem^{ts} as afores^d under the limit'ons contained in the s^d Ind'res th'inbef recited or referred to or some or one of them Sir H^y John Carew St John Mildmay then eldest son not having been entitled to any part or share of the s^d est^e & heredit's & the est^e tail of Paulet St John Mildmay their 2nd son hav^g ceased or determined by reason or in consequence of his hav^g become entitled to the other estates & heredit's in the s^d settlem' mentioned.

And recit^g that the s^d Dame Jane St John Mildmay the W^o of the s^d Sir H^y Paulet St John Mildmay was still living.

And recit^g that s^d Jane Dorothea St John Mildmay one of the Dau^{rs} of the s^d marr'e intermarried with Paul late Lord Methuen then Paul Methuen Esqre & since dec'ed & previously to her marriage the s^d 1/13th part or share of the s^d settled estates & heredit's (a Recovery having been duly suff^d) was by an Ind're of Rel'e of the 30th day of July 1810 & by a Deed Poll or Deed of Appointm^t bear^g date the 12th day of Aug' 1837 limited settled & assured as to 1/16th part or share thereof to the s^d Fred^k H^y Paul Lord Methuen in absolute property & as to the rem^g 15 parts thof to The Honble Jane Matilda now the wife of David Lewis Esqre & The Honble St John George Paul Methuen in equal shares as in the s^d Deed Poll expressed.

And recit^g that Augustus Tucker St John Mildmay, John Fra^s St John Mildmay, Chas Wm Paulet St John Mildmay, Gaulther St John Mildmay, Hugh Cornwall St John Mildmay, & Letitia St John Mildmay being 6 of the s^d 13 younger children as afs^d of the s^d Sir Henry Paulet St John Mildmay & Dame Jane his wife severally some time since died without issue & with' having barred or attempted to bar their s^d resp'ive est^s tail in their s^d resp'ive parts or shares either original or accruing of the s^d settled estates & heredit's And in *{Page 12}* consequence thereof one 7th part or share of & in such sev^l parts or shares as afs^d of the s^d estates & heredit's became vested in the s^d Dame Jane Dorothea Lady Methuen for an estate in tail general & on her decease which happened on or about the 14th day of March 1846 the same 7th part or share descended to or became vested in the s^d Fred^k H^y Paul Lord Methuen as her eldest surviv^g son & heir in tail.

And rect^g that s^d Fred^k H^y Paul Lord Methuen was desirous of raising the sum of £4000 in the security of his s^d several parts or shares of the s^d heredit's & if & in certain monies ment^d in the 2nd Schedule to the s^d abst^g Ind're & the heredit's to be purchased therewith & had applied to & requested the s^d Gabriel Goldney to lend & advance him the same at interest which he had agreed to do on having the repayment th'of secured to him his ex'ors adm'ors & ass^s in manner th'inaf^r mentioned.

It is witn'ed that for effecting the s^d recited agreem' & in cons'on of the sum of £4000 to s^d Fred^k H^y Paul Lord Methuen p^d by the s^d Gabriel Goldney the rec' & for barr^g & destroy^g all est^s & int^{ts} in tail of him the s^d Fred^k H^y Paul Lord Methuen of & in the share and heredit's th'inaf^r granted & rel'ed or int^d so to be & so far as might be & circums' would admit all rem^r & rev'ons estates rights titles and int' expect' or depending upon or to take effect after the determin'on or defeasance of such est^s or int' in tail & for vesting the s^d shares & heredit's in him the s^d Gabriel Goldney his heirs & ass^s He the s^d Fred^k H^y Paul Lord Methuen Did grant release & convey unto the s^d Gabriel Goldney his heirs & assigns.

All the 1/16th part or share of him the s^d Fred^k H^y Paul Lord Methuen of the afs^d 1/13th part or share.

And also all that the 1/7th part or share of & in the s^d 6/13th parts or shares.

And also all other if any the part or share parts or shares of him the s^d Fred^k H^y Paul Lord Methuen of & in All & sing^r the manors mess'es farms lands tenem^{ts} & heredit's sum & sums of money & all o^r prem'es desc^d or ment^d or referred *{Page 13}* to in the s^d 1st & 2nd Schedules to the s^d abst^g Ind're with the appurt's.

And of & in all houses

And of & in all other (if any) the manors & heredit's comprised in or subject to the limit'ons uses or trusts of the s^d th'inbef in part rec^d Ind'res or any or either of them.

And the Rev'on

And all the Estate

To hold the same with the appurt's unto & to the use of the s^d Gabriel Goldney his h'rs & ass^s for ever but subject to the estates for life of the s^d Dame Jane St John Mildmay th'in & subj' also to the prov'o for red'on th'inaf^r contained.

Proviso for red'on of the s^d prem'es on paym' on the 20th Jany 1851 of £4000 & int' at £4.10.0 per cent.

Usual mortgage cov^{ts} but not includ^g powers of sale.

Declaration that the mo^y ultimately recoverable shall not exceed £5000.

The 1st schedule is a copy of the parcels in the settlem' of 20th Novr 1798.

Executed by both parties & duly attested.

Receipt for £4000 endorsed signed & witnessed.

Inrolled in Chancery 7th Aug' 1850 purs'to 3 & 4 W^m 4 C74 P79.

1st June 1854

By Ind're of this date betⁿ the s^d R^t Honble Fred^k H^y Paul Lord Methuen of Corsham Court in the s^d Co^y of Wilts of the one part & s^d Gabriel Goldney of the o^r part.

Recit^g the last abst^d Ind're.

And recit^g that s^d Fred^k H^y Paul Lord Methuen had applied to s^d Gabriel Goldney to advance him the fur^r sum of £2,500 which he had agreed to do & it had been arranged that the repay' with int' at the rate of £5 per cent per ann should be secured in manner th'inaf^r contained.

It was witn'ed that in purs'ce of s^d agreem^t & in cons'on of s^d sum of £2,500 to s^d Fred^k H^y Paul Lord Methuen paid by s^d *{Page 14}* Gabriel Goldney the rec^t the s^d Fred^k H^y Paul Lord Methuen did cov' promise & agree with the s^d Gabriel Goldney his ex'ors adm'ors & ass^s that he the s^d Fred^k H^y Paul Lord Methuen his h'rs ex'ors & adm'ors would pay unto the s^d Gabriel Goldney his ex'ors adm'ors or ass^s the s^d sum of £2,500 with interest for the same at the rate of £5 per cent per ann on the 1st Decr then next without any deduction or abatem' whats^r And in case s^d sum of £2,500 should not be p^d on the s^d 1st day of Decr then next sho^d during the continuance of the abst^g security pay unto the s^d Gabriel Golding his ex'ors adm'ors or assigns interest at the rate aforesaid for such sum of £2,500 or so much th'of as sho^d for the time being remain unpaid by equal half yearly paym^{ts} on the 1st day of Jan^y & the 1st day of Decr in every year.

And it was fur^r witn'ed that in purs'ce of s^d agreem' & for the cons'ons afs^d & for secur^g to s^d Gabriel Goldney his ex'ors adm'ors or ass^s for paym' of s^d sum of £2,500 he the s^d Fred^k H^y Paul Lord Methuen Did th'rby subject & charge the parts shares & int^{ts} of him the s^d Fred^k H^y Paul Lord Methuen of & in the sev^l manors mess'es farms lands & heredit's sum & sums of money conv^d by the last abst^d Ind're subj' to the life int' of the s^d Dame Jane St John Mildmay th'in to & with the paym' to s^d Geo Goldney his ex'ors adm'ors & ass^s of the s^d sum of £2,500 & int' for the same at the rate of £5 per cent at the time & in manner th'inbef appointed for paym' thereof.

Covenant by Lord Methuen to pay premiums of assurance on life policies th'in named in default that mortgagee might pay same & the amounts paid to be a charge upon the s^d premises.

Executed by s^d Fred^k H^y Paul Lord Methuen & duly attested.

Receipt for £2,500 endorsed signed & witn'ed.

3rd March 1855

By Ind're of this date made bet^n s^d Gabriel Goldney of the one part & the Revd James Bliss of Ogbourne St Andrew in the same County Clerk in the other part.

Recit^g s^d abst^d Ind're of the 20th July 1850.

And recit^g s^d abst^d Ind're of the 1st June 1854.

And recit^g that the s^d sums of £4000 & £2,500 were still due & ow^g to s^d Gabriel Goldney from s^d Fred^k *{Page 15}* H^y Paul Lord Methuen but all int' thereon had been fully paid up to the day of the date thereof as s^d Gabriel Goldney did th'rby acknowledge & he having occasion for the same the s^d James Bliss had arranged & agreed to advance & pay to the s^d Gabriel Goldney the s^d p'pal sums of £4000 & £2,500 upon hav^g a transfer to him of the s^d Mortgage debts & the int' to accrue th'ron hav^g a convey'ce & assignm' of s^d sev^l manors heredit's & parts & shares of manors & heredit's in manner thinaf^r expressed.

It is witn'ed that in purs'ce of s^d agreemen' & in cons'on of s^d sev^l sums of £4000 & £2,500 by s^d Ja^s Bliss to s^d Gabriel Goldney in hand well & truly paid the rec' He the s^d Gabriel Goldney Did ass^n & transfer unto s^d Ja^s Bliss his ex'ors adm'ors & assigns

All those the s^d recited principal sums of £4000 & £2,500 resp'ly & all int' thenceforth to accrue due th'on resp'ly but so nev^s that the int' th'on sho^d thenceforth be after the rate at £4.10^s/ per cent per ann in lieu of the rate of interest reserved by the last abst^d Ind're.

To hold the same unto s^d Ja^s Bliss his ex'ors adm'ors &ass^s as his own monies & effects absolutely.

And it is fur^r witn'ed that in fur^r purs'ce of s^d recited agreem' & for the valuable cons'on thr'inbef expr^d He the s^d Gabriel Goldney Did grant & convey unto s^d Ja^s Bliss his heirs & assigns.

All that the s^d 1/16th part or share of him the s^d Fred^k H^y Paul Lord Methuen of & in a certain 1/13th parts or share of 6/13th parts or share & all other (if any) the parts or shares of him the s^d Fred^k H^y Paul Lord Methuen of & in all & sing^r the manors mess'es farms lands tenem^{ts} & heredit's sum & sums of money & all other the prem'es ment^d or referred to in the 1st & 2nd Schedules to the now abst^g Ind're with the appurt's.

And all the estate.

To hold the same to the only proper use & behoof of the s^d James Bliss his heirs & ass^s for ever subject to *{Page 16}* such right & equality of redempt'on as was then subsisting therein under & by virtue of the s^d th'inbef abstracted Ind're of the 20th July 1850.

Covenant by s^d Gabriel Goldney that he had done no act to incumber.

The 1st Schedule contains a short description of the p'cels in the Settlement of 28th November 1789.

Executed by both parties & duly attested.

Receipt for £6,500 indorsed signed & witn'ed.

3rd July 1857

By Ind're of this date made bet'n the s'd R't Fred'k H'y Paul Lord Methuen of Corsham Court in the Co'y of Wilt's of the one part & the Rev'd James Bliss of Ogbourne St Andrew in the same Co'y Clerk of the other part.

Recit'g the s'd abst'd Ind'res of 20th July 1850, 1st June 1854 & 3rd March 1855.

And recit'g that the s'd sums of £4,000 & £2,500 were still due & owing to the s'd James Bliss under & by virtue of the s'd th'inbef rec'd Ind're with some int' thereupon.

And recit'g the death of the s'd Dame Jane St John Mildmay & that th'rupon the s'd Fred'k H'y Paul Lord Methuen became seized of or entitled to the s'd shares heredit's & prem'es comprised in & assured by the s'd sev'l Ind'res th'inbefore resp'ly recited for an estate in tail general or for a base or determinable fee in possession.

And recit'g that for the purpose of confirm'g the s'd rec'd security & of barring, defeat'g & destro'g all estates tail (if any) & all rev'ons & rem'rs expectant or dependant upon or to take effect after the determin'on of such est's tail or after the determin'on or in defeasance of the base fee into which his estate or int' in tail in the s'd shares heredit's & premises was converted or intended to be converted by the s'd first th'inbef recited Ind're the s'd Fred'k H'y Paul Lord Methuen had agreed & determined to make & execute the dispos'on assignm' & assurance of the s'd shares heredit's & prem'es th'inaf'r contained.

{Page 17}

It is witn'ed that for effectua'g the s'd rec'd agreem' and determin'on for barring defeat'g & destroy'g all estates tail (if any) & all rights int'ts & powers expectant or depending upon or to take effect after the determin'on or in defeasance of the s'd estates tail or any of them or after the determin'on or in defeasance of the base fee into which the estate tail of him the s'd Fred'k H'y Paul Lord Methuen was then converted or int'd so to be converted by virtue of the said th'inbef rec'd Ind're of the 20th day of July 1850 & for assuring & confirm'g the s'd shares heredit's & prem'es & the fee simple and inh'ance th'of to the use of the s'd Ja's Bliss his h'rs & ass's & in cons'on of the sum of 10s/ of lawful British money to the s'd Fred'k H'y Paul Lord Methuen paid by the s'd Ja's Bliss the s'd Fred'k H'y Paul Lord Methuen under or by virtue & in pursuance of the powers & prov'ons contained in the s'd Act of Parliam' passed for the abolition of fines & recoveries & for the substitut'n of more simple modes of assurance Did by abst'g Ind're grant convey ass'n & confirm unto the s'd Ja's Bliss his heirs ex'ors adm'ors & assigns.

All & sing'r the parts or shares part or share of him the s'd Fred'k H'y Paul Lord Methuen comprised in & conveyed & assured or int'd or expressed to be cov'd & assured by the s'd h'inbef rec'd Ind're of the 20th day of July

1850 of in to or out of the s^d manors mess'es heredit's sums & sums of money & all o^r the prem'es descr^d or ment^d in the s^d 1st & 2nd Schedules to abst^g Ind're or either of them & of in to or out of all o^r (if any) the heredit's & prem'es comprised in & conveyed & assured by or intended or expressed to be conveyed & assured by the s^d last ment^d Ind're or then subject to the use or limit'on th'in contained with their & every of their rights members & appurt's.

And of & in houses.

And of & in all other if any the manors heredit's & prem'es compr^d in or subject to the *{Page 18}* limit'on uses or trusts of the sev^l Ind'res in the s^d Ind're of the 20th day of July 1850 recited or referred to or any or ei^r of them with their appurt's.

And of & in the Rev'on.

And all the estate.

To hold the s^d parts or shares part or share th'by granted assigned & conv^d or int^d so to be of & in All & sing^r the manors mess'es farms lands tenem^{ts} heredit's sums & sums of money & prem'es th'inbef ment^d or referred to with their & every of their rights members & appurt's.

Unto & to the use of the s^d Ja^s Bliss his heirs ex'ors adm'ors & ass^s And to the intent & so as to ratify & confirm his s^d rec^d security & to vest the absolute int' in the s^d shares heredit's & premises in the s^d James Bliss But subject nev^s to the same or the like right or benefit of redemption in equity as the s^d shares heredit's & prem'es were then subject or liable to under or by virtue of the s^d sev^l Ind'res th'inbef respectively recited or any or either of them & to & for no other use intent or purpose whatsoever.

The 1st Schedule comprises the parcels in the Settlement of the 28th Novr 1789.

Executed by s^d Lord Methuen & att^d by 2 witn^s. Inrolled in Chancery 13th July 1857. 67P

As to the Share to which the s^d Maria St John Mildmay (afterwards Lady Bolingbroke) became entitled of the above Estates

11th May 1812

By Ind're of barg^n & sale of this date made bet^n the s^d Dame Jane St John Mildmay & the s^d Maria St John Mildmay of the 1st part the s^d Edward Bray of the 2nd part & the s^d Wm Bray of the 3rd part.

It is witn'ed that for dock^g barr^g & extinguish^g all estates tail & *{Page 19}* all rem^{rs} & rev'ons th'upon expectant of & in the undivided part or share of the manors & other heredit's th'inaf^r descr^d & for conveying settling & assuring the same part or share t the uses &^{c} th'inafter declared & contained of & concern^g the same. And also in cons'on of 10^s/ a piece to them the s^d Dame Jane St John Mildmay & Maria St John Mildmay resp'ly paid by the s^d Edwd Bray (the rec' &^{c}) The s^d Dame Jane St John Mildmay & Maria St John Mildmay Did & each of them Did grant bargain sell & confirm unto the s^d Edwd Bray & his heirs

All that one undi^d 13th part or share the whole into 13 equal parts or shares to be divided of & in All those the Manors &^{c} by the descript^n in the s^d Ind'res of Lease & Rel'e of 27th & 28th Novr 1789.

And all other the Manors &^{c} in s^d Parishes of Twyford & Owslebury or elsewhere in the s^d Co^y of Southampton if any such were ment^d & comprised in s^d Ind'res of 27th & 28th Novr 1789.

And of & in all houses &^{c}.

And all the Estate &^{c}.

And the Rev'on &^{c}.

To hold the same unto the s^d Edwd Bray his heirs & assigns.

To the use of him the s^d Edwd Bray his h'rs & ass^s for ever to the intent that he might become tenant of the freehold in order that a Common Recovery might be had thereof wh'in s^d Wm Bray sho^d be Demand' s^d Edwd Bray tenant & s^d Dame Jane St John Mildmay & Maria St John Mildmay vouchees to vouch over the Common Vouchee.

Decl'on that s^d Recovery when so suffered sho^d be & enure subt' to the sev^l sums of mo^y then charged on the s^d Manors & o^r heredit's to w'ch the s^d Dame Jane St John Mildmay was entitled in her own right or as ex'trix of the will of Sir H. Paulet St John Mildmay.

To the use of the s^d Dame Jane St John Mildmay & her ass^s for her life sans waste with such powers of *{Page 20}* leasing as to the s^d share as was given to her in the entirety by s^d Ind're of 28th Novr 1789 with Rem^r

To the use of the s^d Wm Bray & his h'rs dur^g the life of the s^d Dame Jane St John Mildmay In trust to preserve the use thinaf^r limited…Rem$^{r.}$

To the use of the s^d Maria St John Mildmay her h'rs & ass^s for ever.

Executed by the s^d Dame Jane St John Mildmay Maria St John Mildmay Edwd Bray & Wm Bray & attested by one witness.

Inrolled in the Common Pleas Easter Term 52nd Geo 3rd Roll 27.

Easter Term 52nd George 3rd Southampton

Exemplification of Recovery wh'in s^d Wm Bray was Demand' s^d Edwd Bray tenant & s^d Dame Jane St John Mildmay & Maria St John Mildmay Vouchees of

One thirteenth part of the Manors of Twyford & Marwell o'rwise Old Marwell with the appurt's & one thirteenth part of 30 mess'es 3 dovehouses one water corn mill 80 gardens 1500 acres of land 300 acres of meadow 300 acres of pasture 400 acres of wood 200 acres of furze & heath & 40^s/ rent common of pasture &^c with the appurt's in Shawford Twyford & Marwell o'rwise Old Marwell & in the Parishes of Twyford & Owslebury and also the Advowsons of the Churches of Twyford & Owslebury.

2nd & 3rd June 1812

By Ind'res of Lease & Rel'e of these dates the latter made bet^n s^d Dame Jane St John Mildmay & s^d Maria St John Mildmay of the first part The Honble Henry St John Eldest Son of the Right Honble Geo Richd Lord Viscount Bolingbroke of the 2nd part & John Clerk of Bugle Hall in the s^d Co^y of Southampton Esqre The Revd Thos Salmon Rector of Dogmersfield afs^d The Honble Fred^k St John of Brockley House in the Co^y of Wilts a Lieut' Genl in His Majesty's Army & Philip Williams of the Temple in the City *{Page 21}* of London Esqre of the 3rd part.

Recit^g inter alia s^d abst^d Ind're of Bargain & Sale of 11th May 1812 & the Recovery in purs'ce th'of & cert^n Ind'res of Lease & Rel'e of the 9th & 11th May 1812 which relate to certain leasehold premises.

And recit^g that a marr'e was int^d to be shortly had & solemn^d bet^n s^d H^y St John & Maria St John Mildmay.

And recit^g that upon the treaty for the s^d marr'e it was agreed that the p'pty of the s^d Maria St John Mildmay be settled in manner th'inaf^r mentioned.

It is witn'ed that in cons'on of the s^d int^d marr'e & of the Settlem' made on the part of the s^d H^y St John as th'in ment^d & also in cons'on of 10^s/ to the s^d Maria St John Mildmay paid by the s^d John Clerk Thos Salmon Fred^k St John & Phillip Williams (the rec' &^c) She the s^d Maria St John Mildmay in purs'ce &performance of the s^d rec^d Agreem' on her part (with the privity & consent of s^d H^y St John test^d by his being a party to & execut^g the now abst^g Indre) Did grant barg^n sell alien rel'e & confirm unto s^d John Clerk Thos Salmon Fred^k St John & Philip Williams (in them then vested or in their actual poss'on &^c) & to their h'rs inter alia

All that the rev'on a rem^r in fee simple expectant upon & to take effect immed'ly after the de'ce of s^d Dame Jane St John Mildmay of in

All that undiv^d 13th part or share (the whole into 13 equal parts or shares to be divided) of & in

All those the Manors or Lordships of Twyford & Marwell &^c before descr^d.

And also of & all o^r the mess'es lands tenem^ts & heredit's in the s^d Parishes of Twyford & Owslebury or elsewhere in the s^d Co^y of Southampton if any such there to be an undiv^d 13th part wh'of the s^d Maria St John Mildmay was entitled in rev'on or rem^r as afs^d under & by virtue of cert^n Ind'res of Lease & Rel'e bearing date

Page | 25

resp'ly the 27th & 28th days of Novr 1789 & also under & by virtue of the sd first th'inbef *{Page 22}* rec'd Ind're of Bargn & Sale & the Recovery suffered in purs'ce th'of And also one undivd 13th part or share of & in all & singr houses &c.

And the Rev'on &c.

And all the Estate &c.

To hold the same with their & every of their rights royalties members & appurt's unto the sd John Clerk Thos Salmon Fredk St John & Philip Williams their h'rs & assigns.

To the use of the sd John Clerk Thos Salmon Fredk St John & Philip Williams their H'rs & asss for ever.

Upon & for the trusts & p'pses & with under & subject to the powers prov'oes & agreemts thinafr expred & declared concerning the same.

Decl'on that the sd undivd parts or shares & heredit's severally th'inbef granted & rel'ed as afsd were so respl'ly granted & rel'ed upon & for the trusts intents & purposes th'inafr exprd & declared of & concerng the same (that is to say) from & immed'ly after the solemnis'on of the sd intended marriage.

Upon trust that they the sd John Clerk Thomas Salmon Fredk St John & Philip Williams & the sur'vor & sur'vors of them & the h'rs & asss of such sur'vor shod when & so soon as sd undivided parts or shares shd come into poss'on with the consent and approb'on of sd Hy St John & Maria St John Mildmay during their lives & after the decease of either of them then with the consent of the sur'vor such consent to be testd as therein mentd & after the decease of such sur'vor then of the proper authy of them the sd tr'ees or the sur'vors or sur'vor of them or the h'rs or asss of such sur'vor make sale & absolutely dispose of the sd undivd parts or shares & heredit's th'rby granted & rel'ed either by Public Auction or Private Contract & eit togr or in lots or p'cels in such manner as they the sd John Clerk Thos Salmon Fredk St John & Philip Williams or the sur'vors or sur'vor of them or the h'rs or asss *{Page 23}* of such sur'vor with such consent or of such authy as afsd should think proper unto any p'son or p'sons who should be willing to become the purchr or purchrs th'of resp'ly for the most moy that could be got for the same if sold by Auctn & if sold by Private Cont' then for such price or prices as by them or him with such consent or of such authy as afsd should be though fit or reasonable & on paymt of the purchase monies for which the same heredit's & prem'es or any of them or any part th'of shod be sold convey & assure the sd undivided parts or shares & heredit's th'rby granted & rel'ed or such of them as shod be sold unto the purchr or purchrs & to his & their h'rs & asss or as he or they should lawfully direct or appt And for the p'pses afsd It was th'r'by declared & agreed by & between all the sd parties thereto that it should & might be lawful for the sd John Clerk Thos Salmon Fredk St John & Philip Williams & the sur'vors & sur'vor of them & the h'rs & asss of such sur'vor with such consent or of such authy as afsd to enter into sign & execute in their his or her names or name any contract or contracts for the sale of the sd parts or shares & heredit's th'rby granted & rel'ed or rel'ed of them or any part th'of to any p'son or p'sons who shod be willing to become the purchr or purchrs th'of or of any part th'of and to receive any sum or sums of money on the exec'on of such cont' or contts resp'ly or any of them by way of deposit & such contts or cont' afterwards to rescind or make void & such deposit money or any part th'of to return to the p'son or p'sons paying the same with int' if it shod be thought advisable so to do And it was th'rby declared & agreed that the rect & rects of the sd John Clerk Thos Salmon Fredk St John and Philip Williams & the sur'vors & sur'vor of them & the h'rs &

ass^s of such sur'vor sho^d be a good & sufficient discharge & discharges to the person or person paying *{Page 24}* such purchase money & deposit as afores^d for so much mo^y as sho^d be expressed in such receipt or receipts resp'ly & such person or persons sho^d not be answerable after any such rec' or rec^ts so given for the misapplic'on or nonapplic'on or in anywise concerned to see to the applic'on of the money for which such rec' or rec^ts should be given.

Declaration that all & every the sum & sums of money which sho^d arise by such sale or sales sho^d with all conv' speed be laid out & invested as th'rin mentioned.

And upon further trust after the death of the s^d Henry St John & Maria St John Mildmay as to for & concern^g the same stocks funds & securities th'inbefore directed or authorised to be purchased with the produce of the s^d freehold est^s for & to be paid or divided to or between or amongst all & every or any one or more child or children of the s^d int^d marr'e (other than & except an eldest or only son) at such age or ages days or times in such parts shares & proportions & under & subject to such limit'ons over such limit'ons over to befor the benefit of some or one of the same children other than & except as afores^d & in such manner as they the s^d Henry St John & Maria St John Mildmay during their joint lives should by any writ^g or writings with or with' power of rev'on & new apptm' to be by them sealed & delivered in the presence of & to be att^d by 2 or more credible wit^s or as the sur'vor of them sho^d by any Deed or Deeds Intrum' or Instrum^ts in writ^g exe'ted & att^d as afs^d or by his or her will or codicil exe'ted as th'rin ment^d direct or app' & in default of such dir'on apptm' or gift & as to all such part or parts of the s^d trust mo^y & securities whereof there sho^d be no such dir'on apptm' or gift the same to be divided bet^n such child^n (other than & except as afs^d) share & share alike the part or parts of such of them as sho^d be a son or sons to be paid or assigned or transferred to him or them at his or their age or *{Page 25}* ages of 21 years & of such of them as sho^d be a Daughter or Daughters at that age or day of marriage which should first happen after the decease of the surviving parent.

Proviso that notwithst^g the postponing of the paym' of the portion or portions of such Son or Sons who sho^d attain the s^d age during the lifetime of the s^d Henry St John or Maria St John Mildmay & of such Daughter or Daughters who should attain the s^d age or be married within that time until after the death of the sur'vor of the s^d H^y St John & Maria St John Mildmay All & every such portion & portions should be deemed vested int^ts in such Son or Sons Daughter or Daughters so as to be transmissable to their resp'ive representative notwithstand^g he she or they should die in the lifetime of the s^d H^y St John or Maria St John Mildmay.

Proviso for survivorship & accruer for maintenance & advancement.

Trusts as to monies in default of issue.

Power to Make partition.

Declaration that until the s^d Sales sho^d be made the rents issues and profits of the heredit's th'rby made saleable as afores^d sho^d from time to time belong to or be rec^d by the person or persons to whom the int' or dividends of the sect^s to be purchased with the monies to arise by such sales would belong & be payable in case the sales had taken place & the mo^y had been invested purs' to the dir'ons th'in contained.

Clause for the Indemnity of Trustees.

Proviso that if the s{^{d}} Jn{^{o}} Clerk Tho{^{s}} Salmon Fred{^{k}} St John & Philip Williams or any or ei{^{r}} of them or any future tr'ee or tr'ees to be appt{^{d}} in the place & stead of them or any or either of them as th'inafter ment{^{d}} sho{^{d}} die or be desirous to quit & be discharged from or become incapable to act in the trusts powers & auth{^{s}} th'rby in them reposed as afs{^{d}} at any time or times before the said trusts powers & auth{^{y}} sho{^{d}} be fully performed & executed or be discharge then & in such case & so often as the same should happen it sho{^{d}} be lawful for the s{^{d}} Henry St John & Maria St John Mildmay or the sur'vor of them & after the decease of both of them & the tr'ees or tr'ee for the time being to be appt{^{d}} in the room of them or any of them resp'ly by any writ{^{g}} or writ{^{gs}} under their his or her *{Page 26}* hands & seals or hand & seal att{^{d}} by 2 or more credible witn{^{s}} to nominate & app' and o{^{r}} p'son or p'sons to be trustee or trustees in place or stead of the tr'ees or tr'ee so dying or desir{^{g}} to be discharged or becom{^{g}} incapable to act as afs{^{d}} & that when & so often as any new tr'ee or tr'ees sho{^{d}} be nominated & appt{^{d}} as afs{^{d}} All & sing{^{r}} the trusts est{^{s}} lands & securities which sho{^{d}} be then legally vested in the tr'ee or tr'ees for the time being sho{^{d}} be conveyed assigned & made over so as to be legally & effectually vested in the surviv{^{g}} or continuing former tr'ee or tr'ees & such new tr'ee or tr'ees jointly or wholly in such new tr'ee or tr'ees as the case sho{^{d}} require to the uses upon the trusts & for the intents & p'pses by the now abst{^{g}} Ind're decl{^{d}} of & concern{^{g}} the same & that all & every such tr'ee or tr'ees sho{^{d}} & might in all things act in the management & exec'on of the trusts & p'pses th'in ment{^{d}} either alone or in conjunction with the surviv{^{g}} or contin{^{g}} tr'ee or tr'ees as the case might require as fully & effectually & sho{^{d}} have & be invested with all such & the same powers & auth{^{s}} to all intents & purposes whats{^{r}} as if they had been originally in & by the now abstract{^{g}} Ind're nominated & appt{^{d}} a tr'ee or tr'ees for the purposes therein aforesaid.

Covenant by the s{^{d}} Maria St John Mildmay that she had good right to convey for quiet enjoym' free from incumb's & for further assurance.

Executed by s{^{d}} Dame Jane St John Mildmay & Maria St John Mildmay & Henry St John & att{^{d}} by two witnesses.

There were 6 Children of the marr'e bet{^{n}} the s{^{d}} H{^{y}} St John Viscount Bolingbroke & Maria St John Mildmay & no more viz The Hon{^{ble}} Maria Jane Louisa St John (aftw'ds Mrs Kneller) The Hon{^{ble}} Anne Jane Charlotte St John (aft'wds Mrs Shaw) The Hon{^{ble}} Isabella Letitia St John The Hon{^{ble}} Emily Arabella St John (aft'wds Mrs Smith) The Hon{^{ble}} Henry St John now The Right Hon{^{ble}} Henry Mildmay Viscount Bolingbroke & The Hon{^{ble}} Spencer Mildmay St John since deceased.

{Page 27}

June 1824. The s{^{d}} Tho{^{s}} Salmon died.

5th Nov{^{r}} 1842. The s{^{d}} John Clerk died.

14th Oct{^{r}} 1843. The s{^{d}} Phillip Williams died.

19th Nov{^{r}} 1844. The s{^{d}} Fred{^{k}} St John died.

11th August 1841

Will of the s^d Fred^k St John Whereby after certⁿ specific devises & bequests th'in he gave & bequeathed unto Chas Geo Beauclere since dec'ed (in the sd will called Charles Beauclerk) & Thos Baverstock Merriman of Marlborough in the Co^y of Wilts Esqre (in the s^d Will called Thos Merriman) their ex'ors adm'ors & assigns.

All his monies in the funds ready monies & securities for money & all o^r his personal est^e & effects whats^r & whereso^r not th'inbefore specifically disposed of

Upon certⁿ trusts th'in declared.

All & sing^r the mess'es lands tenem^{ts} & heredit's & other real estates which were vested in him upon any trusts or by way of mortgage & which he had power to dispose of by that his will with their & every of their appurt's And all his est^e & int^{ts} th'in resp'ly.

Unto the s^d Chas Geo Beauclerk & Thos Baverstock Merriman their h'rs ex'ors adm'ors & ass^s accord^g to the nature & quality th'of resp'ly.

Upon trust to hold & dispose of the s^d trusts est^{es} in the manner in which the same ought accord^g to the trusts th'of to be held & disposed of & to convey the est^s in mortgage unto such p'son or p'sons or otherwise dispose of the same in such manner as by the rules of Law & Equity they or he ought to do.

And the s^d test'or appointed the s^d Chas Geo Bauclerk & Thomas Bavistock Merriman ex'ors of his s^d will.

Proved with 2 Codicils in the Prerogative Court *{Page 28}* of the Archbishop of Canterbury on the 10th Feby 1845 by both executors.

25th Decr 1845. The s^d Chas Geo Beauclerk died.

5th June 1847. The late Lady Bolingbroke died.

9th Octr 1851. The late Lord Bolingbroke died.

As to the accrued shares vested in the s^d Henry Mildmay Viscount Bolingbroke in lieu in tail of his mother the Lady Bolingbroke

6th March 1858

By Ind're of this date betⁿ The Right Honble H^y Mildmay Lord Viscount Bolingbroke & St John of the 1st part Sir Henry Bouverie Paulet St John Mildmay Bar' of the 2nd part & James Wickens Gent^m of the 3rd part.

Recit^g (amongst other things not relat^g to the estate comprised in this Abstract) the settlm' of the 27th & 28th Novr 1789.

And that since the date & exec'on th'of o^r heredit's than those compr^d th'in had been settled & assured upon or had otherwise become subject to such & the same uses trusts intents & p'pses & under & subject to such & the same powers prov'oes cond'ons & limit'ons as were th'rby declared of the prem'es thereby granted & rel'ed or in case of copyholds as near th'rto as the Rules of Law & Customs of the Manors of which they were resp'ly holden & the nature of the tenure & intervening circumstances would admit of.

And stat^g the Issue of the s^d marr'e bet^n the s^d Sir H^y Paulet St John Mildmay & Dame Jane St John Mildmay.

And recit^g that in contempl'on of the marr'e of the s^d Maria St John Mildmay with the Honble St John af'rwds Lord Viscount Bolingbroke in the year 1812 All the orig^l one 13th share of the s^d Maria St John Mildmay of & in the s^d heredit's in the co^y of Southampton was settled & assured by the s^d Maria St John Mildmay with the concurrence of the s^d Dame Jane St *{Page 29}* John Mildmay & with the privity of the s^d Henry St John discharged from the estate tail of the s^d Maria St John Mildmay to the use of trustees upon cert^n trusts by way of Settlement on the s^d marriage.

And recit^g that the s^d Chas Wm Paulet St John Mildmay John Francis St John Mildmay Gualtier St John Mildmay Aug^s Tucker St John Mildmay Hugh Cornwall St John Mildmay & Letitia St John Mildmay all died without issue & with' having done any act to bar their resp'ive est^s tail in their resp'ive shares of & in the s^d heredit's & prem'es wh'rby their resp'ive shares ultimately devolved under the limit'ons afs^d by way of accruer in 7 shares upon the surviv^g issue inheritable under the entail created by way of cross rem^rs as aforesaid.

And recit^g that the s^d Maria St John Mildmay died on or about the [blank space] day of dec^r 1836 leav^g the s^d H^y Mildmay Lord Viscount Bolingbroke her eldest son & heir at Law her surviv^g but with' hav^g barred her est^e tail on rem^r in the shares which accrued upon the resp'ive deaths with' issue of her s^d last ment^d Brothers & Sisters.

And that the s^d H^y Lord Viscount Bolingbroke the father of the s^d H^y Mildmay Lord Viscount Bolingbroke died on or about the 1st day of Octr 1851.

And that the s^d Dame Jane St John Mildmay died on or about the 6th day of May 1857 intestate as to real estate held by her as trustee leaving her Grandson the s^d Sir H^y Bouverie Paulet St John Mildmay her heir at Law in whom the legal estate in the freehold heredit's which by an Ind're of Enfranchisem' of the 24th day of Aug' 1804 th'inbefore recited were conveyed to the s^d Sir H^y Paulet St John Mildmay had become vested.

And recit^g that the s^d H^y Mildmay Viscount Bolingbroke had attained his age of 21 years & being desirous of barring all est^s tail in all heredit's of which he was tenant in tail & all rem^rs over the s^d Sir H^y Bouverie Paulet St John Mildmay had at his request agreed to concur in convey^g the s^d Viscount Bolingbroke's share of the s^d freehold heredit's in manner *{Page 30}* thereinafter appearing.

It is witn'ed that in order to defeat all est^s tail at law & in equity as to heredit's of freehold tenure of the s^d H^y Mildmay Lord Viscount Bolingbroke & in equity as to heredit's of copyhold tenure of the s^d H^y Mildmay Lord Viscount Bolingbroke in the parts or shares original and accruer which devolved on the s^d Maria St John Mildmay or on the said H^y Mildmay Lord Viscount Bolingbroke upon the resp'ive deaths of the s^d Chas Wm Paulet St John Mildmay John Francis St John Mildmay Gualtier St John Mildmay Aug^s Tucker St John Mildmay Hugh Cornwall St John Mildmay & Letitia St John Mildmay or any of them as afs^d & in all o^r if any parts or shares of the entirety of any manors & other heredit's in the sev^l Counties of Southampton & Middlesex resp'ly or either of them or elsewhere to which the s^d H^y Mildmay Lord Viscount Bolingbroke was entitled by any means whatsoever for an estate in tail & all est^s rights interests & powers to take effect after the determin'on or in defeasance of such est^s tail the s^d H^y Mildmay Lord Viscount Bolingbroke Did thereby grant & convey unto the s^d Ja^s Wickens & his heir

All & sing^r the undiv^d part or share parts or shares of & in the s^d several manors & heredit's in the several Counties of Southampton and Middlesex resp'ly or elsewhere (including such heredit's as were copyhold or customary holden of the Manor of Marwell in the Co^y of Southampton afs^d) which were comprised in or rel'ed & assured or covenanted to be settled & assured by the s^d Ind're of the 28th day of Novr 1789 or which were then subject to the limit'ons th'of or which were by any acts & deeds & means made subject to the same or the like limit'ons And all o^r the heredit's whether freehold or copyhold or customary in the Counties of Southampton & Middlesex resp'ly or ei^r of them or elsewhere in England to which the s^d H^y Mildmay Lord Viscount Bolingbroke was either at Law or in equity entitled for any estate tail with their rights members & appurtenances.

{Page 31}

And all the Estate &^{c}.

To hold the s^d parts & shares heredit's & prem'es with their appurt's unto the s^d James Wickens & his h'rs freed & discharged from all est^s tail of the s^d H^y Mildmay Lord Viscount Bolingbroke & from all est^s rights int' and powers subsequent to or in defeasance of the s^d estates tail subj' nev^s to their liability to make up a proportionate part or share or proportionate parts or shares of the sev^l sums of mo^y & int' resp'ly charged th'ron in priority to such est^e in tail & to the resp'ive est^s terms & trusts respectively created therein for secur^g the paym' of the s^d sums of mo^y & interest.

To the use of the s^d H^y Mildmay Lord Viscount Bolingbroke his h'rs & ass^s for ever.

And the s^d H^y Mildmay Lord Viscount Bolingbroke did thereby declare that if the sho^d die leav^g a Widow she sho^d not be entitled to dower or freebench out of or in respect of the s^d heredit's.

Executed by the s^d H^y Mildmay Viscount Bolingbroke & Sir Henry Bouverie Paulet St John Mildmay & attested.

Inrolled.

As to the share to which Judith Anne St John Mildmay (afterwards Lady Radnor) became entitled of the above Estates

20th May 1814

By Ind're of Barg^n & Sale of this date made bet^n the said Dame Jane St John Mildmay & Anne Judith St John Mildmay of the 1st part the s^d Wm Pleydell Bouverie Viscount Folkestone of the 2nd part the s^d Wm Bray of the 3rd part the s^d Augustus Warren of the 4th & Richd White th'in descr^d of the 5th part.

Recit^g the s^d Ind're of 27th & 28th Novr 1789.

And recit^g that there were 13 Children of the s^d Dame Jane St John Mildmay by the s^d Sir Henry Paulet St John Mildmay (besides her two eldest Sons) of which s^d 13 Children the said Anne Judith St John Mildmay was one.

{Page 32}

And recit^g that a marr'e had been agreed upon & was intended shortly to be had bet^n S^d Wm Pleydell Bouverie Viscount Folkestone & Anne Judith St John Mildmay & that upon the treaty for s^d int^d marr'e it was agreed that s^d Viscount Folkestone should make a provision by way of pin mo^y & jointure for s^d Anne Judith St John Mildmay & that in cons'on th'of she sho^d suffer a recovery of all & every her share or shares in the afs^d manors & other heredit's as well present as future expectant or reversion^y & sho^d settle & assure such share or shares to such uses for the benefit of Vis' Folkstone as th'in mentioned.

And recit^g that in purs'ce of s^d agreem' of Viscount Folkestone he had previously to the exec'on of the abst^g Ind're made such provision by way of pin money & jointure for s^d Anne Judith St John Mildmay as was agreed upon between the parties.

And recit^g that in order to enable s^d Judith Anne St John Mildmay to suffer such Recovery as afs^d she had applied to & requested s^d Dame Jane St John Mildmay to execute such conveyance as th'inaf^r expressed which she had accordingly agreed to.

It was witn'ed that for docking barring & extinguish^g all estates tail of her life s^d Anne Judith St John Mildmay & all rem^{rs} & rev'ons th'rupon of & in the manors & heredit's th'in described & for settling the same to the uses th'in desc^d & in cons'on of 10^s/ to the s^d Dame Jane St John Mildmay p^d by the s^d Wm Bray (the rec' &^{c}) She the s^d Dame Jane St John Mildmay Did grant barg^n sell & confirm unto the s^d Wm Bray & his ass^s dur^g the joint lives of him & of the s^d Dame Jane St John Mildmay.

All those the manors &^{c} in the s^d Co^y of Southampton by the descript^n in the s^d abst^d Ind're of 27th & 28th days of Novr 1789 And also all other manors mess'es lands tenem^{ts} & heredit's situate in the s^d Parishes of Twyford & Owslebury or elsewhere in the s^d Co^y of Southampton (if any such there were) ment^d & comprised in the s^d Lease & Rel'e of 27th & 28th Novr 1789.

And all houses &^{c}.

{Page 33}

And the Rev'on &ᶜ.

And all the Estate &ᶜ.

Saving & reservᵍ to sᵈ Dame Jane St John Mildmay her ex'ors adm'ors & assˢ all sums of money to which she was in anywise entitled eiʳ in her own right or as ex'trix of her sᵈ dec'ed Husband & which were charged upon the sᵈ prem'es or any part thereof.

To hold the sᵈ Manors &ᶜ unto sᵈ Wᵐ Bray & his assˢ.

To the use of the sᵈ Wᵐ Bray & his assˢ durᵍ the joint lives of the sᵈ Wᵐ Bray & sᵈ Dame Jane St John Mildmay .

To the intent that the sᵈ Wᵐ Bray might become tenant of the freehold in order that a Common Recovery might be suffered th'of wh'in the sᵈ Augˢ Warren might be Demand' the sᵈ Wᵐ Bray tenant & the sᵈ Anne Judith St John Mildmay Vouchee to vouch the Common Vouchee.

Decl'on that sᵈ Recovery when so suffered shoᵈ be & enure.

To the uses that were the subsistᵍ in the sᵈ prem'es until the sᵈ marr'e & after the solemnis'on thereof.

To the use of the sᵈ Dame Jane St John Mildmay & her assˢ for her life sans waste with such powers &ᶜ & after her decease.

Then as to all & every the present & immediate & also all every the future expectant eventual reversᵍ share or shares right title or int' of the sᵈ J. A. St John Mildmay.

To such uses &ᶜ as the sᵈ Wᵐ Pleydell Bouverie Viscount Folkston by deed sealed & delivered in the presence of and attested by 2 or more credible witnesses shoᵈ from time to time direct or appoint…Remʳ

To the use of the sᵈ Wᵐ Pleydell Bouverie Visc' Folkstone & his assigns…Remʳ

To the use of the sᵈ Rᵈ White & his h'rs durᵍ the life of the sᵈ Wᵐ Pleydell Bouverie Viscount Folkstone in bar of dower…Remʳ

To the use of the h'rs & assˢ of the sᵈ Wᵐ Pleydell Bouverie Visc' Folkstone for ever.

{Page 34}

Exe'ted by the s^d Dame Jane St John Mildmay & Anne Judith St John Mildmay & att^d by 2 witn^s Also by the s^d Wm Bray & Aug^s Warren Junr & att^d by 1 witness.

Inrolled in the Court of Common Pleas Easter Term 54 Geo 3 Roll 74.

Easter Term 54th George 3rd Southampton

Exemplification of Recovery wh'in the s^d Aug^s Warren Junr was Demandant the s^d Wm Bray tenant & the s^d Anne Judith St John Mildmay Vouchee of

The Manors of Twyford & Marwell otherwise Old Marwell with the appurt's & 30 mess'es 3 dovehouses one water corn mill 80 gardens 1,500 acres of land 300 acres of meadow 300 acres of pasture 400 acres of wood 2000 acres of furze & heath & 40^s/ rent common of pasture &^c with the appurt's in Shawford Twyford & Marwell or o'rwise Old Marwell & in the Parishes of Twyford and Owslebury.

23rd & 24th May 1814

By Ind're of Lease & of Apptm' & Release the latter made bet^n the Right Honble Jacob Earl of Radnor Viscount Folkstone Baron of Longford in the Co^y of Wilts, Baron Pleydell Bouverie of Coleshill in the Co^y of Berks & Baronet & The Right Honble Wm Pleydell Bouverie commonly called Viscount Folkstone Eldest Son & heir apparent of the s^d Jacob Earl of Radnor of the 1st part the s^d Anne Jane St John Mildmay of the 2nd part the Right Honble Cropley Earl of Shaftesbury & Sir Philip Hales of Brymore in the County of Somerset Bart' of the 3rd part Chas H^y Bouverie of Betchworth in the Co^y of Surrey Esqre & Sir H^y St John Carew St John Mildmay of Dogmersfield Park in the Co^y of Southampton Bart' of the 4th part The Right Honble Charles Earl of Romney & John Clerk of Shawford House in the s^d Co^y of Southampton Esqre of the 5th part & The Honble P. P. Bouverie of Craven Street in the County of Middlesex & Paulet St John Mildmay of Dogmersfield Park afs^d Esqre of the 6th part.

{Page 35}

After recit^g (inter alia) that a marr'e had been agreed upon & was int^d to be shortly solemn^d bet^n the s^d Wm Viscount Folkstone & Anne J. St John Mildmay.

And recit^g that the s^d Anne J. St John Mildmay was entitled ei^r in poss'on or in rem^r or expectancy to cert^n real estates of considerable value & she was also entitled in poss'on to certain shares of the Parliamentary Stocks or Public Funds of Great Britain & she was under the Will of Judith Smith dated the [Blank space] day of [Blank space] also entitled in poss'on to 1/7th Share of the monies to arise from the sale of an estate in the Island of Antigua directed to be sold by the s^d Judith Smith but which sale had not then taken place.

And recit^g that upon the treaty for the marriage it was agreed that the s^d Jacob Earl of Radnor & Wm Viscount Folkstone should appoint & convey certain of the family est^s of the Earl of Radnor To the uses & upon the trusts th'in declared & that in cons'on th'of the s^d Anne Judith St John Mildmay sho^d forthwith convey or o'rwise assure all such part of the real est^e to which she was entitled in poss'on as afs^d & not in rem^r or expectancy to him the s^d Wm Viscount Folkstone & his h'rs for his & their own absolute use & benefit & that she should also forthwith convey or o'rwise assure all such part of the real est^e to which she was entitled in rem^r or expectancy & not in poss'on as afs^d to him the s^d Viscount & his h'rs upon this express condition nev^s that he the said Viscount sho^d immed^{ly} aftw'ds convey the same To the uses upon the trusts & in manner th'inaf^r ment^d & that all & sing^r the s^d shares of the s^d Ann Judith St John Mildmay in the afs^d Parliamentary Stocks or Public Funds of Great Britain sho^d be permitted to vest in the s^d Wm Vis' Folkestone by the rights of marriage & that she sho^d ass^n her 1/7th share in the monies to arise from the sale of the s^d estates in the Island of Antigua so directed to be sold as afs^d unto the s^d Viscount for his absolute use & benefit.

And recit^g that in part performance of the s^d Agreement the s^d Ann Judith St John Mildmay had immed'ly previously *{Page 36}* to the exec'on of the now abst^g Ind're converted or otherwise assured all the heredit's & real est^e to which she was so entit^d in poss'on & not in rev'on rem^r or expectancy as afs^d unto the s^d Viscount & his h'rs for his & their own use & benefit as he the s^d Viscount did th'rby ackn'ge & in further performance of the s^d agreem' the s^d Anne J. St John Mildmay had also at or immed'ly before the exec'on of the now abst^g Ind're conveyed or o'rwise assured all the heredit's & real est^e to which she was so entitled in rem^r or expectancy & not in poss'on as afs^d unto the s^d Viscount & his heirs Nev^s to be by him forthwith conveyed to the uses upon the trusts & in the manner th'inaf^r ment^d & expressed.

It is witn'ed that in cons'on of the prem'es & in pursuance of the s^d Agreem' on the part of the s^d Earl of Radnor & Viscount Folkestone & in cons'on of the s^d int^d marr'e The s^d Earl & Viscount Did appoint & convey

Certain Estates belong^g to the s^d Earl of Radnor & Viscount Folkestone.

To the s^d Earl of Shaftsbury & Sir Philip Hales heir & ass^s

To such uses as were in s^d heredit's immediately previously to the exec'on of the Ind're now being abst^d until such marr'e but s^d Viscount Folkestone & Anne J. St John Mildmay should be solemnised and after the solemnis'on therof.

To the use of other tr'ees for 99 years sans waste

In trust to secure pin money & after the determin'on of s^d term & in the meantime subject th'rto & to the trust thereof.

To the use that s^d Anne J. St John Mildmay might receive a jointure & subject as afs^d the apptm' & convey'ce th'rby made should enure & the heredit's remain.

To the use of tr'ees for 100 years sans waste

In trust to secure jointure & after the determin'on of s^d term & subject th'rto & to the trusts thereof.

To the uses of o[r] tr'ees for 200 years from the death of s[d] W[m] Viscount Folkestone in case he should die *{Page 37}* in the lifetime of the s[d] Earl of Radnor & after the expir'on of s[d] term & subject thereto & to the trusts th'of.

To the use of the s[d] Earl of Radnor & his ass[s] for his life sans waste…Rem[r]

To the use of tr'ees during the life of s[d] Earl to preserve contingent remainders…Rem[r]

To the use of s[d] W[m] Pleydell Bouverie Vis' Folkestone & his ass[s] for life sans waste…Rem[r]

To the use of tr'ees during the life of s[d] Viscount Folkestone to preserve contingent remainders with divers remainders over.

And it is moreover witn'ed that with respect to such part of the Real Est[s] of the s[d] Anne J. St John Mildmay to which previously to the exec'on of the now abst[g] Ind're she was so entitled in rem[r] or expectancy & not in poss'on as afs[d] & which immed'ly previous to the date th'of had been so conveyed to the s[d] W[m] Viscount Folkestone & his h'rs as th'inbef was ment[d] & rec[d] He the said Viscount did th'rby for himself his heirs ex'ors adm'ors & ass[s] cov' promise & agree with & to the s[d] Cropley Earl of Shaftsbury & Sir Philip Hales their ex'ors adm'ors & ass[s] that the s[d] Viscount would immed'ly after the exec'on of the now abst[g] Ind're well & effectually convey & assure all such part of the real estate of the s[d] Anne Judith St John Mildmay as lastly th'inbefore was expressed unto & to the use of the s[d] Cropley Earl of Shaftsbury & Sir Philip Hales their h'rs & ass[s] for ever

Upon trust to sell the same either by Public Auction or Private Contract at such convenient time or times with such consent as in the s[d] convey[ce] or assurance or convey'ces or assurances sho[d] be expressed & to give rec[ts] for the money to arise from such sale or sales & to stand poss'ed of the mo[y] which sho[d] arise therefrom & the int' & accumul'ons th'of.

Upon trust in the first place to pay off any charges or incumb's which might then affect the s[d] Manors & o[r] heredit's th'inbef ment[d] to be th'rby appointed & rel'ed or any of them & to stand poss'ed of the surplus of the *{Page 38}* same money (if any) upon the same trusts & for the same intents & purposes in all respects as are th'inbefore expressed & declared of & concern[g] the monies which should arise & be produced from the sale of all or any part of the manors & o[r] heredit's th'rby appointed & released & which should be sold & disposed of in exercise of the power of sale th'inbef expr[d] & contained.

And that in the meantime & until such convey'ce or assurance sho[d] be executed by the s[d] W[m] Viscount Folkestone as afs[d] he the s[d] Viscount & his heirs should & would stand & be seized of the s[d] last ment[d] est[s] & of the rents issues & profits thereof upon the same trusts as are th'inbefore declared of the monies which should arise or be produced from the sale of the same estates.

Declaration that the receipt or receipts in writ[g] of the s[d] sev[l] tr'ees or tr'ee for the time being acting under or by virtue of the now abst[g] Ind're for any sum or sums of money payable to them or him by virtue of the same should be a good & sufficient discharge or good and sufficient discharges for such monies resp'ly & that the person or persons paying such sum or sums of money & taking such rec' or rect[s] for the same sho[d] not aft'wrds be answerable for any loss misapplic'on or nonapplic'on or be in anywise bound or concerned to see to the applic'on of the monies therein ment^d & acknowledged to be received.

Proviso that if the sev^l tr'ees th'rby appointed or any of them their or any of their heirs ex'ors adm'ors or ass^s or any future tr'ees to be appt^d as th'in ment^d their or any of their h'rs ex'ors adm'ors or ass^s should die or desire to be discharged or refuse or be incapable to act in the trusts or powers th'rby in them reposed before the s^d trusts sho^d be exe'ted it sho^d be lawful for the s^d Jacob Earl of Radnor dur^g his life & after his decease for the s^d Viscount Folkstone & the sev^l other persons to whom the s^d Manors & heredit's were th'rby or by the powers th'rby created sho^d be th'inaf^r limited when in poss'on of the s^d heredit's be entitled to the rents & profits th'of being of full age & for the Guardian or Guardians of any such person as afs^d being a minor during such minority by writ^g under hand & seal from time to time to nominate substitute or app^r any o^r person or person to be a tr'ee or tr'ees in their place & that on every such apptm^r the s^d heredit's th'rby appt^d & all the trust est^{es} & prem'es sho^d be with all convenient speed *{Page 39}* conveyed & transferred in such manner & so as that the same wo^d be legally vested in the surviv^g or cont^g tr'ee & tr'ees such new or o^r tr'ee or tr'ees or if there sho^d be no contin^g tr'ee or tr'ees then in such new tr'ees only to the same uses & upon the same trusts as were th'inbefore declared concern^g the same heredit's trusts est^s & prem'es resp'ly the tr'ee or tr'ees whereof sho^d so die be discharged from or refuse or be incapable to act or such of them as sho^d be then subsist^g or capable of taking effect And it was agr^d that such new tr'ee or tr'ees sho^d in all things act in the execution of the afores^d trusts ei^r jointly with any continuing tr'ee or tr'ees or solely as afs^d as fully & effectually & with the same powers of consent approb'on descret^n calling in laying out & invest^g giv^g rec^s & disch^s to purch^{rs} m'gees & all other powers as if he or they had been originally appt^d a tr'ee or tr'ees by the now abst^g Indenture.

Executed by Lords Radnor & Folkestone & Judith St John Mildmay Charles H^y Bouverie Philip Pleydell Bouverie & Paulet St John Mildmay and att^d by 2 witn^s & by the Earl of Shaftsbury & att^d by one witness.

Inrolled in the Common Pleas at Westminster Easter Term 58 Geo 3rd Roll 149.

22nd & 23rd August 1825

By Ind'res of Lease & Release indorsed upon the last abst^d Ind're of Settlem' the Release made bet^n the s^d Jacob Earl of Radnor of the 1st part the s^d Wm Pleydell Bouverie Viscount Folkstone of the 2nd part the s^d Cropley Earl of Shaftsbury of the 3rd part Richd White of Essex Street Strand in the Parish of St Clement Danes in the Co^y of Middlesex Gent^n of the 4th part & the s^d Cropley Earl of Shaftsbury & Robt Marsham of the Inner Temple London Barrister at Law of the 5th part.

Recit^g that the marr'e bet^n s^d Viscount Folkstone & Anne Judith St John Mildmay had been duly solemnised.

And recit^g the death of Sir Philip Hales in the year 1824 and that s^d Jacob Earl of Radnor with the consent & approb'on of s^d Viscount Folkstone was desirous of appoint^g the s^d Robt Marsham a tr'ee in the place of the s^d Sir Philip Hales dec'ed for the p'pses for which under last abst^d Ind're of Rel'e S^d Sir Philip *{Page 40}* Hales was a trustee jointly with the s^d Cropley Earl of Shaftsbury

It is witn'ed that in consequence of the death of the s^d Sir Philip Hales in pursuance & exercise of the power & auth^y given to the s^d Jacob Earl of Radnor by the last ment^d Ind're the s^d Jacob Earl of Radnor by the last ment^d Ind're the s^d Jacob Earl of Radnor with the approb'on of the s^d Pleydell Bouverie Viscount Folkestone did nominate substitute & app' the s^d Rob' Marsham to be a tr'ee in the place or stead of Sir Philip Hales to the intent that s^d Robert Marsham by virtue of such apptm' might in conjunction with s^d Cropley Earl of Shaftsbury in all things act & assist in the exec'on of the trusts &^{c} by the last mentioned Ind're limited & declared to all intents & p'pses as he might have done if he had been originally named a trustee by the same Ind're jointly with s^d Cropley Earl of Shaftsbury.

And it is fur^r witn'ed that s^d Cropley Earl of Shaftsbury in cons'on of 10^s/ to him p^d by s^d Richd White did (at the request & by the dir'on of s^d Jacob Earl of Radnor & Wm Viscount Folkestone) grant^n sell release & convey unto s^d R^d White (in the actual poss'on &^{c}) & his heirs and assigns.

All & sing^r the Castle, Hundreds, Royalty, Barony, Manors, Lands & o^r the freehold heredit's & prem'es comprised in & appt^d granted & rel'ed by the last abst^d Ind're of Release.

And the Rev'on &^{c}.

And all the Estate &^{c}.

To hold the same unto & to the use of the s^d Richd White his heirs & assigns.

In trust by certain Ind'res of Lease & Release next h'inaf^r abst^d to convey & assure the s^d heredit's unto said Cropley Earl of Shaftsbury & Rob' Marsham their heirs & ass^s to the use of the last abst^d Indenture.

Executed by Lords Radnor Folkestone and Shaftsbury & att^d by 2 witn^s & by s^d Richd White & att^d by 1 witness.

24th & 25th August 1825

By Ind'res of Lease & Release (also endorsed on the s^d last abst^d Ind're of Rel'e & Settlem') the Rel'e made bet^n the s^d R^d White of the one part & the s^d Cropley Earl of Shaftsbury & Rob' Marsham of the o^r part

{Page 41}

It is Witn'ed that the s^d Richd White in purs'ce of the trust reposed in him by last abst^d Ind're & in cons'on of 5^s/ to him p^d by the s^d Cropley Earl of Shaftsbury & Rob' Marsham did grant bargain sell alien & release unto s^d Cropley Earl of Shaftsbury & Rob' Marsham in the poss'on &^{c} & their heirs & assigns.

All & Sing^r the Castle Hundred Royalty Barony Manors Farms Lands & other freehold heredit's & premises comprised in last abst^d Ind're of Release with the appurt's.

And the Rev'on &ᶜ.

And all the Estates &ᶜ.

To hold the same unto said Cropley Earl of Shaftsbury & Robᵗ Marsham & their heirs for all such estate as was then vested in sᵈ Richᵈ White.

To the uses & upon & for the trusts &ᶜ subject to which the same prem'es would stand limited to in case last abstᵈ Ind're of Release had not been executed & the name of the sᵈ Robᵗ Marsham had in sᵈ Ind're of Settlem' of 24ᵗʰ May 1814 been inserted instead of the name of the sᵈ Philip Hales deceased.

Cov' by sᵈ Richᵈ White that he had done no act to incumber.

Executed by sᵈ Richᵈ White & Earl of Shaftsbury & attested.

Jacob Earl of Radnor died in January 1828 leavᵍ Ann Countess of Radnor his Widow surviving him who died in Octʳ 1829.

December 1857 (Number One)

By Ind're endorsed on the before abstᵈ Ind're of 24ᵗʰ May 1814 & made betⁿ the sᵈ Wᵐ Pleydell Earl of Radnor of the 1ˢᵗ part the sᵈ Philip Pleydell Bouverie the younger of the 2ⁿᵈ part the sᵈ Robᵗ Marsham of the 3ʳᵈ part Hʸ Tylee of Essex Street Strand in the Coʸ of Middlesex of the 4ᵗʰ part & the sᵈ Philip Pleydell Bouverie the youʳ & Robᵗ Marsham of the 5ᵗʰ part.

Recitᵍ that Ann Judith Countess of Radnor died in the year.

And that sᵈ Cropley Earl of Shaftsbury died in the same year.

{Page 42}

And recitᵍ that the sᵈ Wᵐ Earl of Radnor was desirous of apptᵍ the sᵈ Philip Pleydell Bouverie the youʳ to be a tr'ee in the place of the sᵈ Cropley late Earl of Shaftsbury deceased for the p'pses for which under the within written Ind're the sᵈ Cropley late Earl of Shaftsbury was a tr'ee jointly with the within named Sir Philip Hales or such of the same purposes as were then subsisting & capable of taking effect.

It is witn'ed that the sᵈ Wᵐ Earl of Radnor for effectuating the sᵈ desire in this behalf & in pursuance & exercise of the powers & authʸ given to him by the sᵈ Ind're of the 24ᵗʰ May 1814 and of every or any other power in anywise enabling him in this behalf Did by the now abstᵍ writing under his hand & seal nominate substitute & appoint the sᵈ Philip Pleydell Bouverie the youʳ to be a tr'ee in the place or stead of the sᵈ Cropley late Earl of Shaftsbury dec'ed for the p'pses for which the sᵈ Cropley late Earl of Shaftsbury was by the within written Ind're appt^d a tr'ee jointly with the s^d Sir Philip Hales or such of the same purposes as are now subsist^g or capable of taking effect.

And it is fur^r witn'ed that in purs'ce of the direction in that behalf in the s^d Ind're of the 24th May 1814 contained & in cons'on of the prem'es the s^d Rob' Marsham at the request & by the dir'on of the s^d Wm Earl of Radnor Did grant & convey unto the s^d H^y Tylee & his heirs

All & Sing^r the Castle, Hundreds, Royalty, Barony Manors Farms Lands & other freehold heredit's & prem'es comprised in & appt^d & released by the s^d Ind're of the 24th May 1814 except such of the same heredit's as had been sold or conveyed away in exchange & also by way of conveyance & not of exception all & singular the heredit's purchased or acquired in exchange since the date of the last mentioned Ind're in pursuance of powers for such p'pses in the same Ind're contained or the trusts of the will of the s^d Jacob late Earl of Radnor or o'rwise howsoever & now vested in the s^d Rob' Marsham as a tr'ee under the s^d Ind're of the 24th May 1814 & the above abst^d Ind'res of the 22nd 23rd 24th & 25th *{Page 43}* days of Aug' 1825 or any of them And all & sing^r other if any the heredit's vested in the s^d Rob' Marsham as such tr'ee as afs^d with their rights casements & appurt's.

And all the Estate &^{c}.

To hold the same with the appurt's unto & to the use of the s^d H^y Tylee his heirs & assigns for ever.

To the intent that the s^d H^y Tylee might by the Ind're next th'runder written & intended to be executed immed'ly after the execution of the now abst^g Ind're grant & convey the same heredit's & prem'es unto the s^d Philip Pleydell Bouverie the you^r & Rob' Marsham their h'rs & assigns.

To the uses upon & for the trusts intents & purposes & with under & subject to the powers provisos agreements & decl'ons to for upon with under & subject to which the same heredit's & premises would now under & by virtue of the s^d Ind're of the 24th May 1814 stand & be limited or subject in case the now abst^g Ind're & the above abst^d Ind'res of the 22nd & 23rd 24th & 25th days of Aug' 1825 had not been made & exe'ted & the s^d Philip Pleydell Bouverie the you^r & Rob' Marsham resp'ly had been originally made parties to the s^d Ind're of the 24th May 1814 & the Lease for a year whereon the same is grounded instead of the s^d Cropley late Earl of Shaftsbury & the s^d Sir Philip Hales resp'ly & accordingly the names of the s^d Philip Pleydell Bouverie the younger & Rob' Marsham resp'ly had in the s^d last ment^d Ind're & the Lease for a tear whereon the same is grounded been inserted throughout instead of the names of the s^d Cropley late Earl of Shaftsbury & Sir Philip Hales.

Cov' by Rob Marsham that he had not incumbered.

Duly exe'ted & attested.

December 1857 (Number 2)

By Ind're also endorsed on the s^d Ind're of the 24th of May 1814 & made bet^n the s^d H^y Tylee of the one part & the s^d Sir Philip Pleydell Bouverie the younger & Rob' Marsham of the o^r part.

{Page 44}

It is witn'ed that the s^d H^y Tylee in purs'ce of the trust reposed in him by the lastly recited Ind're did by the now abst^g Ind're grant & convey unto the s^d Philip Pleydell Bouverie & Rob' Marsham & their heirs & assigns.

All & Sing^r the Castle, Hundreds, Royalty, Barony, Manors, Farms, Lands & o^r the freehold heredit's & prem'es comprised in & conveyed & assured by the s^d lastly above abst^d Ind're with the rights members & appurt's.

And all the Estate &^c.

To hold the same with the appurt's unto the s^d Philip Pleydell Bouverie the you^r & Rob' Marsham & their heirs for all such estate as is now vested in the said Henry Tylee.

To the uses upon & for the trusts intents & p'pses & with under & subject to the powers prov'oes agreem^ts & decl'ons to for upon with under & subject to which the same heredit's & prem'es would now under & by virtue of the s^d Ind're of the 24th day of May 1814 stand & be limited or subject in case the now abst^g Ind're & the above abst^d Ind'res of the 22nd 23rd 24th & 25th days of Jany 1825 & of even date herewith had not been made & executed & the s^d Philip Pleydell Bouverie the younger & Robert Marsham resp'ly had been originally made parties to the s^d Ind're of the 24th day of May 1814 & the Lease for a year whereon the same is grounded instead of the s^d Cropley late Earl of Shaftsbury & Sir Philip Hales resp'ly & accordingly the names of the s^d Philip Pleydell Bouverie the younger & Rob' Marsham resp'ly had in the s^d Ind're of the 24th May 1814 & the Lease for a year whereon the same is grounded been inserted throughout instead of the names of the s^d Cropley late Earl of Shaftsbury & Sir Philip Hales.

Executed & att^d.

December 1857 (Number 3)

By Ind're endorsed on the h'inbefore abst^d Ind're of the 20th May *{Page 45}* 1814 made bet^n the s^d Wm Earl of Radnor of the one part & the said Philip Pleydell Bouverie the you^r & Rob' Marsham of the other part.

Recit^g the abst^d Recovery suffered in or as of Easter Term in the 54 Geo 3rd in the Co^y of Southampton.

And recit^g the above abst^d Ind're of the 24th of May 1814 so far as the same relates to such part of the real estates of the s^d Anne Judith Countess of Radnor to which previously to the execution of the Ind're now in recital she was entitled in rem^r or expectancy & not in possession.

And recit^g that sev^l of the 13 younger Children of the s^d Dame Jane St John Mildmay by the s^d Sir Henry St John Mildmay died without issue & without having barred the estates tail limited to them.

And recit^g the death of the s^d Philip Hales.

And recit[g] the above abst[d] Ind're of the 22nd day of Aug' 1825 whereby the s[d] Rob' Marsham was duly appt[d] a tr'ee of the s[d] Ind're of Settlement in his place.

And recit[g] that the s[d] Dame Jane St John Mildmay died in the year 1857.

And that the s[d] Ann Judith Countess of Radnor & Cropley Earl of Shaftsbury died resp'ly in the year 1857.

And recit[g] the above abst[d] Ind're whereby the s[d] Philip Bouverie the younger was duly appointed a tr'ee of the s[d] Ind're of Settlement of the 24th day of May 1814 in the place of the S[d] Cropley late Earl of Shaftsbury.

And recit[g] that no convey[ce] or assurance in pursuance of the s[d] recited cov' in this behalf in the s[d] Ind're of Settlem' contained had been made by the s[d] W[m] Earl of Radnor of the shares which by the s[d] first Ind're of the 24th day of May 1814 & the s[d] Recovery suffered in purs'ce th'of were cov[d] to or to the uses in favour of the s[d] W[m] Earl of Radnor of & in the manors mess'es lands & herem[ts] described or referred to and which same shares was previously to the exec'on of the same Ind're & Recovery part of the real est[e] of the s[d] Anne Judith Countess of Radnor & as such were or were intended in the s[d] recited cov' for the convey'ce & assurance by the s[d] William Earl of Shaftsbury & Sir Philip Hales their heirs & ass[s] of the part to *{Page 46}* which previously to the execution of the s[d] Ind're of Settlem' she the s[d] Anne Judith Countess of Radnor was entitled in remainder or expectancy & which immed'ly to the date thereof had been conveyed to the s[d] real estate of the s[d] Anne Judith Countess of Radnor.

It is witn'ed that in purs'ce of the s[d] recited cov' in this behalf in the s[d] Ind're of Settlem' contained & in cons'on of the premises

The s[d] W[m] Earl of Radnor in exercise & exec'on of the power or auth[y] to him given or limited by the s[d] first h'inbefore abst[d] Ind're of the 20th May 1814 & the Recovery suffered in pursuance th'of & of all other powers or authorities in anywise enabling him in this behalf Did direct limit & appoint that

All & Sing[r] the share h'inaf[r] expr[d] to be granted of & in the manors & heredit's th'inafter described or referred to with their rights members & appurt's sho[d] thenceforth remain & be (subj' nev[s] as th'inaf[r] mentioned.

To the use of P.P. Bouverie the you[r] & Rob' Marsham their heirs & assigns.

Upon & for the trusts intents p'pses & with under & subject to the powers prov'oes & decl'ons thinaf[r] expr[d] & decl[d] or referred to concerning the same.

And it is also witn'ed that in fur[r] pursuance of the s[d] rec[d] cov' in this behalf the s[d] W[m] Earl of Radnor by way of further assurance only did grant & convey unto the s[d] P.P Bouverie the younger & Rob' Marsham their heirs & assigns

All & Sing[r] the share & shares as well originally as accruing which by under or by virtue of the s[d] h'inbefore abst[d] Ind're of the 20th May 1814 & the Recovery suffered in purs'ce thereof became vested at Law or in Equity in him the s[d] W[m] Earl of Radnor or over which by under or by virtue of the same Ind're & Recovery he then had any power of disposition of & in all & sing^r the manors mess'es lands tenem^{ts} & heredit's comprised or ment^d in the s^d *{Page 47}* last rec^d Ind're except such of the same mess'es lands tenem^{ts} & heredit's if any as had been sold or conveyed in exchange but including such mess'es lands tenem^{ts} & heredit's if any as had been purchased or acquired in exchange.

And also of & in all & singular other (if any) the manors mess'es lands tenem^{ts} & heredit's any undivided share or shares whereof was or were subject at Law or in Equity to the subsisting uses of the s^d Ind're with their rights members & appurt's.

And all the estate &^{c}.

To hold the same unto & to the use of the s^d Philip Pleydell Bouverie the you^r & Robt Marsham their h'rs & ass^s (subject nev^s to such of the charges in the s^d Ind're of the 20th May 1814 mentioned or referred to as are now subsisting).

Upon & for the trusts intents & p'pses & with under & subject to the prov'oes & decl'ons in & by the s^d Ind're of Settlement expr^d & declared of such part of the s^d real est^e of the s^d Ann Judith Countess of Radnor as were in & by the same Ind're covenanted to be conveyed & assured by the s^d Wm Earl of Radnor unto & to the use of the s^d Cropley late Earl of Shaftsbury & Sir Philip Hales their heirs & ass^s for ever or such of the same trusts intents & purposes powers provisoes & decl'ons as are now subsist^g or capable of taking effect.

Cov' by the s^d Wm Earl of Radnor that he had done no act to incumber.

Executed by the s^d Wm Earl of Radnor and attested by 2 witnesses.

As to the share to which the s^d George William St John Mildmay became entitled of the above Estates

26th & 27th April 1832

By Ind'res of Lease & Release bet^n S^d Dame Jane St John Mildmay of the 1st part s^d Sir Geo W^m St John Mildmay of 2nd part Mary Morritt of Upper Grosvenor St Co^y Middlesex Widow & Relict of John Morritt Esqre dec'ed of the 3rd part Augustus Warren the you^r of Great Russell Street Bloomsbury co^y Middlesex Gent^n of the 4th part James Leman of Lincolns *{Page 48}* Inn Fields Co^y Middlesex Gent^n of the 5th part & Humphrey St Jno Mildmay of Piccadilly in s^d Co^y of Middlesex & James Evan Baillie of Seymour Place Mayfair Co^y Middlesex of the 6th part.

After recit^g the abst^d Ind'res of 27th & 28th Novr 1789 & the Common Recovery suffered in Hants in Mich'as Term 30th Geo 3rd the will of s^d Sir Henry Paulet St John Mildmay his death and probate And stating the issue of the marriage.

That s^d Sir H^y St John Carew St John Mildmay became entitled to the devised estates of s^d Carew Hervey Mildmay & s^d Paulet St John Mildmay to the estates settled by the s^d Ind're of 21st June 1786 in manner before abstracted.

And also stat^g the deaths of s^d Augustus Tucker St John Mildmay & John Francis St John Mildmay & s^d Charles Wm Paulett St John Mildmay.

And that under the limit'ons contained in s^d Ind're of 28th Novr 1789 & in consequence of the deaths with' issue of s^d Augustus Tucker St John Mildmay John Francis St John Mildmay and Chas Wm Paulett St John Mildmay s^d Geo W^m St John Mildmay was tenant in tail in remainder immed'ly expectant on the decease of s^d Dame Jane St John Mildmay of one undivided tenth part or share of & in All the manors & heredit's in the Counties of Southampton & Middlesex th'in comprised & th'rby settled.

And recit^g that a marr'e had been agreed upon & was int^d to be shortly solemnised bet^n said George W^m St John Mildmay & Mary Morritt & upon the treaty for s^d marr'e it was (amongst o^r things) agreed that the manors & heredit's after ment^d with their appurt's sho^d be discharged from all est^s tail of s^d Geo W^m St John Mildmay th'in & from the rem^rs & rev'ons thereon expectant or depending & sho^d be assured & limited to the uses &^c after expressed concerning the same.

It was witn'ed that in purs'ce of s^d agreem' & in cons'on of s^d int^d marr'e & of 10^s/ to s^d Dame Jane St John Mildmay by s^d Augustus Warren p^d s^d Dame Jane St John Mildmay (with the privity of s^d Geo W^m St John Mildmay & Mary Morritt test^d &^c) Did grant bargain sell & confirm unto s^d Augustus Warren & his heirs

All that the one undivided tenth part or share *{Page 49}* (the whole into 10 equal parts or shares to be divided) of which s^d George W^m St John Mildmay was tenant in tail in remainder immed'ly expectant on the decease of s^d Dame Jane St John Mildmay of & in All the manors & heredit's comprised in the Schedule thereto annexed.

And also of & in All other the heredit's & heredit's in the Counties of Southampton & Middlesex to one undivided tenth part or share of which said Geo W^m St John Mildmay was entitled for an est^e tail in rem^r immed'ly expectant on the decease of s^d Dame Jane St John Mildmay.

And also of & in All houses &^c.

And the Rev'on &^c.

And all the Estate &^c.

To hold unto & to the use of s^d Augustus Warren & his ass^s during the joint lives of s^d Augustus Warren & Dame Jane St John Mildmay.

To the intent that s^d Augustus Warren might be immediate tenant of the actual freehold of s^d undivided tenth part or share heredit's & prem'es so that two or more Common Recoveries with double Voucher might be suffered thereof.

Decl'on that it sho[d] be lawful for s[d] James Leman or some o[r] p'son or p'sons at the costs of s[d] Geo W[m] St John Mildmay before the end of then Easter Term or in any o[r] subsequent term to prosecute against s[d] Augustus Warren out of Chancery 2 or more Writs of entry sur disseisen en le post returnable in the Common Pleas & to demand th'rby of s[d] Augustus Warren s[d] 10th part heredit's & prem'es by apt descriptions to pass the same And that s[d] Augustus Warren sho[d] in person or by Attorney appear to each of s[d] Writs and vouch to warranty s[d] Geo W[m] St John Mildmay & that s[d] Geo W[m] St John Mildmay should in p'son or by Attorney appear gratis & freely enter on the Warranty of s[d] Aug[s] Warren & take the same upon himself & vouch over to warrant the Common Vouchee who should th'rupon appear gratis and freely enter into the Warranty of s[d] Geo W[m] St John Mildmay & take the same on himself & imparte & then make *{Page 50}* default so that judgm' might be given on s[d] Writs for s[d] Ja[s] Leman or o[r] the Demandant to recover against s[d] Augustus Warren & for s[d] Aug[s] Warren to recover against s[d] Geo W[m] St John Mildmay & for s[d] Geo W[m] St John Mildmay to recover over in value against s[d] Common Vouchee as usual in such cases And that th'rupon execution might be sued & seisin delivered unto s[d] Ja[s] Leman or other the Demandant accordingly & that all other acts & things necessary sho[d] be done for the purpose suffer[g] & perfect[g] two or more Common Recoveries of s[d] 10th parts heredit's & prem'es with double voucher to dock all est[s] tail th'in of s[d] Geo W[m] St John Mildmay & the rem[rs] thr'on expectant or depending.

Decl'on that s[d] Recoveries & all o[r] & all convey'ces & assurances whats[r] of s[d] undiv[d] 10th part heredit's & prem'es thr'by rel'ed so far as they comprise same undiv[d] 10th part heredit's & prem'es or any of them & so far as the parties to the Ind're now being abst[d] could lawfully direct the uses th'of sho[d] enure (subj' as to s[d] undiv[d] 10th part of & in the manors & heredit's comprised in the first part of the Schedule th'rto annexed to one equal 10th part of the s[d] 3 sums of £1,500 £1,500 & £1,500 payable to s[d] Dame Jane St John Mildmay Ann Mildmay & Letitia Mildmay as in s[d] rec[d] Ind're of Release of 28th Nov[r] 1789 & th'inbefore was ment[d] & of the int' th'of resp'ly And to the term of years for raising the same And also to one equal 10th part of the two sev[l] sums of £6,000 & £6,000 to be raised for the portion of s[d] Ann Mildmay & Letitia Mildmay under the trusts of s[d] term of 1000 y'rs created by the th'inbefore rec[d] Ind'res of 27th & 28th Nov[r] 1789 & of the int' thereof & s[d] term of 1000 yrs for raising the same & also to 1/10th part of all other sums then charged on s[d] heredit's to which s[d] Dame Jane St John Mildmay was entitled in her own right or as executrix of the Will of the s[d] Sir Henry Paulet St John Mildmay And also subj' to the Leases under which any part of the manors & heredits comprised in s[d] Schedule were then held & as to s[d] undivided 10th part of & in the mess'es lands & heredit's comprised in the 2nd part of the s[d] Schedule subj' as in s[d] lastly rec[d] Ind're of Lease as th'inbefore was mentioned

To the use of s[d] Dame Jane St John Mildmay and her ass[s] for life by way of restoration & confirmation of her est[e] for life in s[d] undiv[d] 10th part heredit's & prem'es & of all powers & privileges annexed or belonging to her s[d] estate *{Page 51}* & subject th'rto & to s[d] powers & privileges & to the powers of leasing & other powers contained in s[d] Act of Parliam' & which were to be exercised after the decease of s[d] Dame Jane St John Mildmay.

To the use of s[d] George W[m] St John Mildmay his h'rs & ass[s] until s[d] int[d] marriage between him & s[d] Mary Morritt should be solemnised & after the solemnisation thereof

To the use of s[d] Humphrey St John Mildmay & Ja[s] Evan Baillie their heirs & assigns for ever.

Upon trust that they the s[d] Humphrey St John Mildmay & Ja[s] Evan Baillie & the sur'vor of them & the heirs & assigns of such survivor sho[d] with all convenient speed after the decease of the survivor of s[d] Dame Jane St John Mildmay George W[m] St John Mildmay & Mary Morritt or in the lifetime of them or the sur'vors or sur'vor of them with their his or her consent in writing at such price or prices as they or he should think proper absolutely sell &

dispose of s^d undivided tenth part or share heredit's & prem'es either altogether or in one lot or in several lots & either by Public Auction or Private Contract with liberty to buy in the same & resell the same or any future Auction or by Private Contract with' being liable to answer for any loss or price by such re-sale.

And upon this fur^r trust that s^d tr'ees or tr'ee for the time being did & sho^d at any time or times at the request in writing of s^d Dame Jane St John Mildmay & George W^m St John Mildmay during their joint lives & of s^d George W^m St John Mildmay alone after her decease in case he should survive her & before any sale or sales sho^d have been made under the trusts afs^d levy & raise by way of m'tge any sum or sums not exceeding in the whole the sum of £3,000 & pay the sum or sums so to be raised to s^d Geo W^m St John Mildmay his ex'ors adm'ors or ass^s for his or their own absolute use and benefit.

Declaration that for effectuating such sale or sales m'tge or m'tges s^d *{Page 52}* tr'ees or tr'ee for the time being sho^d enter into make & execute all such contracts agreem^ts acts deeds conveyances & assurances as to them or him sho^d seem necessary & proper And that the rec' or rec^ts of s^d tr'ees or tr'ee for the time being sho^d effectually discharge the p'son or p'sons pay^g the monies arising from such Sale or Sales Mortgage or Mortgages as afs^d from being answerable or accountable for the misapplic'on or nonapplic'on or from being obliged or concerned to see to the applic'on of the monies in such rec' or rec^ts expressed or acknowledged to be received.

Declaration that s^d tr'ees or tr'ee for the time being sho^d out of the mo^s arising from such Sales or Sales pay to & reimburse themselves & himself all the costs charges & expenses which they or he sho^d incur or sustain in carrying the trusts th'rby created into execution And also pay & satisfy the charges & incumb's affect^g the prem'es sold & disch^d from which they might be sold by s^d tr'ees or tr'ee under the trusts afs^d & also pay to s^d Geo W^m St John Mildmay his ex'ors adm'ors or ass^s for his or their own absolute use & benefit the sum of £3000 or so much thereof as might not be previously raised by m'tge under the trusts afs^d it being th'rby intended that not more than £3000 in the whole sho^d be paid to s^d W^m St John Mildmay his ex'ors adm'ors or assigns.

Declaration that s^d tr'ees or tr'ee sho^d stand & be possessed of & interested in so much of the monies to be raised by such sale or sales as afs^d as sho^d not be required for the p'pses afs^d upon & for such trusts intents & p'pses & with under & subj' to such powers prov'oes agreem^ts & decl'ons as were or sho^d be expr^d & decl^d of & concern^g the same in & by an Ind're already prepared & engrossed & bear^g or int^d to bear even date with the now abst^g Ind're & made or int^d to be made bet^n Dame Jane St John Mildmay of 1st part s^d Geo W^m St John Mildmay of 2nd part s^d Mary Morritt of 3rd part & s^d Humphrey St John Mildmay & James Evan Baillie of 4th part.

Proviso that after the decease of s^d Dame Jane St John Mildmay & in the meantime & until s^d undiv^d 10th part or share sho^d be sold it sho^d be lawful for s^d tr'ees or tr'ee for the time being with the consent in writ^g of s^d George W^m St John Mildmay & Mary Morritt or the sur'vor of them & after the decease of such sur'vor at the discretion of s^d tr'ees or tr'ees to demise or lease s^d tenth part or share for any term not exceeding *{Page 53}* 21 years.

Power of appoint^g new tr'ees & clauses of indemnity against involuntary losses & for allowance of expenses.

Cov^ts by s^d Geo W^m St John Mildmay for the title.

Executed by all parties except s^d Humphrey St John Mildmay & Ja^s Evan Baillie & attested.

The 1st Schedule contains a copy of the parcels contained in the abstracted Ind'res of 27th & 28th Novr 1789.

Easter Term 2 William 4th Southampton

Exemplification of Recovery wherein s^d James Leman was Demandant s^d Augustus Warren Tenant & George William St John Mildmay Vouchee who Vouched over the Common Vouchee of

One 10th part of

The Manors of Twyford & Marwell otherwise Old Marwell with the appurt's & one 10th part of 30 mess'es 3 dovehouses one water corn mill 80 gardens 1,500 acres of land 300 acres of meadow 300 acres of pasture 400 acres of wood 2,000 acres of furze & heath & 40^s/ rent & common of pasture with the appurt's in Shawford Twyford & Marwell o'rwise Old Marwell & in the Parishes of Twyford & Owslebury & also the advowsons of the Churches of Twyford & Owslebury.

23rd & 24th November 1832

By Ind're of Lease & Release between s^d Humphrey St John Mildmay & James Evan Baillie of 1st part s^d Geo W^m St John Mildmay of 2nd part s^d Dame Jane St John Mildmay of the 3rd part & Lewis Vulliamy of Regent Street in the Parish of St Marylebone in the s^d Co^y of Middlesex esquire of the 4th part.

Recit^g the s^d Lease & Release of the 26th & 27th days of April 1832.

And recit^g that no sale had been made by the s^d Humphrey St John Mildmay & Ja^s Evan Baillie in purs'ce of the s^d in part recited Indenture.

And recit^g that the s^d Humphrey St John Mildmay & Ja^s Evan Baillie at the request of the s^d Dame Jane St John Mildmay & George W^m St John Mildmay testified &^{c} had requested the s^d Lewis Vulliamy *{Page 54}* to lend & advance the sum of £3000 which he had agreed to do upon having the repaym' thereof with int' secured to him in manner th'inafter mentioned & the s^d Dame Jane St John Mildmay & George W^m St John Mildmay had agreed to join in now abst^g Ind're for the purposes & in manner th'inafter mentioned.

It is witn'ed that in purs'ce of s^d agreem' & in cons'on of the sum of £3,000 to the s^d Humphrey St John Mildmay & Ja^s Evan Baillie at or before the sealing & delivery of s^d abst^g Ind're with the privity of s^d Dame Jane St John Mildmay test^d &^{c} p^d by the s^d Lewis Vulliamy the rec' &^{c} They the s^d Humphrey St John Mildmay & James Evan Baillie in purs'ce of the trust reposed in them by the s^d in part rec^d Ind're & accord^g to the est^e & int' of them the s^d Humphrey St John Mildmay & Ja^s Evan Baillie Did & each of them Did barg^n sell & rel'e the s^d George W^m St John Mildmay Did grant release & confirm unto the s^d Lewis Vulliamy (in his actual poss'on &^{c}) & to his heirs & assigns

All that one undivided equal 10th part or share by the s^d Ind'res of the 26th & 27th days of April 1832 conveyed or expressed to be conveyed to the use of the s^d Humphrey St John Mildmay & Ja^s Evan Baillie their heirs & ass^s upon the trusts & in manner th'inbefore ment^d of & in all the manors mess'es lands & other heredit's the par'lars wh'of were specified in the Schedule th'runder or th'runto annexed & of & in all other the heredit's (if any) of which one undiv^d 10th part or share was by the s^d in part recited Ind're conveyed or expressed to be conveyed to the use of s^d Humphrey St John Mildmay & Ja^s Evan Baillie their heirs & ass^s upon the trusts & in manner afs^d of & in all & sing^r houses &^{c}.

And the Rev'on &^{c}.

And all the Estate &^{c}.

To hold the s^d undiv^d 10th part or share heredit's & all & sing^r other the prem'es th'rby granted & rel'ed unto the s^d Lewis Vulliamy his heir & assigns.

To the use of the s^d Lewis Vulliamy his heirs & ass^s for ever subj' to the est^e for life of the s^d Dame Jane St John *{Page 55}* Mildmay & to the powers & charges which are in s^d in part recited Ind're ment^d to precede the use or estate thereby limited to the use of the s^d Humphrey St John Mildmay & Ja^s Evan Baillie their heirs & ass^s & subj' to redemption.

Cov^t by s^d Humphrey St John Mildmay & Ja^s Evan Baillie that they had not incumbered.

Proviso for red'on on paym' by s^d George W^m St John Mildmay his heirs ex'ors adm'ors or ass^s unto s^d Lewis Vulliamy his ex'ors adm'ors or ass^s of the sum of £3,000 & int' as th'in mentioned.

Cov^{ts} by s^d Geo W^m St John Mildmay for paym' of s^d m'tge mo^y & int' that s^d Humphrey St John Mildmay & Ja^s Evan Baillie & Geo W^m St John Mildmay had good right to convey for quiet enjoym' after default (except s^d Dame Jane St John Mildmay & her ass^s claim^g in respect of her s^d life estate & except any person or persons claim^g in respect of the charges & incumb's th'in & th'inbefore referred to) free from incumb's (except s^d life est^e & s^d charges amount^g in the whole to £32,000 & then vested in Sir Charles Morgan & o'rs for fur^r assurance (save as afs^d)

Proviso for quiet enjoym' by the s^d Humphrey St John Mildmay & Ja^s Evan Baillie until default.

And s^d Dame Jane St John Mildmay Geo Wm Mildmay & Mary his wife did by the s^d abst^g Ind're consent to such sales as the s^d tr'ees or tr'ee of the s^d Ind're of 27th April 1832 might at any time or times th'rafter make in purs'ce of the trusts for sale in the same Ind're contained in the lifetime of the s^d Dame Jane St John Mildmay & Geo Wm Mildmay & Mary his wife or the sur'vor of them to the intent that any such sale or sales might be made with' any fur^r consent of the s^d Dame Jane St John Mildmay Geo W^m St John Mildmay & Mary his wife.

The first part of the schedule comprises the premises in Hants by the same description as before.

Executed by s^d Humphrey St John Mildmay Ja^s Evan Baillie Geo W^m St John Mildmay Mary St John Mildmay & Dame Jane St John Mildmay & duly att^d. Receipt for £3000 endorsed signed & witnessed.

Registered 5th March 1833 B.2. N°.322.

{Page 56}

4th December 1849

By Memorandum under the hand of s^d Lewis Vulliamy ind^d on last abst^d Ind're it is ackn'ged that £1000 part of the £3000 by s^d Ind're int^d to be secured had been paid & s^d Lewis Vulliamy did declare that the p'pal of £2000 alone then remained due on the security of s^d abst^d Indenture.

30th August 1830

By Ind're of this date made bet^n s^d Geo W^m St John Mildmay of the 1st part s^d Dame Jane St John Mildmay of the 2nd part The Right Honble Lord James Fitzroy of Clarges S^t in the Co^y of Middlesex of the 3rd part Thos Thompson of the Abbey Road St John's Wood in the Parish of St Marylebone in the s^d Co^y of Middlesex Esqre of the 4th part & Edwd Thompson of Barnsbury Terrace in the Parish of St Mary Islington in s^d Co^y of Middlesex Gen^t of the 5th part.

Recit^g that s^d George W^m St John Mildmay was entitled as one of the younger children of his late father Sir Henry Paulet St John Mildmay by Dame Jane his widow to one equal undiv^d share with the o^r younger children of his late father of and in the manors lands tenem^ts & heredit's th'inaf^r descr^d subject only to the life est^e th'in of his mother.

And rect^g s^d Thos Thompson had agreed with s^d Geo W^m St John Mildmay for the absolute purchase of an Annuity of £128 to be p^d to s^d Thos Thompson dur^g the life of s^d Geo Wm John Mildmay redeemable as th'inaf^r mentioned.

And recit^g that it was agreed upon the treaty for the purchase that s^d Annuity sho^d be charged upon such parts of s^d manors & heredit's thinaf^r descr^d in which the s^d Geo W^m St John Mildmay had any est^e or int' & that the same sho^d be demised unto s^d Edwd Thompson for 99 years if s^d Geo W^m St John Mildmay sho^d so long live upon the trusts th'inaf^r expressed.

It is witn'ed that in cons'on of £1,150 to s^d Geo W^m St John Mildmay p^d by s^d Thos Thompson the rec' &c He s^d Geo W^m St John Mildmay Did give grant barg^n sell & confirm unto s^d Thos Thompson his ex'ors adm'ors & ass^s during the natural life of him s^d Geo W^m St John Mildmay.

One Ann^y of £128 to be yearly issuing and payable to him s^d Thos Thompson his ex'ors adm'ors *{Page 57}* & ass^s out of & charged upon all & every the parts & shares part & share of him the s^d Geo W^m St John Mildmay as one of the younger children of s^d Sir Henry Paulet St John Mildmay & Dame Jane St John Mildmay of & in the manors of Twyford & Marwell heredit's to them severally belong^g sit^e within the Parishes of Twyford & Owslebury in the Co^y of Southampton.

And the Rev'ons &^c.

Subjec' nev^s to the est^e & int' of s^d Dame Jane St John Mildmay his mother therein.

To hold receive & take s^d Annuity of £128 unto s^d Thos Thompson his ex'ors adm'ors & ass^s dur^g the life of s^d Geo W^m St John Mildmay to be p^d as th'in mentioned.

Powers of distress & entry.

Cov' by s^d George W^m St John Mildmay to pay s^d Annuity.

And it is fur^r witn'ed that in purs'ce of s^d Agreem' & in cons'on of s^d sum of £1,150 to s^d Geo W^m St John Mildmay by s^d Thomas Thompson p^d & for fur^r & better secur^g the paym^t of s^d Ann^y of £128 in manner afs^d And also in cons'on of 10^s/ to s^d Geo W^m St John Mildmay in hand p^d by s^d Edwd Thompson the rec' &^c He the s^d Geo W^m St John Mildmay at the request & by the dir'on of s^d Thos Thompson test^d &^c Did grant barg^n sell & demise unto s^d E^d Thompson his ex'ors adm'ors & assigns.

All & every the parts & shares part & share of him the s^d Geo W^m St John Mildmay as one of the younger children of s^d Sir Henry Paulet St John Mildmay dec'ed & Dame Jane St John Mildmay or o'rwise of him s^d Geo W^m St John Mildmay of & in the s^d Manors of Twyford & Marwell & the heredit's to them severally belonging situate & within the Parishes of Twyford & Owslebury in the Co^y of Southampton th'inbefore charged with the paym' of s^d Annuity.

Tog^r with all house &^c.

And the Rev'on &^c.

{Page 58}

To hold the same with their appurt's unto the s^d Edwd Thompson his ex'ors &^c from the day next before the day of the date of now abst^g Ind're for 99 years without impeachment of waste if s^d Geo W^m St John Mildmay sho^d so long live.

Yielding & Paying yearly during the continuance of that demise unto s^d Geo W^m St John Mildmay the rent of One Pepper Corn (if demanded) subj' to the life estate of s^d Dame Jane St John Mildmay therein.

Upon trust for better securing the s^d Annuity th'inafter expressed.

Power for the s^d George W^m St John Mildmay to repurchase the s^d Annuity as th'in mentioned.

Executed by all parties and attested.

Receipt for £1,150 signed & witnessed.

1st December 1832

Ind're indorsed on last abst^d Ind're bet^n s^d Thos Thompson of 1st part s^d Edwd Thompson of 2nd part s^d Geo W^m St John Mildmay of 3rd part s^d Dame Jane St John Mildmay & Lord Ja^s Fitzroy of the 4th part.

It is witn'ed than in cons'on of £1,208 to s^d Thos Thompson p^d by s^d Geo W^m St John Mildmay the rec' &^c the s^d Thos Thompson did remise release & quit claim unto s^d George W^m St John Mildmay his ex'ors adm'ors & assigns.

The within ment^d Ann^y or annual sum of £128 & all arrears th'of & all & sing^r the powers of entry & distress & other powers upon the share heredit's' & prem'es comprised in the th'in within written Ind're & thereby charged with the payment thereof.

And all the estate &^c.

To the intent that the same Annuity powers & remedies might be extinguished.

Cov' by s^d Thos Thompson that he had done no act whereby he was prevented from releasing.

It was by the s^d Ind're fur^r witn'ed that for the nom^l cons'on th'in ment^d to s^d Edwd Thompson p^d by s^d Geo W^m St John Mildmay *{Page 59}* s^d Edwd Thompson at the request of the s^d Thos Thompson test^d &^c Did sur^r & yield up unto s^d Geo W^m St John Mildmay his heirs & assigns

All & every the parts & shares part & share of & in the manors & heredit's by the th'in within written Ind're demised to s^d Edwd Thompson as th'in within ment^d with their appurt's.

And all the estate &^c.

To the intent that the th'in within ment^d term of 99 years or the then residue thereof might be merged & extinguished in the freehold & inh'ance of s^d parts or shares heredit's & prem'es or o'rwise extinguished & annihilated.

Cov' by s^d Edwd Thompson that he had done no act to incumber.

Executed by s^d Thos Thompson & Edward Thompson & George W^m St John Mildmay & duly att^d.

Receipt for cons'on money indorsed signed & witn^d.

14th December 1832

Ind're indorsed on s^d Ind're of 30th Augt 1830 bet^n s^d Geo W^m St John Mildmay 1st part Lewis Vulliamy Esqre of 2nd part & George Ward Esqre of 3rd part.

Recit^g the before abst^g Ind'res of the 26th & 27th April 1832 & 23 & 24th Novr 1832.

And recit^g that s^d abst^d Ind're of 1st Decr 1832 was not an effectual surrender of s^d term of 99 years.

It was witn'ed that for the cons'ons th'in ment^d s^d Geo W^m St John Mildmay at the request & on the nomination of s^d Lewis Vulliamy test^d &^{c} did assign & transfer unto the s^d George Ward his ex'ors adm'ors & assigns

All & every the parts & shares part & share & o^r heredit's by s^d Ind're of 1st December 1832 expr^d to be surrendered & yielded up to s^d Geo W^m St John Mildmay as th'in mentioned.

And all the Estate &^{c}.

To hold the same unto the s^d Geo Ward his ex'ors adm'ors & assigns for all the residue then to come of the s^d term of 99 years.

In trust for s^d Lewis Vulliamy his h'rs & ass^s & to *{Page 60}* dispose of the same as he or they sho^d direct or appoint & in the meantime

Upon trust to permit the residue of s^d term to attend the freehold & inh'ance of the prem'es th'in comprised & to protect the same from all incumb's (if any) But subj' as to the same term to the same equity of redempt^n as to the fr'hold & inh'ance of the same heredit's were or sho^d be liable to by virtue of the s^d Ind're of the 24th day of Novr 1832.

Cov' by s^d George W^m St John Mildmay that he had done no act to incumber.

Executed by s^d Geo W^m St John Mildmay & Lewis Vulliamy & duly att^d. Registered in Middlesex 5th March 1833. B.2. N°. 320.

The s^d Geo Ward died on the 22nd July 1840 intestate.

23rd November 1840

Letters of Administration of the goods & chattels & credits of s^d Geo Ward were granted by the Prerogative Court of the Archbishop of Canterbury to Henry Ward of Lincolns Inn Fields in the Co^y of Midd'x Gen^t the Bro^r & a Creditor of the dec'ed (Harriet Ward ~"~ Widow the Relict & John Ward the Father & next of kin having renounced).

9th August 1845

The s^d Geo W^m St John Mildmay by Will of this date after dispos^g of certain 6 per cent Ohio stock gave & devised All the residue of his property to his Wife for her life & at her death to be divided between his Children equally.

In the event of the Children dying under 21 he left all he might die possessed of as in the s^d Will mentioned.

Adm'on with the Will annexed was on the 11th March 1851 granted by the Prerogative Court of Canterbury to Mary St John Mildmay Widow the Relict of s^d Testator.

14th February 1851

The s^d Geo W^m St John Mildmay died leav^g Herbert Alex^r St John Mildmay his only Son.

{Page 61}

22nd June 1858

By Ind're of this date (endorsed on the abst^d Ind're of Rel'e of 27th Novr 1832) bet^n Mary St John Mildmay of 1st part s^d Lewis Vulliamy of 2nd part & s^d Ja^s Evan Baillie of 3rd part.

Recit^g the paym^t of £1,000 part of the s^d m'tge debt of £3,000 by s^d Geo W^m St John Mildmay out of his own p'per mo^y.

And recit^g his death & the grant of Letters of Adm'on to the s^d Mary St John Mildmay.

And recit^g the deaths of the s^d Humphrey St John Mildmay & Dame Jane St John Mildmay.

And recit^g a convey'ce of part of the s^d m'tged estate to a purch^r & dated the 23rd day of June 1858 whereby the s^d Lewis Vulliamy in cons'on of £1,199.18.0 sterling p^d to him Did by the dir'on of the s^d Ja^s Evan Baillie & Mary St John Mildmay grant the equal undiv^d part of the prem'es comprised in such convey'ce to the purchaser.

And also recit^g a further conv'ce of fur^r part of s^d m'tged est^e to a purch^r dated the [Blank space] day of [Blank space] wh'rby the s^d Lewis Vulliamy & Ja^s Evan Baillie with the consent of the s^d Mary St John Mildmay accord^g to their resp'ive est^e & int^{ts} granted rel'ed & conveyed the s^d prem'es th'in described to the purchaser.

And recit^g that the s^d James Evan Baillie had p^d to the s^d Mary St John Mildmay the s^d sum of £1,000 so p^d by the s^d Geo W^m St John Mildmay & to which the s^d Mary St John Mildmay was entitled as such administratrix as afs^d & has p^d to the s^d Lewis Vulliamy the sum of £800.1.6 being the balance of the same principal sum or m'tge debt of £3000 & also all int' in respect of the same p'pal sum of £3000.

It was witn'ed that in cons'on of the sum of £1000 so as afs^d p^d to the s^d Mary St John Mildmay & also of the s^d sum of £800.1.6 & int' so as afs^d p^d to the s^d Lewis Vulliamy the rec' &^{c} She the s^d Mary St John Mildmay Did release & the s^d Lewis Vulliamy Did grant release & convey unto the s^d Ja^s Evan Baillie (as the surviv^g trustee of the s^d therein ment^d Ind'res of the 26th & 27th days of April 1832 & his heirs.

All & such part & parts of the undivided 10th part or share & all & sing^r other the prem'es by the th'in within written Ind'res rel'ed unto & to the use of the s^d Lewis Vulliamy his h'rs *{Page 62}* & ass^s as were not comprised in the th'inbef in part rec^d Ind'res of the 23rd day of June 1858 & the [Blank space] day of [Blank space] 1858.

And all the Estate &^{c}.

To hold the same part or share & prem'es unto & to the use of the s^d Ja^s Evan Baillie his h'rs & ass^s freed & discharged of & from the s^d p'pal sum or m'tge debt of £3000 secured or int^d to be secured by the th'in within written Ind're & of & from all int' in respect th'of & all claims & demands whats^r in respect of the same sum & int^t or any part or parts th'of resp'ly & of & from all the trusts powers & remedies in & by the th'in within written Ind'res reserved given & contained for securing the paym' of the s^d p'pal sum & int' th'of but subject to the powers & charges preceding the use & estate by the th'in within ment^d Ind'res of the 26th & 27th days of April 1832 limited to the s^d Humphrey St John Mildmay & James Evan Baillie or such of the same prem'es & charges as were the subsist^g & capable of taking effect.

Sev^l Cov^{ts} by the s^d Mary St John Mildmay & Ja^s Evan Baillie that they had not incumbered.

Executed by Mary St John Mildmay & Lewis Vulliamy & attested.

As to the accruing shares vested in Herbert Alexander St John Mildmay Esqre as heir in tail to his father the late Geo W^m St John Mildmay

23rd July 1857

By Ind're inrolled in Chancery 24th July 1857 & made betn the sd Herbert Alexr St John Mildmay Esqre a Lieut' in the 2nd Battalion of the Rifle Brigade of the one part & Fras Robt Warren Gentn of the or part

Recitg that under & by virtue of the before abstd Ind'res of the 27th & 28th Novr 1789 & Common Recovery duly suffered in purs'ce of the sd Ind're of Release Mich'as term 30th Geo & a Common Recovery duly suffered at a Court holden in & for the Manor of Newington *{Page 63}* Barrow o'rwise Highbury in Islington & certn Surrs & Admittances duly made & had at the same Court & an Ind're of Apptmt & Release by way of Enfranchisem' bearing date the 24th day of Aug' 1804 or under or by virtue of some or one of the sd Ind'res or Assurances the Manors of Twyford & Marwell & divers freehold mess'es lands tenemts & heredit's site in the sevl Parishes of Marwell Owslebury & Twyford in the County of Southampton formally the property of Carew Mildmay Esqre dec'ed & divers heredit's in the Coy of Middlesex with their resp'ive appurt's became & stood limited & settled (after & subject to certain limitations to or for the benefit of the sd Sir Hy Paulet St John Mildmay & Dame Jane St John Mildmay for their respective lives successively) to the use of all & every the younger Son & Sons & the Daur & Daurs of the sd Sir Hy Paulet St John Mildmay on the body of the sd Dame Jane St John Mildmay lawfully to be begotten (other than & except an only or or Son entitled in poss'on or remr immed'ly expectant on his Mother's decease to certain Estates devised by the Will of Carew Hervey Mildmay Esqre dec'ed under the limit'ons th'of contained in that Will & also except such Son as should by virtue of the limit'ons contained in the Ind're of 21st June 1786 h'inbefore referred to or of any apptm' by the sd Sir Hy Paulet St John Mildmay pursuant to the power th'in likewise contained be entitled to certn heredit's & prem'es th'rby granted & released either in poss'on or remr expectant on his Father's decease equally to be divided among them if more than one as tenants in common & not as joint tenants & of the sevl & resp'ive heirs of his her or their body or resp'ive bodies & in default of lawful issue of the body or bodies of any such your Son or Daur younger Sons or Daurs then as to the share or shares as well origl as accruing of such younger Son or Sons Daur or Daurs whose issue shod so fail to the use of the remg or other or others of them except as afsd equally to be divided between them if more than one as tenants in common & of the sevl & resp'ive heirs of the body & bodies of such remg & other younger Son or Sons Daur or Daurs (except as before excepted)

And recitg that there was issue of the marriage betn the sd Sir Hy Paulet St John Mildmay & the sd Dame Jane St John Mildmay 11 Sons & 4 Daughters.

{Page 64}

And recitg that the eldest Son Hy St John Carew St John Mildmay af'twds Sir Hy St John Carew St John Mildmay Bart' & since dec'ed became entitled in remr immed'ly expectant upon the decease of the sd Dame Jane St John Mildmay to the este devised by the sd Will of the sd Carew Hervey Mildmay & the second son Paulet St John Mildmay became entitled in poss'on to the heredit's settled by the sd Sir Hy Paulet St John Mildmay dec'ed by the afsd Ind're of the 21st June 1786 & that the sd ests site in the Counties of Southampton & Middlesex accordingly became divisible under the afsd limit'on thereof th'inbefore recited in equal shares between the 13 younger Sons & Daurs of the sd Sir Paulet St John Mildmay & Dame Jane St John Mildmay his wife.

And recitg that sd Augustus Tucker St John Mildmay, John Francis St John Mildmay, Charles Wm Paulet St John Mildmay, Gualtier St John Mildmay, Hugh Cornwall St John Mildmay & Letitia St John Mildmay 6 of the sd younger Sons & Daurs of the sd marr'e had died without issue & with' having done any act to bat their sd resp'ive ests tail on the remrs expectant th'ron & accordingly the sd ests in the Counties of Southampton & Midd'x had become divisible under the afsd limit'ons in equal shares betn the remg 7 younger Sons & Daurs of the sd Sir Hy

Paulet St John Mildmay & Dame Jane St John Mildmay his wife of which remain^g younger Sons Geo Wm John Mildmay was one.

And recit^g that by virtue of the before abst^d Ind'res of 26th & 27th April 1832 & Common Recoveries suffered in purs'ce of the Agreem^t for that p'pse contained in the s^d Ind'res of Release the undiv^d 10th part or share to which the s^d Geo W^m St John Mildmay was then entitled of & in the s^d est^e in the Counties of Southampton & Midd'x were discharged from all est^s tail of the s^d Geo W^m St John Mildmay th'in & all rem^{rs} & rev'ons th'ron expectant or depend^g.

And recit^g that the s^d Geo W^m St John Mildmay died on or about the 14th day of Feby 1851 with' having done any act to bar his estate tail or the rem^{rs} expectant th'ron in the part or share of the s^d est^s in the Counties of Southampton & Middlesex to which he the s^d Geo W^m St John Mildmay became entitled by accruer or o'rwise after the date & execution of the s^d Ind'res of the 26th *{Page 65}* & 27th days of April 1832.

And recit^g that the s^d Herbert St John Mildmay was the eldest son of the body & heir at Law of the s^d Geo Wm St John Mildmay & as such entitled under the limit'ons before recited to the part or share parts or shares of the s^d est^s in the Counties of Southampton & Middlesex to which the s^d Geo W^m St John Mildmay became entitled as afs^d subsequently to the date & exec'on of the s^d Ind'res of the 26th & 27th days of April 1832.

And recit^g that the s^d Dame Jane St John Mildmay died on the 6th May 1857.

And recit^g that the s^d Herbert St John Mildmay had attained the age of 21 years.

It is witn'ed that in order to bar & defeat the est^e tail of him the s^d Herbert St John Mildmay created by the before abst^d Ind're of Rel'e & Settlem^t of the 28th Novr 1789 & every other (if any) estate tail of him the s^d Herbert St John Mildmay in all & every the then present & immediate & future expectant eventual & reversionary share or shares of him the s^d Herbert St John Mildmay in the manors & heredit's comprised in or which were then subject to the uses of the s^d Ind're of Release & Settlem^t & all rem^{rs} rev'ons est^s rights int^{ts} & powers to take effect after the determin'on or in defeasance of the s^d estate tail & of every other (if any) est^e tail of him the s^d Herbert St John Mildmay in the s^d parts or shares part or share & prem'es & to limit & assure the same in manner th'inafter ment^d He the s^d Herbert St john Mildmay Did by the now abst^g Ind're grant bargain sell & release unto the s^d Fra^s Robt Warren & his heirs

All & every the then present & immediate & future expectant eventual & reversionary share or shares of him the s^d Herbert St John Mildmay in all & sing^r the manors & heredit's comprised in the s^d Ind're of the 28th Novr 1789 except such parts of the s^d heredit's (if any) as have been sold or given in exchange & also in all & sing^r the lands tenem^{ts} & heredit's (if any) which had been taken in exchange or purchased of which had been allotted in respect of any of the lands or heredit's comprised in the s^d Ind're or so purchased *{Page 66}* or taken in exchange as afs^d by the Award under any Inclosure Act & in all other the lands tenem^{ts} & heredit's (if any) which had been settled by reference to the s^d Ind're of Release & Settlement or by any other means were then subject to the subsisting uses thereof.

Tog^r with all rights &^{c}.

And all the estate &^{c}.

To hold the s^d share or shares heredit's & all & sing^r other the prem'es thereby assured freed & discharged from the s^d estate tail created by the s^d Ind're of the 28th Novr 1789 & every other estate tail of him the s^d Herbert St John Mildmay therein And all estates rights titles interests and powers to take effect after the determination or in defeasance of such est^s tail unto the s^d Francis Robert Warren and his heirs.

To the use of the s^d Herbert St John Mildmay his h'rs & assigns for ever.

Decl'on that no wife of s^d Herbert St John Mildmay who should survive him should be entitled to dower out of s^d heredit's or any part th'of.

Executed by Herbert St John Mildmay & attested.

As to the share to which Humphrey St John Mildmay & Edward St John Mildmay resp'ly became entitled of the above estates

4th November 1824

By Ind're of Bargain & Sale inrolled in the Common Pleas Hilary Term 5 & 6 Geo 4 bet^n the s^d Dame Jane St John Mildmay & Humphrey St John Mildmay & Edwd St John Mildmay of 1st part said Augustus Warren the you^r of 2nd part Wm Bray Esqre of 3rd part & Paulet St John Mildmay Esqre of 4th part.

After recit^g the abst^d Ind'res of 27th & 28th Novr 1789.

And stat^g the issue of the marriage (viz' 13 children besides the eldest two Sons two of which 13 children had died & that s^d Humphrey St John Mildmay & Edwd St John Mildmay were two *{Page 67}* of such sur'vors & younger sons) & that s^d Humphrey St John Mildmay & Edwd St John Mildmay being desirous of suffering a Common Recovery & their shares in the s^d mess'es & other heredit's as well present as future expectant eventual or reversionary & to settle & assure such shares to such uses for the resp'ive benefit of s^d Humphrey St John Mildmay & Edwd St John Mildmay as were th'inaf^r expr^d & in order to enable them to suffer such Recoveries they had applied to & requested s^d Dame Jane St John Mildmay to execute such conveyance or assurance as th'inaf^r was expr^d which she the s^d Dame Jane St John Mildmay had accordingly agreed to do.

It was witn'ed that in pursuance of s^d agreem' & for barring all est^s tail of them the s^d Humphrey St John Mildmay & Edwd St John Mildmay & all rem^{rs} & rev'ons th'ron expectant or depend^g of & in the mess'es & other heredit's after descr^d & for settling the same to the uses &^{c} after contained & in cons'on of 10^s/ to s^d Dame Jane St John Mildmay p^d by s^d Augustus Warren S^d Dame Jane St John Mildmay Did grant barg^n sell & confirm unto s^d Augustus Warren & his ass^s during the joint lives of him s^d Augustus Warren & s^d Dame Jane St John Mildmay

The Manors of Twyford & Marwell & other the heredit's comprised in s^d Ind'res of the 27th & 28th Novr 1789.

And all houses &c.

And the Rev'on &c.

And all the Estate &c.

Excepting to s^d Dame Jane St John Mildmay her ex'ors adm'ors & ass^s all sums of mo^y to which she was entitled either in her own right or as executrix of her s^d deceased Husband & which were charged upon same prem'es.

To hold unto & to the use of the s^d Augustus Warren & his ass^s during the joint lives of him the Augustus Warren & Dame Jane St John Mildmay.

To the intent that the s^d Augustus Warren might become & be a good & perfect tenant of the freehold & inh'ance of the same manors & o^r heredit's in order that one or more *{Page 68}* perfect Common Recovery or Recoveries with double Voucher might be thereof had & suffered in manner after ment^d for which p'pse it was th'rby agreed & declared that it sho^d be lawful for s^d Wm Bray as next Mich'as Term or some subsequent term to sue out one or more Writ or Writs of Entry Sur disseisin le post returnable before the Justices of Common Pleas thereby demanding against the s^d Aug^s Warren the s^d Manors & other heredit's with their appurt's by such descriptions as sho^d be sufficient to ascertain the same to which Writ or Writs s^d Augustus Warren sho^d appear gratis in person or by Attorney & vouch to warranty s^d Humphrey St John Mildmay & Edwd St John Mildmay who sho^d also appear gratis in person or by Attorn^s & enter into warranty & vouch over to warranty the Common Vouchee of the s^d Court of Common Pleas who sho^d in like manner appear & imparle & after imparlance make default to the end that judgm^t might be th'rupon given & such further proceedings be had in the prem'es that one or more perfect Common Recov^y or Recoveries with double Voucher be perfected of the premises according to the usual course of Common Recoveries with double Voucher for assurance of lands.

Decl'on that s^d Common Recovery or Recoveries when so suffered as afs^d & all o^r recoveries fines & assurances th'tofore barred suffered or exe'ted of s^d Manors & o^r heredit's bet^n s^d parties th'rto or whereunto they or any of them were or was parties or privies or a party or privy sho^d be & enure & the Recoveror & Recoverors in s^d Recovery or Recoveries to be named & his & their h^rs sho^d stand & be seized of s^d Manors & other heredit's.

To the use of s^d Dame Jane St John Mildmay & her ass^s for life sans waste in corroboration & confirmation of the life est^e limited to her by s^d Ind're of 28th Novr 1789 & of the powers of leasing & other powers to such life estate appending or annexed & after the decease of s^d Dame Jane St John Mildmay

Then as to for & concern^g all & every the present & immediate & *{Page 69}* also all & every the future expectant eventual & reversionary share or shares right title & int' of s^d Humphrey St John Mildmay of & in s^d Manors & other heredit's.

To such uses upon & for such trusts intents & p'pses & with under & subject to such powers provisoes agreem^ts & decl'ons as the s^d Humphrey St John Mildmay by any deed or deeds instrum^t or intrum^ts in writ^g with or with' power of revoc'on to be by him sealed & deliv^d in the presence of & att^d by two or more credible witn^s sho^d from time to time direct or app' & in default of & until such dir'on & apptm' & so far as no such dir'on or apptm' should extend.

To the use of s^d Humphrey St John Mildmay & his assigns for life…Rem^r

To the use of s^d Paulet St John Mildmay & his h'rs during the life of s^d Humphrey St John Mildmay.

In trust for him & to prevent the present or any future wife of s^d Humphrey St John Mildmay from being dowable out of s^d shares & prem'es And after decease of s^d Humphrey St John Mildmay.

To the use of the heirs & ass^s of s^d Humphrey St John Mildmay for ever.

And as to for & concern^g All & every the present & immediate & also all & every the future expectant eventual & reversionary share or shares right title & interest of s^d Edward St John Mildmay of & in said manors & other heredit's.

To such uses upon & for such trusts intents & p'pses & with under & subject to such powers prov'oes agreem^ts & decl'ons as said Edwd St John Mildmay by any deed or deeds intrum^t or instrum^ts in writ^g with or with' power of revoc'on to be by him sealed & delivered in the presence of & att^d by two or more credible witn^s sho^d from time to time direct or app' & in default of & until such dir'on or apptm' & so far as no such dir'on or apptm' should extend.

To the use of s^d Edwd St John Mildmay & his *{Page 70}* assigns for life…Rem^r

To the use of s^d Paulet St John Mildmay & his h'rs during the life of s^d Edward St John Mildmay.

In trust for him & to prevent the present or any future Wife of s^d Edwd St John Mildmay from being dowable out of s^d shares & premises & after the decease of s^d Edward St John Mildmay.

To the use of the heirs & ass^s of s^d Edwd St John Mildmay for ever.

Executed by Dame Jane St John Mildmay Humphrey St John Mildmay Edward St John Mildmay Aug^s Warren Junr & Wm Bray & att^d.

Michaelmas Term 5th George 4th

Exemplification of Recovery wherein the s^d Wm Bray was Demandant the s^d Aug^s Warren the You^r tenant & the s^d Humphrey St John Mildmay & Edwd St John Mildmay Vouchees who vouched over the Common Vouchee of

Two 11th parts of the Manors of Twyford & Marwell o'rwise Old Marwell with the appurt's and two 11th parts of 30 mess'es 3 dovehouses 1 water corn mill 80 gardens 1500 acres of land 300 acres of meadow 300 acres of pasture 400 acres of wood 2000 acres of furze & heath & 40s/ rent & common pasture for all manner of Cattle View of Frankpledge Courts Leets Courts Baron goods & chattels of felons & felons of themselves fugitives estrays deodands customs franchises liberties & privileges with the appurt's in Shawford Twyford & Marwell o'rwise Old Marwell & in the Parishes of Twyford & Owslebury & also the advowsons of the Churches of Twyford and Owslebury.

{Page 71}

As to the share to which Humphrey St John Mildmay became entitled of the above Estates

2nd July 1850

The sd Humphrey St John Mildmay by his Will after giving various pecuniary & specific Legacies gave devised & bequeathed All his real estate in the Coy of Kent or elsewhere & all the rest & residue of his p'sonal este &p'pty whatsr & wheresor to his eldest Son Humphrey Francis Mildmay & in the event of his death in tes'tor's lifetime tes'tor gave same to his second son Henry Bingham Mildmay And tes'tor declared that what he gave to his sd two sons shod be in addition to such sum as they would be resp'ly entitled to under the Settlem' made on his marr'e with their mother it not being his intention of making an unequal division.

The above abstd Will (with a Codicil dated 3rd July 1852) which gave an additional Legacy to testor's wife was proved in the Prerogative Court of Canterbury on the 8th Octr 1853.

9th August 1853

The sd Humphrey St John Mildmay died leavg his eldest son sd Humphrey Francis St John Mildmay him surviving.

As to the share to which Edward St John Mildmay became entitled of the above Estates

11th June 1818

Bond from Edwd St John Mildmay a Cornet in His Majesty's 22nd Regim' of Dragoons then stationed at Bangalore in the East Indies to Rob' Sherson of Chittoor Esqre in the Civil Service of the Honble the East India Company under their Presidency of Fort St Geo in £10,000 with the condition of which the following is a copy

"Whereas the above bounden Edwd St John Mildmay will on the death of his mother under a Marr'e Settlem' be entitled either to the rents & profits of certain est^s thereby settled or to a share of money to be raised for the benefit of the s^d Edward St John Mildmay & his younger Brothers & Sisters.

And whereas a Marriage is shortly to be had & solemnised between the s^d Edwd St John Mildmay & Marianne Catherine *{Page 72}* Sherson Spinster one of the Dau^{rs} of the above named Robert Sherson.

And whereas in order to make a provision for the s^d Marianne Catherine Sherson (in case she sho^d survive the said Edward St John Mildmay) & for the Children of the s^d intended Marriage The s^d Edward St John Mildmay hath proposed & agreed to enter into the Bond or Obligation above written to be conditioned as hereinafter is mentioned that is to say

Now the Condition of the before written obligation is such that if the s^d Edward St John Mildmay his h'rs ex'ors or adm'ors shall after the s^d intended marr'e between him & the s^d Marianne Catherine Sherson has been duly had & solemnised & when th'runto required by the s^d Rob' Sherson his ex'ors or adm'ors by one or more Deed or Deeds Writing or Writings to be by him duly executed & attested in the manner required by Law settle & effectually secure the rents issues & profits of all such messes lands tenem^{ts} & heredit's as he the s^d Edwd St John Mildmay may or shall become possessed of or entitled to under the provisions or limit'ons in such Settlem' contained or if the s^d Edwd St John Mildmay shall on the death of his mother under such settlem' be entitled to any sum of money or o^r p'pty or effects then in like manner to settle & secure such sum of money & its int' & produce & such property & effects to & for the use & benefit of the s^d Marianne Catherine Sherson (in case she shall survive the s^d Edward St John Mildmay) & the children of the s^d intended marriage then the written Bond or Obligation to be void otherwise to be & remain in full force & virtue."

20th & 21st December 1826

By Ind're of Lease & Release the Release bet^n the s^d Edwd St John Mildmay of the one part & s^d Humphrey St John Mildmay & the s^d Carew Anthony St John Mildmay described as Rector of Chelmsford in the Co^y of Essex Clerk of the other part.

Recit^g (inter alia) the abst^d Ind're of Bargain & Sale of 4th Novr 1824 & the Recovery in pursuance thereof.

And that by a Writing under the hand of s^d Edwd St John Mildmay & dated 29th Octr then last he did agree that s^d rec^d Deeds sho^d remain in the custody of s^d Wm Bray & Reginald Bray & Aug^s Warren for securing to them the repaym' of £250 which they had advanced to him on 3rd July then last.

{Page 73}

And that s^d Edwd St John Mildmay was desirous of making a settlem' of two thirds of his reversionary share & int' under & by virtue of s^d Ind're of Bargain & Sales & Recovery of & in said manors heredit's & prem'es in manner after expressed but discharged from all claims as to s^d £250 & interest.

It was witn'ed that in cons'on of 10^s/ to s^d Edwd St John Mildmay p^d by s^d Humphrey St John Mildmay & Carew Anthony St John Mildmay s^d Edward St John Mildmay in purs'ce of the power to him given by s^d rec^d Ind're of Barg^n & Sale & of every o^r power &^{c} Did by that Deed sealed & delivered by him in the presence of the two credible p'sons whose names were int^d to be th'rupon indorsed as witn^s attesting such sealing & delivery direct limit & appoint that

The rem^r or rev'on of him s^d Edwd St John Mildmay subj' as in s^d Ind're of Barg^n & Sales was ment^d & to take effect in poss'on after the decease of s^d Dame Jane St John Mildmay of & in two equal 3rd parts or shares the whole into 3 equal parts or shares being divided of all & every the present & immediate & also all & every the future expectant eventual & reversionary share or shares right title & int' of him s^d Edwd St John Mildmay of & in the Manors &^{c} after ment^d with the appurt's.

And the Rev'ons &^{c}.

Should thenceforth remain & be & that s^d Recovery sho^d touching s^d 2/3rd parts enure.

To the use & behoof of s^d Humphrey St John Mildmay & Carew Anthony St John Mildmay their h'rs & ass^s for ever

Upon the trusts after expressed.

And it was fur^r witn'ed that for the cons'on before ment^d & by way of fur^r assurance s^d Edwd St John Mildmay Did grant barg^n sell alien release & confirm unto s^d Humphrey St John Mildmay & Carew Anthony St John Mildmay (in their actual poss'on &^{c}) their heirs & assigns

Said rem^r or rev'on of & in s^d two third parts of and in All those the Manors of Twyford & *{Page 74}* Marwell & all o^r the property in the County of Southampton as before described.

And also of & in All & sing^r o^r manors mess'es farms tenem^{ts} & heredit's in the s^d parishes of Twyford & Owslebury or elsewhere in the Co^y of Southampton (if any such there were) ment^d and comprised in the abst^d Ind'res of 27th & 28th Novr 1789.

And all houses &^{c}.

And the Rev'on &^{c}.

And all the Estate &^{c}.

To hold subject to the sev^l sums of mo^y charged on the entirety of s^d heredit's & to which s^d Dame Jane St John Mildmay was entitled as afs^d & with^t prejudice to the estate of s^d Dame Jane St John Mildmay for her life in same heredit's unto & to the use of s^d Humphrey St John Mildmay & Carew Anthony St John Mildmay their heirs and assigns.

Upon trust that the s^d Humphrey St John Mildmay & Carew Anthony St John Mildmay or the sur'vor of them their heirs or ass^s sho^d after the decease of s^d Dame Jane St John Mildmay or in her lifetime with her consent and the consent of s^d Edwd St John Mildmay if he sho^d be then living such consent resp'ly to be test^d by some writ^g under the hands or hand of the persons or person whose consent was or were th'rby made necessary sell & dispose of or join in selling & disposing of the s^d heredit's & prem'es th'inbefore appt^d & rel'ed with the appurt's th'rto respectively belong^g either tog^r or in p'cels & either by Public Sale or Auction or by Private Contract or both to any person or persons willing to become the purch^r or purch^rs th'of for such price or prices or sum or sums of money as to them the s^d Humphreys St John Mildmay & Carew Anthony St John Mildmay or the survivor of them his heirs or ass^s sho^d seem reasonable with full power & authority to & for the tr'ees or trustee for the time being of the settlem' now being abstracted *{Page 75}* to buy in the s^d shares & prem'es at any such Auct^n or Sale & to rescind any contract or agreem' which should or might have been entered into by them or him & to put up the same again for or o'rwise make sale thereof with' being answerable for and difference or diminution in the produce thereof And do & share for the purposes afs^d or any of them enter into make & execute all such contracts agreem^ts acts deeds matters & things conveyances & assurances in the law as to them the s^d trustees or trustee for the being sh^d seem proper.

Declaration that s^d Humphrey St John Mildmay & Carew Anthony St John Mildmay & the survivor of them his ex'ors &^c sho^d stand poss'ed of s^d sale monies

Upon trust to pay to or permit the int' & dividends thereof to be received by s^d Edwd St John Mildmay & his ass^s during his life And after his decease.

Upon trust to assign the securities & to pay the dividends & int' which sho^d grow due after his decease to Marianne Catherine the wife of s^d Edwd St John Mildmay & all or any one or more exclusive of the o^rs or o^r of the children of the s^d Edwd St John Mildmay by his then present or any future marriage in such manner & form & if more than one in such shares & proportions with such limit'ons as substitutions in favor of one or more of the other of the objects of that power & either by way of Legacy portion present or remote int' or o'rwise to be paid or transferred at such time or times age or ages & upon such contingencies & subject to such dir'ons & regulations for maintenance education & advancem' & such conditions as s^d Edwd St John Mildmay at any time or times & from time to time during his life by any deed or deeds intrum' or instum^ts in writ^g with or with' power of revoc'on & new apptm' to be sealed & delivered by him in the presence of two or more credible witn^s or by his last will & testam' in writ^g or by any writ^g purport^g to *{Page 76}* be in the nature of his last will & testam' or any codicil or codicils th'rto to be resp'ly signed & published by him as th'in ment^d sho^d direct or appoint & in default of such apptm' & so far as the same did not extend.

Upon trust to pay the dividends & int' to the separate use of the s^d Marianne Catherine for her life without being subject to the control of any Husband she might thereafter happen to marry & after the decease of the survivor.

Upon trust to pay & assign the securities & dividends & annual produce to the child if only one & if more than one among all the children of the s^d Edwd St John Mildmay & Marianne Catherine his wife at the times & in manner th'in ment^d And in case there sho^d be no child of s^d Edwd St John Mildmay by s^d Marianne Catherine his wife or no child who being a son sho^d attain 21 or die under that age leaving issue at his death or being a Daughter should attain that age or be married.

Upon trust to stand the poss'ed of s^d trust funds accumul'ons & interest.

In trust for s^d Edwd St John Mildmay his ex'ors adm'ors & assigns.

Declaration that the purch^r or purch^rs of the s^d 2/3rd parts or shares heredit's & prem'es & other the person or persons comp^y of comp^s who sho^d become liable to the paym' of the s^d trust mo^s or who from time to time sho^d have all or any part th'of in their his or her hands or hand or upon securities as afs^d sho^d not be obliged or required to see to the applic'on or disposition of the same mo^s or any thereof or the int' dividends or annual income th'of or of any part th'of after paym' of the same to the person or persons who for the time being should be the acting tr'ees or tr'ee of the settlem' now being abst^d or be answerable or accountable for the misapplic'on or nonapplic'on of the same or any part th'of & that all & every receipt which should be given for the s^d purchase & trust moneys or any part thereof or the int' dividends & income of the same by the person or persons *{Page 77}* who for the time being sho^d be such acting trustee or trustees sho^d be a good & effectual discharge or sev^l good & effectual discharges for all & every sum & sums of money th'in & th'rby expressed & acknowledged to be or to have been received

Signed sealed & delivered by s^d Edwd St John Mildmay & att^d by 2 witnesses.

1 William 4 1830

By An Act of Parliam' entitled "An Act to dissolve the marr'e of Captn Edwd St John Mildmay with Marianne Catherine his now Wife to enable him to marry again & for o^r p'pses th'in ment^d". It was amongst other things enacted that the bond of Matrimony bet^n the s^d Edwd St John Mildmay & the s^d Marianne Catherine his Wife be & the same was th'rby from thenceforth dissolved annulled vacated & made void to all intents constructions & p'pses whatso^r & that it should be lawful for the s^d Edwd St John Mildmay at any time th'raf^r (as well in the lifetime of s^d Marianne Catherine as after her decease) to marry with any other Woman or Woman with whom he might lawfully marry in case the s^d Marianne Catherine his then Wife were not living.

And it was fur^r Enacted that the s^d Marianne Catherine sho^d be & she was th'rby barred & excluded from all dower freebench & thirds at Common Law or by custom or o'rwise & of & from all other est^e rights titles claims & demands whatso^r of in to or out of all or any of the manors messes lands tenem^ts & heredit's whereof or wh'runto the s^d Edwd St John Mildmay then was or any time or times since the s^d marr'e had been or at any time th'raf^r sho^d or might be seized or entitled for any est^e of inh'ance & of & from all rights titles claims & demands whatso^r in to or out of all or any of the goods chattels personal est^e & effects whats^r of or to which the s^d Edwd St John Mildmay then was possessed of or entitled ei^r in poss'on or rem^r or to wch he sho^d or might at any time or times th'rafter become poss'ed or entitled by any ways or means whatsoever.

20th March 1832

By Ind're between s^d Dame Jane St John Mildmay of 1st part s^d Edwd St John Mildmay 2nd part Henrietta Roscoe of Tavistock Square in the Co^y of Middlesex Widow of the 3rd part & Lewis Peacock Gent^n of the 4th part.

{Page 78}

Recit^g (inter alia) the Ind'res of 27th & 28th Novr 1789 the Recovery suffered in Mich'as Term 30th Geo 3rd the Ind'res of Le' & Rel'e of 23rd & 24th Aug' 1804 the Will of Sir H^y Paulet St John Mildmay dated 6th July 1808 & noticing his death & the probate of his Will leaving the s^d Dame Jane St John Mildmay his Widow Sir H^y St John Carew St John Mildmay Bar^t his eldest Son & Heir & 14 Dau^{rs} & younger Sons him surviving.

And recit^g that the s^d Edwd St John Mildmay about the year 1818 intermarried with his present Wife the Marianne Cath^e Sherson Sp^r & that previously to & in cons'on of such marr'e he on the 11th day of June 1818 executed a Bond (which is set out in the earlier part of this Abstract).

And recit^g that the before abst^d Bargain & Sale of 4th Novr 1824 & Common Recovery of the 5th Geo 4th.

And recit^g that s^d Edwd St John Mildmay on or about the 29th Octr 1826 delivered the s^d Ind'res of Barg^n & Sale before recited & the Exemplification of the Recoveries unto the s^d Wm Bray Augustus Warren & Reginald Bray Gent^n by way of equitable mortgage to secure to them repaym^t with int^t of £250 which was then due with some arrear of interest.

And recit^g the Ind'res of Le' & Rel'e of 20th & 21st Decr 1826.

And recit^g that the s^d Chas Wm Paulett Mildmay died 20th Jany 1830 without issue whereby 1/10th part of this reversionary share in the s^d sev^l heredit's th'inbef ment^d became vested in the s^d Edwd St John Mildmay & the heirs of his body in rem^r immed'ly expect^t on the death of the s^d Dame Jane St John Mildmay subj' to the grant made of two thirds thereof in & by the s^d rec^d Ind're of Rel'e of the 21st day of Decr 1826.

And recit^g the s^d Henretta Rosco had contracted with the s^d Dame Jane St John Mildmay & Edwd St John Mildmay for the purchase of an Annuity of £74 for the term of 99 years if the s^d Edwd St John Mildmay sho^d so long live as is th'inaf^r ment^d subject to such redempt^n or repurchase of the same Annuity as th'inaf^r ment^d provided.

And recit^g that upon the treaty for the purchase it was agreed that the same sho^d be charged & secured in manner *{Page 79}* th'inaf^r ment^d as well upon the life est^e of the s^d Dame Jane St John Mildmay of & in all & sing^r the sev^l heredit's th'inbef ment^d as also upon the estate in remainder expectant upon the decease of or to which the s^d Edwd St John Mildmay was seized or entitled of & in one third of one tenth of the same heredit's as th'inbefore ment^d or such other part or share th'in as he might be entitled to in such rem^r as afs^d & also upon the interest both during his life & in rem^r which in &by the s^d Ind'res of the 21st day of Decr 1826 was reserved to the s^d Edwd St John Mildmay in the monies to arise from the sale of the heredit's th'in comprised & directed to be sold as aforesaid.

It was witn'ed that in pursuance of the s^d Agreem' & in cons'on of £600 the rec' &^{c} The s^d Dame Jane St John Mildmay in respect of her life est^e in the heredit's th'inaf^r charged during her life And he the s^d Edwd St John Mildmay in respect of his afs^d est^e in rem^r in one third of one tenth of the same heredit's & in respect of all such other estate share & int' th'in to which he was or might be entitled in rem^r expectant on the death of his s^d mother Did & each of them did grant And also he the s^d Edwd St John Mildmay in purs'ce & exercise of the sev^l powers of apptm' to him given by the s^d Ind'res of Barg^n & Sale of the 4th day of Novr 1824 & of all o^r powers &^{c} as to the heredit's or parts or shares of heredit's to which s^d powers resp'ly extended Did appoint unto the s^d Henrietta Rosco her ex'ors adm'ors & ass^s thenceforth for 99 years if the s^d Edwd St John Mildmay sho^d so long live

One Annuity of £74 to be issuing during so many years of the s^d term determinable as afs^d as the Dame Jane St John Mildmay should happen to live out of & to be charged upon All & sing^r the s^d sev^l manors mess'es advowsons lands tenem^{ts} & heredit's in the sev^l Counties of Southampton & Middlesex comprised in s^d Ind'res of the 27th & 28th days of Novr 1789 & th'rby resp'ly rel'ed & covenanted to be surv^d And which heredit's were more fully descr^d in the sev^l Schedules to the Ind're now being abst^d with their resp'ive appurt's subj' to the prior charges affect^g the same resp'ly & th'inbef ment^d And also to be issuing at all *{Page 80}* times dur^g the continuance of the s^d Ann^y out of & to be charged upon All that one third part of one tenth part or share & all & every other part or parts share or shares of & in the same several manors mess'es advowsons lands tenem^{ts} & heredit's of or to which he the s^d Edwd St John Mildmay under the limit'ons in the s^d Ind're of the 28th Novr 1789 or under or by virtue of any o^r of the deeds instrum^{ts} & assurances th'inbef ment^d was seized or entitled for an est^e in fee simple or in fee tail or for life in rem^r expectant upon the death of his s^d Mother together with one third part of one tenth part or share or such other part or parts share or shares as afs^d & of & in the appurt's to the s^d heredit's belong^g or in anywise appertaining.

And the Reversions &^{c}.

But subject to the prior charges th'inbef ment^d

To hold receive & take s^d Ann^y of £74 & every part thereof unto the s^d Henrietta Rosco her ex'ors adm'ors & ass^s thenceforth dur^g the term of 99 years if the s^d Edwd St John Mildmay sho^d so long live to be paid as therein mentioned.

Powers of distress & entry in case of nonpaym' of the s^d Annuity.

It is fur^r witn'ed that in fur^r purs'ce of the s^d agreem' & for the cons'on afs^d & of 5^s/ the rec' &^{c} He the s^d Edwd St John Mildmay at the request & by the dir'on of the s^d Henrietta Rosco Did grant barg^n sell & demise & also in exercise of the powers of apptm' given or reserved to him by the s^d rec^d Ind're of the 4th Novr 1824 & of all o^r powers &^{c} Did limit & appoint unto the s^d L. Peacock his ex'ors adm'ors & assigns.

All that one third part or share of & in the one tenth part or share of him the s^d Edwd St John Mildmay of & in the sev^l manors messuages advowsons lands tenem^{ts} & heredit's th'inbefore ment^d or referred to & all & every other part or parts share or shares of him the s^d Edwd St John Mildmay *{Page 81}* of & in the same heredit's which was or were th'rby charged by the s^d Edwd St John Mildmay with the paym' of the s^d Annuity th'rby granted tog^r with the same one third of one tenth & other parts or share parts or shares of & in the appurt's .

And the Rev'on &^{c}.

To hold (subject to the sev^l prior charges & incumb's affect^g the same as th'inbef ment^d) Unto the s^d Lewis Peacock his ex'ors adm'ors & ass^s from the decease of the s^d Dame Jane St John Mildmay for the term of 100 years thence next ensuing if he the s^d Edwd St John Mildmay sho^d so long live at the rent of one peppercorn if demanded upon the trusts th'inaf' declared.

And it is further witn'ed that in fur' purs'ce of the s^d Agreem' & for the cons'on expr^d & of the fur' sum of 5^s/ He s^d Edwd St John Mildmay Did grant bargain sell assign transfer & set over unto the s^d Lewis Peacock his ex'ors adm'ors & assigns

All & Sing^r the net monies to arise & be produced by & from the sale or sales of the heredit's or share or shares of heredit's comprised in & conveyed by the s^d rec^d Ind're of the 21st Decr 1826 & th'rby directed to be sold as afs^d & to which net monies the s^d Edwd St John Mildmay was under & by virtue of the trusts of the same Ind're entitled during his life & absolutely in the events th'in specified together with all int' dividends & annual income to arise from or be produced by the same.

To hold receive & take same unto the s^d Lewis Peacock his ex'ors adm'ors & ass^s upon trusts thereinafter declared concern^g the same.

Decl'on that he the s^d Lewis Peacock his ex'ors adm'ors & ass^s sho^d stand poss'ed of the parts or shares of heredit's th'inbef appt^d or demised to him for 100 years determinable as afs^d & also the net mo^s dividends & int' th'rby assigned to him as afs^d upon trust for better secur^g the s^d Ann^y of £74 as th'in mentioned.

{Page 82}

Agreement & Declaration that in case the s^d Dame Jane St John Mildmay & Edwd St John Mildmay or ei^r of them sho^d at any time th'raf^r be desirous of repurchas^g the s^d Ann^y of £74 & of such their his or her desire sho^d give unto the s^d Henrietta Rosco her ex'ors adm'ors or afs^d or leave at her or their usual place of residence or abode 21 days notice in writ^g she the s^d Henrietta Rosco her ex'ors adm'ors or ass^s wo^d at the end of the s^d 21 days for which such notice sho^d be given as afs^d on receiv^g from the s^d Dame Jane St Jn° Mildmay & Edwd St John Mildmay or one of them all sums of mo^y whats^r which sho^d be then due for the arrears of the s^d Annuity & also a proportionate part th'of from the last quarterly day of paym' preceding such repurchase up to & inclusive of the day of repurchas^g the same and all costs which the s^d Henrietta Roscoe her ex'ors adm'ors or ass^s should have incurred on account of the nonpayment of the s^d ann^y accept £620 in full for the redempt^n or repurchase of the s^d Ann^y & upon rec' of the s^d £620 & of all arrears of the s^d Ann^y & of such proportional part th'of as afs^d & of all such costs as afs^d she the s^d Henrietta Rosco her ex'ors adm'ors or ass^s & also the s^d Lewis Peacock his ex'ors adm'ors & ass^s wo^d at the request cost & charges of the s^d Dame Jane St John Mildmay & Edwd St John Mildmay or one of them do everything which sho^d be necessary for the releas^g assign^g vacating & discharg^g as well the s^d Ann^y of £74 as the s^d sev^l securities given & exe'ted for the paym' th'of as afs^d &which by the s^d Dame Jane St John Mildmay & Edwd St John Mildmay or ei^r of them or their resp'ive heirs ex'ors adm'ors or ass^s or his or their Counsel in the Law sho^d be reasonable advised & required.

Executed & attested.

Receipt for £600 endorsed signed & witnessed.

Inrolled in Chancery.

The schedule to which the foregoing Ind're refers

Twyford and Owslebury Estate, Hampshire

The Manors of Twyford and Marwell

5th July 1856

By Ind're made bet{n} Wm Palmer 1st part the sd Lewis Peacock 2nd part the sd Geo Ashwell 3rd part & Charles Stewart Hawthorne 4th part *{Page 83}* (which same Ind're is indorsed on sd Ind're of 20th March 1832).

 Will dated 4th March 1843 whereby she gave her residue unto The Reverend Thomas Harrison his heirs ex'ors &{c} for ever for his own use & benefit as therein mentioned And she appointed him and Leigh Churchill Smyth Executors.

 And recit{g} that sd Thomas Harrison & Leigh Churchill Smyth both survived sd Testatrix & that sd Thomas Harrison on the 9th Aug' 1849 died having by his Will appointed the sd Wm Palmer & Thomas Chadwick Executors.

 And recit{g} that sd Leigh Churchill Smyth survived sd Thomas Harrison & duly renounced Probate of sd Will & Codicil of sd Henrietta Rosco deceased & Letters of Administration dated 23rd Octr 1851 of the personal estate of the sd Henrietta Rosco deceased were granted to sd William Palmer & Thomas Chadwick by the Prerogative Court of the Archbishop of Canterbury.

 And recit{g} that the sd Thomas Chadwick died in the month of May 1854 leaving the sd William Palmer his sd co-administrator him surviving.

 And recit{g} that sd William Palmer as surviv{g} administrator of the 7th May then last caused sd Annuity & the policy therein ment{d} to be put up to sale by Public Auction in one lot and that at such sale the sd George Ashwell as the highest bidder was duly declared the purchaser at £960.

 It was witn'ed that for & in consideration of the sum of £960 the sd Wm Palmer granted & assigned unto the sd George Ashwell his ex'ors adm'ors & assigns

 The sd Annuity of £74 granted & secured by the sd hereinbefore recited Indenture & the growing payments thereof from the 20th day of June 1856 & all rights & powers for better securing payment of the same & all covenants and other securities for the sd Annuity or yearly rent & growing payments thereof & also the sd sum of £620 to be p{d} for the red'on of the sd Annuity & of £74.

{Page 84}

And also the policy th'in ment^d being a policy on the life of the s^d Edwd St John Mildmay effected by the s^d Henrietta Roscoe as in the s^d Ind're mentioned.

To hold the s^d Annuity of £74 unto the s^d Geo Ashwell his ex'ors adm'ors & ass^s for the then residue of the s^d term of 99 years if the s^d Edwd St John Mildmay sho^d so long live.

And to hold the s^d growing payments redemption money policy & sum of £620 & other monies thereby assigned & the rights powers covenants securities & premises thereby also assigned unto the s^d George Ashwell his ex'ors ad'mors & ass^s as his & their own monies together with full power to sue for recover & receive & give good discharges for the same as therein mentioned &^c.

Cov^t by Palmer that he had not incumbered.

And by the same Indenture the s^d Lewis Peacock (at the request & by the dir'on of the s^d Wm Palmer & on the nomination & appointm' of the s^d Geo Ashwell did assign unto the s^d C. S. Hawthorn his ex'ors ad's & ass^s

The s^d 1/3rd part or share of 1/10th part or share & all & sing^r other the part or parts share or shares of him the s^d Edwd St John Mildmay by said h'inbef rec^d Ind're demised.

To hold the same with the appurt's (subject only to the several prior charges & incumbrances affecting the same as in the s^d thereinbefore recited Ind're mentioned or such of them as were then still subsisting unto the s^d C. S. Hawthorne his ex'ors ad'mors & ass^s from the day of the decease of the s^d Dame Jane St John Mildmay for the then residue of the s^d term of 100 years if the s^d Edwd St John Mildmay sho^d so long live upon the trusts th'inaf^r referred to concern^g the same.

It is fur^r witn'ed that he the s^d Lewis Peacock (at such requests and by such direction and on such nomination and appointm' as aforesaid Did assign unto the s^d Chas S. Hawthorne his executors & ad'mors.

All & singular the net monies to arise and *{Page 85}* be produced from the sale of the heredit's or share or shares of heredit's assigned by the s^d th'inbefore recited Ind're of the 21st Decr 1826 & int' dividends & annual proceeds by the same Ind're also assigned or int^d so to be

To hold the same unto the s^d C. S. Hawthorne his ex'ors adm'ors & ass^s as his & their own monies upon the trusts th'inaf^r referred to concerning the same (Tog^r with full power &^c)

And it is by the same Indenture declared & agreed that the s^d C. S. Hawthorne his ex'ors ad'mors & assigns should stand possessed of the sev^l heredit's thereby assigned for the residue of the s^d term of 100 years determinable as afs^d & of the s^d net monies & premises th'rby also assigned upon the trusts & with under & subject to the powers provisos & decl'ons & agreem^ts in the s^d th'inbef ment^d Ind're expressed & declared concerning the same.

Cov' by s^d Lewis Peacock that he had not incumbered.

Executed by s^d W. Palmer L. Peacocke & Geo Ashwell & attested.

Receipt for £960 endorsed signed & witnessed.

1856

By Ind're bet^n s^d Geo Ashwell 1st part s^d Chas Stewart Hawthorne of 2nd part Dame Jane St John Mildmay 3rd part & s^d Edwd St John Mildmay 4th part.

Recit^g the abst^d Ind'res of the 20th March 1832 & the 5th July 1856.

And recit^g that the s^d Dame Jane St John Mildmay & Edwd St John Mildmay had given to the s^d G. Ashwell notice in writ^g of their desire to repurchase the s^d Ann^y of £74 in exercise of the power for that purpose reserved to them by the th'inbef rec^d Ind're of 20th March 1832.

And recit^g that the th'inbefore rec^d Ind're of 5th July 1856 which included an assignm' of a policy or assurance on the life of the s^d Edwd St John Mildmay hav^g been endorsed upon the th'inbefore rec^d Ind're of the 20th March 1832 it had been agreed that the same Ind'res sho^d remain in the custody of s^d Geo Ashwell until 6 months after the decease of s^d Edwd St John Mildmay or the amount which sho^d become due upon s^d policy sho^d be sooner paid or s^d policy be surr^d & that s^d George Ashwell sho^d enter into the cov' th'inaf^r contained concern^g the same

And recit^g that s^d Ann^y & also a proportionate part th'of from last quarterly day of paym' up to & inclusive of the day of the date of the Ind're now being abst^d had been fully paid as s^d George *{Page 86}* Ashwell thereby acknowledged.

It is witn'ed than in cons'on of £620 p^d by s^d Dame Jane St John Mildmay & E^d St John Mildmay to the s^d Geo Ashwell the rec' wh'of & that the sa: was in full for the repurchase & extinguishm' of the s^d Ann^y of £74 & of all arrears thereof & of all claims & demands for or respecting the same under the s^d Ind're of the 20th March 1832 or any cov' Warrant of Attorney Judgm' or o^r security made given or exe'ted for paym' th'of as afs^d the s^d Geo Ashwell did th'rby acknowledge &^{c} He the s^d Geo Ashwell Did for himself his h'rs ex'ors ad'mors rel'e & for ever quit claim unto the s^d Dame Jane St John Mildmay & Edwd St John Mildmay their h'rs ex'ors & ad'mors.

All that the s^d Ann^y of £74 granted & appt^d to the s^d H. Rosco her ex'ors ad's & ass^s in or by the s^d rec^d Ind're of the 20th March 1832 as aforesaid.

And also a proportionate part of the s^d Annuity from the last preceding quarter day up to the decease of the s^d Edwd St John Mildmay.

And all powers of distress & entry upon all or any of the prem'es compr^d in the same Ind're th'rby charged with the paym' th'of & all o^r powers cov^{ts} & remedies given by the s^d th'inbef rec^d Ind're of the 20th March 1832.

And all the Estate &^{c}.

To the end & intent that the same Ann^y of £74 & all powers & remedies for recover^g the same or enforc^g or compell^g paym' th'of might be extinguished & annihilated & that the s^d Dame Jane St John Mildmay & E^d St John Mildmay & each of them their & each of their ex'ors adm'ors & ass^s & the heredit's & prem'es by the s^d th'inbef rec^d Ind're of the 20th Mar 1832 charged with the paym' th'of & O^r their & each & every of their lands tenem^ts goods & chattels might be for ever exonerated & disch^d of & from the same & also of & from all actions suits cov^ts Warrants of Attorney judgm^ts executions acc^ts suits claims & demands whats^r of him the s^d Geo Ashwell his ex'ors adm'ors or ass^s for or in respect th'of or any part th'of or any deed instrum' or security made or given for or relat^g to the same.

And it is fur^r witn'ed that for the cons'ons afs^d He the s^d C. S. Hawthorne by the dir'on of the s^d Geo Ashwell & at the request of the s^d Edwd St John Mildmay test^d &^c Did assign surrender & yield up unto the s^d Edwd St John Mildmay & his h'rs

{Page 87}

All & sing^r the part or share parts or shares of & in all & sing^r the manors mess'es advowsons lands tenem^ts & heredit's by the s^d Edwd St John Mildmay granted & demised & appointed by the s^d th'inbef rec^d Ind'res of the 20th March 1832 with the appurt's.

And all the Estates &^c.

In such manner & to & for the end intent & purpose that the s^d term of 100 years determinable as afs^d might become merged & extinguished in & consolidated with the freehold of the same prem'es & the s^d part or share parts or shares & prem'es be had holden & enjoyed by the s^d Edwd St John Mildmay freed & discharged of & from all & sing^r the trusts decl'ons & agreem^ts in & by the s^d th'inbefore rec^d Ind're of the 20th March 1832 declared of or concerning the same.

And it is fur^r witn'ed that for the cons'on afs^d he the s^d C. S. Hawthorne by the dir'on of the s^d Geo Ashwell & at the request of the s^d Edwd St John Mildmay test^d as afs^d Did assign & transfer unto the s^d Edwd St John Mildmay his ex'ors adm'ors & assigns.

All & sing^r the net monies to arise & be produced by & from the sale or sales of the h'dts or share or shares of heredit's comprised in & conv^d by the s^d Ind're of Release of the 21st Decr 1826 rec^d or referred to in the s^d thereinbefore rec^d Ind're of the 20th March 1832 which were granted & assured by the s^d th'inbef rec^d Ind're of the 20th March 1832.

Together with all int' dividends & annual income granted & assigned by the last ment^d Ind're to arise from or be produced by the same net mo^s or any stocks funds or securities in or upon which the same should or might be invested.

And all the right &^{c}.

To hold receive & take the s^d net monies interest dividends & all & singular the premises lastly thereby assigned unto the s^d Edwd St John Mildmay his ex'ors adm'ors or ass^s to & for his & their own proper use & benefit wholly absolutely freed exonerated & discharged of & from all & sing^r *{Page 88}* the trusts decl'ons & agreem^{ts} in or by the s^d th'inbef recited Ind're of the 20th March 1832 declared of or concern^g the same.

Cov' by the s^d C. S. Hawthorne that he had not incumbered.

Cov' by the s^d Geo Ashwell that he had not done any act wh'rby he was prevented from releasing as th'inbefore mentioned.

It is fur^r witn'ed that in pursuance of the s^d agreem' s^d Geo Ashwell did cov' to produce & furnish copies of the s^d th'inbef rec^d Ind'res of the 20th March 1832 & the 5th July 1856 or ei^r of them And within 6 calander months from the decease of the s^d Edwd St John Mildmay or within one cal^r month from the day on which the amount which sho^d become due upon the s^d policy sho^d be paid or the s^d policy sho^d be surrendered whichever sho^d first happen to deliver up to the s^d Dame Jane St John Mildmay & Edwd St John Mildmay their ex'ors adm'ors or ass^s the s^d th'inbef rec^d Ind'res & in the meantime to keep the same whole uncancelled & undefaced unless prevented from so doing by fire or other inevitable accident.

Executed by all parties & attested.

The schedules are copies of the schedules to the lastly before abst^d Ind're of the 20th March 1832 & are ref^d to in the recital of the Deed.

As to the interest of Mrs Marianne Jane Barnett formally Miss Mary Anne Jane Mildmay one of the Daughters of the s^d Edward St John Mildmay in her Father's share

16th April 1847

By Ind're between Charles George Barnett of Lombard Street Banker of the 1st part s^d Marianne Jane St John Mildmay Spinster of the 2nd part s^d Edwd St John Mildmay of the 3rd part & H^y Barnett of Lombard Street aforesaid Banker & The Honble Edwd Pleydell Bouverie of Chester Street in the Parish of St George Hanover Square Middlesex of the 4th part.

Recit^g that a marriage had been agreed upon between the s^d Chas George Barnett & Marianne St John Mildmay.

And recit^g by virtue of the before abst^d Ind'res of 27th & 28th of Novr 1789 the sev^l manors &^{c} comprised in the schedule thereto were settled subj' to cert^n charges in the s^d Ind're of Release ment^d to the use of Henry Peters & Wm Bragge their ex'ors adm'ors & ass^s for 100 years upon cert^n trusts for raising two sev^l sums of £6000 each And also upon *{Page 89}* certain other trusts in the s^d Ind're of Release ment^d & subj' th'rto to the use of Dame Jane St John Mildmay & her ass^s for her life with rem^r To the use of all the Sons & Dau^{rs} of the s^d Dame Jane St John Mildmay by the s^d Sir H^y Paulet St John Mildmay (except the 2 eldest of such sons) as tenants in common in tail with cross rem^{rs} between or among them in tail with divers remainders over.

And recit^g that besides the 2 eldest Sons of the s^d Dame Jane St John Mildmay by the s^d Sir Henry Paulet St John Mildmay there was 13 other Children of whom the s^d Edwd St John Mildmay was one.

And recit^g the before abst^d Bond of the 11th June 1818.

And recit^g that s^d Bond was executed by the s^d Edwd St John Mildmay for the purpose of settling & assuring All the real & personal estate rights & interests whatsoever in poss'on rev'on rem^r or expectancy or o'rwise howsoever of him the s^d Edwd St John Mildmay under or by virtue of the s^d th'inbefore ment^d Ind'res as he the s^d Edwd St John Mildmay did acknowledge.

And recit^g that the s^d Dame Jane St John Mildmay & also the s^d Marianne Catherine Sherson af'twds Marianne Catherine Mildmay were both then living And that there had been issue of the s^d marr'e bet^n the s^d Edwd St John Mildmay & Marianne Catherine Sherson 4 Children & no more one of whom died under age unmarried & 3 of whom were then living & had attained 21.

And recit^g that it was considered that under the s^d Bond the s^d M Jane St John Mildmay was as one of such 3 Children as afs^d entitled to a share of all the real and personal estate to which the s^d Edwd St John Mildmay was entitled or interested under the said th'inbefore mentioned Indentures.

And recit^g (inter alia) that upon the treaty for the s^d marr'e it was amongst other things agreed that all the real & personal estate whatso^r of her the s^d Marianne Jane St John Mildmay under the s^d th'inbef recited Bond should be settled to the uses upon the trusts & in the manner thinaf^r mentioned.

It is witn'ed that in purs'ce of the s^d Agreem' & in cons'on of the s^d int^d marriage & of 10^s/ She the s^d Marianne St John Mildmay with the privity & consent of the s^d Charles G. Barnett (test^d &^{c}) Did grant bargain sell & release unto the s^d Henry Barnett & Edwd Pleydell Bouverie *{Page 90}* and their heirs.

All that & those the part or share parts or shares & interests whatsoever of her the said Marianne Jane St John Mildmay of and in All & Sing^r the Manors or Lordships messuages or tenements farms advowsons & heredit's ment^d and comprised in the schedule to the Ind're now being abstracted annexed.

And also of & in All & Sing^r other (if any the freehold heredit's compr^d in & conveyed & assured by the s^d Ind're of 28th Novr 1789.

Page | 73

And also of & in All & singular other the heredit's whatso' & wheresoever which by virtue of any Inclosure Act or Acts or by purchase & exchange allotm' substitution or o'rwise howsever then were either at Law or in Equity subject to be holden upon or liable to the uses trusts limit'ons & decl'ons decl'd & contained in & by the s^d Ind're of the 28th day of Novr 1789.

And also all & sing^r other (if any) the part or share parts or shares & int^{ts} whatso^r of her the said Marianne Jane St John Mildmay of & in any other heredit's whatso^r or whereso^r under or by virtue of the s^d rec^d Bond.

Tog^r with all & singular houses &^{c}.

And the Rev'on &^{c}. And all the Estate &^{c}.

To hold the s^d part or share parts or shares & heredit's & all & sing^r other the prem'es th'rby granted & rel'ed or o'rwise assured with their appurt's unto the s^d H^y Barnett & Edwd Pleydell Bouverie & their heirs.

To the use of the s^d Marianne Jane St John Mildmay her h'rs & ass^s until the solemnisation of the s^d int^d marr'e & from & after the solemnisation thereof.

To the use of the s^d H^y Barnett & Edward Pleydell Bouverie their heirs and assigns for ever upon the trusts and purposes & with under and subject *{Page 91}* to the powers provisos agreements and decl'ons thrinaf^r declared and contained of and concerning the same (that is to say)

Upon trust that they the said trustees or trustee sho^d immed'ly or as soon as conveniently might be after the solemnisation of the s^d intended marriage absolutely sell and dispose of the said part or share parts or shares and hereditaments thereby granted & released or o'rwise assured or intended so to be and the inh'ance th'rof in fee simple & unless authorised to postpone such sale under the power thereinaf^r contained to any person or persons whomsoever for such price or prices in money as to the said trustees or trustee for the time being should seem reasonable.

Agreement and Declaration that the heredit^s for the time being sold or offered for sale under the provisions afs^d might be sold either together or in lots by Public Auction or Private Contract and either with or without special cond'ons of sale as to title or to the evidence to be given of title & generally in such manner as the said trustees or trustee for the time being should think proper or deem most advisable and with a view to any such sale or sales they or he might enter into & make such Contracts or Agreements as might seem necessary or expedient and that they or he the said trustees or trustee for the time being might buy in the hereditaments offered for sale at any such auction or auctions as aforesaid and rescind abandon or modify any contract or contracts for sale and resell the hereditaments for the time being sold or offered for sale without being liable to answer for any loss or damage occasioned thereby and that when all or any part of the said part or share parts or shares & hereditaments thereby granted and released or o'rwise should have been sold for a valuable cons'on in money the s^d Henry Barnett & Edwd Pleydell Bouverie or other the trustee or trustees for the time being their ex'ors adm'ors & assigns should *{Page 92}* and be possessed of and interested in the the monies to arise by any such sale as aforesaid upon and for the trusts intents & purposes & with under and subject to the powers provisos agreements and declarations thereinafter declared and contained of and concerning the same .

Declaration & Agreement that said Henry Barnett & Edwd Barnett Edward Pleydell Bouverie and the survivor of them and their or his executors administrators & assigns (as the case might be) should stand possessed of & interested in all & singular the monies to arise by sale disposition or conversion into money under all or any of the trusts powers & provisions thereinbefore contained & also of other monies and properly in the Indenture now being abstracted.

Upon trust to lay out and invest and vary the investment thereof in manner therein mentioned and to pay the interest of so much of said monies as was not required for keeping certain policies of assurance on foot unto said C. G. Barnett and his assigns for his life and after his decease to pay the interest of the whole to s^d Marianne Jane St John Mildmay for her life and after the decease of the survivor the said trust monies funds & securities and the interest dividends & annual produce th'rof should be in trust for the child or children of the said marriage as therein ment^d And in case there should be no child or children in whom the s^d monies should become absolutely vested under the trusts therein declared the same trust monies funds and securities & the annual produce th'rof should from and after the decease of the survivor of the s^d C. G. Barnett & Marianne Jane St John Mildmay and such failure of their children as aforesaid but subject and without prejudice to the trusts & purposes aforesaid be upon the trusts if the said Marianne Jane St John Mildmay should survive the s^d Charles Geo Barnett then in trust for the *{Page 93}* said Marianne Jane St John Mildmay her executors administrators & assigns for her and their absolute benefit But if the said Marianne Jane St John Mildmay should die in the lifetime of the said Chas George Barnett then as the s^d Marianne Jane St John Mildmay by Deed or Will should appoint and in default of such appointm' & so far as any such appointment if incomplete should not extend in trust for the person or persons who under or by virtue of the statutes made for the distribution of the estate of intestates would upon her decease & such failure of her children by the s^d Chas Geo Barnett as aforesaid be intitled in case the said M. J. St John Mildmay having survived the said Charles Geo Barnett were then to die possessed of and intestate.

Power for the said trustees or trustee for the time being with the consent of the said Chas Geo Barnett & Marianne Jane St John Mildmay during their joint lives & after the decease of either of them with the consent of the survivor of them during his or her life and after the decease of such survivor then at the discretion of the said trustee or tr'ees for the time being to postpone the sale & conversion into money of all or any of the freehold copyhold or customary & leasehold hereditaments property effects and premises th'inbef^r resp'ly granted & released as afores^d for such period or periods as they or he might think fit.

Power if default sho^d be made by the s^d Chas Geo Barnett in payment of the s^d premiums payable in respect of certain policies of assurance in the Indenture now being abstracted before mentioned the s^d trustees or trustee for the time being out of the annual produce which sho^d accrue during the life of the s^d Chas Geo Barnett of the said trust monies stocks funds & securities thereinbefore settled to raise such money as should be necessary for keeping on foot the s^d several policies of assurance and *{Page 94}* for defraying all costs and expences which should be sustained on account of any such default as aforesaid.

Declaration that the receipt or receipts in writing of the said Henry Barnett and Edward Pleydell Bouverie or the survivor of them or the executors or adm'ors of such survivor or other the s^d trustees or trustee for the time being of any money payable to them or him under or in exercise of the powers of sale or partitioning or otherwise payable to them or him under or by virtue of these present or any provision herein contained should be a good and sufficient discharge or good & sufficient discharges for the same and that the person or persons to whom such receipt should be resp'ly given should not be ans'wble for the loss misapplication or nonapplic'on or be in anywise bound or concerned to see to the application of the money in such receipt or receipts acknowledged to be received and should exonerate every purchaser or other person from enquiring into & ascertaining the regularity & propriety of any sale or sales or other disposition or dispositions which might be made or purported to be made under or by virtue of the said powers & provisions for that purpose therein contained

 Covenant by said C. G. Barnett & M. a. j. St John Mildmay for further assurance

 Executed by the parties of the first 3 parts and attested.

 The schedule contains a Copy of the Parcels in the Release of 28th November 1789.

As to the interest of Mrs Jane Catherine Vernon formally Miss Jane Catherine St John Mildmay another of the Daughters of the said Edwd St John Mildmay in her Fathers share

18th April 1849

By Ind're between the Revd Evelyn Hardoff Harcourt Vernon *{Page 95}* Rector of Grove in the County of Nottingham Clerk of the first p^t Granville Harcourt Vernon Esquire the Father of the said Evelyn Hardoff Harcourt Vernon of the 2 part s^d Jane Catherine St John Mildmay Spinster of the 3^d part the s^d Edward St John Mildmay of the 4th part The Honorable Edward Pleydell Bouverie and Granville Edwd Harcourt Vernon of Grove afs^d Esqre of the 5th part

 Reciting that a marriage was intended to be shortly solemnised between the said Evelyn Hardoff Harcourt Vernon & Jane Catherine St John Mildmay.

 And reciting the before abst^d Indentures bearing date the 27th and 28th November 1789 & the Common recovery suffered in pursuance thereof.

 And reciting that there was Issue of Marriage between the said Sir Henry Paulet St John Mildmay and the said Dame Jane St John Mildmay 11 Sons and 4 Daughters.

 And reciting that the eldest son Henry St John Carew St John Mildmay af'twds Sir Henry St John Carew St John Mildmay Bart' since deceased became entitled in remainder imm'dly expectant upon the decease of the said Dame Jane St John Mildmay to the estates devised by the said will of the said Carew Hervey Mildmay before referred to and the second son Paulet St John Mildmay became entitled in possession to the hereditaments settled by the said Sir Henry Paulet St John Mildmay deceased by the aforesaid Indenture of the 21st June 1786 before referred to and the said estates situate in the counties of Southampton & Middlesex before mentioned acc'dly became devisable under the aforesaid limitations thereof before recited in equal shares between the 13 younger sons and dau'rs of the said Sir Henry Paulet St John Mildmay & Dame Jane St John Mildmay his wife.

 And reciting that augustus Tucker St John Mildmay Charles William Paulet St John Mildmay Gualtier St John Mildmay Hugh Cornwall St John Mildmay and *{Page 96}* Letitia St John Mildmay 6 of the said 13 younger sons and dau'rs of the said marriage had died without issue and without having done any act to bar their said respective estates tail or the remainders expectant thereon and accordingly the said estates in the said Counties of Southampton and Middlesex before mentioned had become divisible in equal shares between the seven surviving younger son and daughters of which remaining younger sons the said Edward St John Mildmay was one

And reciting the before abstracted Bond of 11th June 1818

And reciting (inter alia) that by virtue of the before abstracted Ind're of 4th November 1824 and the Common Recovery 5 George 4 and the sett[t] of 21st December 1826 All and every the then present and immediate and future expectant eventual and reversionary share or shares of him the said Edward St John Mildmay of and in the manors & hereditaments in the County of Southampton thrinbef mentioned were freed & disc'ged from the said estate or estates tail limited to the said Edward St John Mildmay therein as aforesaid and two equal third parts or shares of such share or shares were vested in or assured unto and to the use of the said Humphrey St Jno Mildmay & Carew Anthony St John Mildmay their heirs and assigns (subject to the estate for life therein of the said Dame Jane St John Mildmay) Upon certain trusts for sale of the said premises and for investment of the proceeds and payment of the income thereof unto the said Edward St John Mildmay during his life and after his decease for payment & division of such monies or proceeds unto & amongst the said Marianne Catherine his wife and all or any one or more exclusively of the others or other of his children by his then present or any future marriage in such manner as he should appoint and in default of appointment Upon trust to pay the income unto the *{Page 97}* said Marianne Catherine St John Mildmay during her life and after her decease to pay and transfer the trust funds to the children of the marriage in equal shares as tenants in common.

And reciting the said Indentures of the 2nd & 3rd Nov[r] 1824 – 4th November 1824 and 21st December 1826 were respectively made and executed without reference to the said Bond of 11th June 1818 or the agreement or stipulation for executing a settlement therein contained but that it was considered that the aforesaid one undivided 7th p[t] or share of the said Edward St John Mildmay and every other (if any) his share in the said Manors & hereditaments comprised in the said several last ment[d] Indentures were subject in equity to the said recited bond and to the articles or agreement for a settlement therein contained or thereby entered into

And reciting that there had been issue of the s[d] marriage between the said Edward St John Mildmay and Marianne Catherine his wife 4 children (that is to say) Edward Wheatley St John Mildmay, Arthur George St John Mildmay, Marianne Jane St John Mildmay then the wife of said Charles George Barnett and the said Jane Catherine St John Mildmay.

And reciting that the said Edw[d] Wheatley St John Mildmay died under 21 and without having been married leaving his father the said Edward St John Mildmay his heir at Law.

And reciting that it was considered that under the settlement which would or ought to have been made in pursuance of the agreement in the aforesaid Bond the said share or shares of the s[d] Edward St John Mildmay thereby agreed to be settled would have been settled so that the share thereunder of the said Edward Wheatley St John Mildmay deceased would upon his death under age and unmarried as aforesaid become vested in equal shares in his surviving Brothers & Sister *{Page 98}* the said Arthur George St John Mildmay, Marianne Barnett and Jane Catherine St John Mildmay who had severally attained 21 years & accordingly the settlem[t] now being abstracted was agreed to be made upon the understand[g] between the s[d] Jane Catherine St John Mildmay & her Father the s[d] Edw[d] St John Mildmay that she the s[d] Jane Catherine St John Mildmay was then entitled in equity to one undivided third part of the share or shares which by the agreem^t cont^d in the s^d Bond were agreed to be settled as afores^d subj^t to the life interests th'rin of the s^d Edward St John Mildmay & Marianne Catherine his wife as well as the life interest in the entirety of the said heredit's of the s^d Dame Jane St John Mildmay.

And reciting that it had been agreed that the one undivided third part or share of the said Jane Catherine St John Mildmay under the s^d equitable settlem^t of & in the s^d one undivided seventh part or share and all and every other part or share parts or shares of the said Edwd St John Mildmay in the s^d manors & heredits in the County of Southampton thrinbef ment^d should be conveyed & assured unto & to the use of the s^d Edwd Pleydell Bouverie & G. E. H. Vernon their heirs & ass^s upon the trusts thrinafter expressed.

And reciting that for strengthening & confirming the s^d settm^t agreed to be made on the part of the s^d Jane Catherine St John Mildmay the s^d Edwd St John Mildmay had agreed to concur in the Ind're now being abstracted as such heir at Law of the s^d Edwd Wheatley St John Mildmay deced and as having such power of appointm^t under the s^d Ind're of 21st December 1826 afores^d in manner after appearing

It is witnessed that in cons'on of the s^d intended marriage & in pursuance of the s^d agreem^t in that behalf & in cons'on of the cov'ts on the part of the s^d G. E. H. Vernon thrinafter contained she the s^d Jane Catherine St John Mildmay with the privity & appr'on of the s^d Evelyn H. H. Vernon (testified &^c) Did by the Ind're now being abstracted grant b'gain sell alien convey & confirm & the s^d Edwd St John Mildmay as such heir at Law of *{Page 99}* the said Edwd Wheatley St John Mildmay dec'ed as afores^d & in respect of all the estate & interest which vested in the s^d Edward Wheatley St John Mildmay deced under the said thrinbefore ment^d equitable settlem^t Did grant b'gain sell alien convey & confirm unto the s^d Edwd Pleydell Bouverie & Granville Edwd H Vernon their heirs & ass^s

All that one full equal undivided third part or share of & in the one equal undivided seventh part or share of & in every other the share & shares as well contingent as vested of or to which the s^d Edwd St John Mildmay had thr'tofore or should thrafter become poss'ed or entitled under or by virtue of the afs^d limitations thrinbef^e recited in favor of the younger Sons & Daughters of the s^d Sir H^y Paulet St John Mildmay dec'ed & Dame Jane St John Mildmay his wife of & in

All those the s^d several manors lands tenem^ts heredits & all and singular other the premises comprised in & assured by s^d Indres of 27th & 28th Novr 1789 & 24th aug^t 1804 or expressed or intended so to be thrin comprised or thereby assured & of & in all & every other the manors & heredit's whatsoever & wheresoever then subject (by any manner or means whatsoever) to the uses or limitations of s^d Ind'res and of & in the appurt's

And of & in the reversions &^c

And all the estate &^c

To hold the s^d part or share heredits & all & singular other the premises thrinbef^e expressed to be thereby granted & conveyed or otherwise assured (subject to the estate for life thrin of the s^d Dame Jane St John Mildmay & subject also to the equitable estates of the s^d Edwd St John Mildmay & Marianne Catherine Mildmay respectively thrin under the afores^d equitable settlem^t

{Page 100}

Unto & to the use of the s^d Edwd P Bouverie & G. E. Harcourt Vernon their heirs & assigns for ever

Upon trust for the s^d Jane Catherine St John Mildmay her heirs & ass^s until the s^d intended marriage between the s^d Jane Catherine St John Mildmay & Evelyn H H Vernon should be solemnised and after the solemnisation of such marriage upon the trusts following (that is to say) Upon trust that they s^d E. P. Bouverie & G. E. H. Vernon or the survivor of them or his heirs or their or his assigns should as conveniently might be after the decease of the survivor of them s^d Dame Jane St John Mildmay & Edwd St John Mildmay or in the lifetime of them or the survivor of them with their his or her consent in writing absolutely sell & dispose of all & every s^d share heredits & premises & the inh'ance th'rof in fee simple either together or in parcels & either at one time or at several times to any person or persons whomsoever for such price or prices in money & under & subject to such conditions of sale & generally & in all respects in such manner & under such arrangem^{ts} as to them s^d E. P. Bouverie & G. E. H. Vernon or the survivor of them or the heirs exors or admors of such sur'vor or their or his assigns should seem reasonable or otherwise should concur with the person or persons entitled to any other undivided shares or interests in all or any of the manors lands heredit's & premises a part or share th'rof was thrby conveyed in selling & disposing of such premises or any part or share or parts or shares throf in such manner as should be thought fit.

And upon fur^r trust that they or he might upon paym^t of the money to arise by sale of s^d share h'dits & premises or any part throf sign & give receipts for the money for which same should be sold which receipts should be sufficient discharges to the person *{Page 101}* or persons paying same respectively for the money for which the same should be so given or for so much throf as in such receipts should be resply acknowlg^d to be received & that the person or persons paying same resply & taking such receipt or receipts for same resply as afores^d should not afterwards be answerable or accountable for the loss misapplion or nonappl'on or be in anywise obliged to see to the applon throf or any part throf resply.

Declaration that the s^d Edwd Pleydell Bouverie & G. E. H. Vernon their heirs executors adm'ors & ass^s should stand possessed of the monies which should be received by them resply upon or for any sale or sales to be made in pursuance of the trusts & provisions before cont^d after thereout discharging all incidental expenses upon the trusts & for the purposes thinaf^r declared & contained concern^g same

It is fur^r witnessed that for strengthening & confirming the settlem^t intended to be thrby made of one undivided 3 part of all & every such share & shares as afs^d & in pursuance of the afores^d agreem^t & in cons'on of s^d intended marriage He s^d Edwd St John Mildmay in pursuance of the power to him for that purpose given by s^d Indenture of 21st Decr 1826 Did by that Deed or Instrument in writing by him sealed & delivered in the presence of the two credible persons &^{c} irrevocably direct and appoint that

One equal undivided 3rd part of the monies arising or to arise by any sale of s^d two third parts or shares & premises by s^d Ind're of 21st Decr 1826 conveyed unto or vested in s^d Humphrey St John Mildmay & Carew Anthony St John Mildmay their heirs & assigns.

Upon trust for sale as afores^d or expressed or intended so to be should from & immediately after the dec'e of the s^d Edwd St John Mildmay go & be paid unto the s^d Jane Catherine St John Mildmay her exors admors or assign^s subject to the paym^t th'rout unto the s^d Marianne Catherine Mildmay her ex'ors adm'ors or ass^s of the sum *{Page 102}* of £1 which was th'rby appointed unto her for her absolute benefit.

  Proviso that nothing thrin cont^d should be deemed to establish or set up the settlem^t made or purported or intended to be made or the trusts created or expressed or int^d to be created by the s^d Indre of 21st Decr 1826 so far as the s^d equitable settlem^t made by virtue of the s^d Bond of the 11th June 1818 had legal or equitable precedence or priority to or over the s^d settlem^t or the s^d trusts made or created by the s^d Indre of 21st Decr 1826 or int^d so to be the intention of the s^d parties to the Indre now being abstracted being merely to make use of the afs^d power of appointm^t cont^d in the s^d last ment^d Indre so far as the same might be subsisting & capable of being exercised for the purpose of strengthening perfecting & confirm^g the settlem^t int^d to be th'rby made as afores^d

  Declon that the s^d E. P. Bouverie & G. E. H. Vernon their exors adm'ors & ass^s should stand possessed of the monies which should arise by virtue of the sale of the s^d share & heredit's thrby conveyed under the trusts th'rinbef^e cont^d And also of & in the one third share thinbef^e expressed to be appointed by the s^d Edwd St John Mildmay in pursu'ce of the s^d power thinbef^e ment^d (if & so far as such appointm^t should or might or could have any effect or be acted upon under the cir'ces afores^d which share the s^d Jane Catherine St John Mildmay did thereby assign unto the s^d E. P. Bouverie & G. E. H. Vernon their ex'ors ad's & ass^s & did direct the same to be paid & assigned to them

  Upon trust to lay out the same in their or his name or names upon some or one of the Parliamentary stocks or public funds of Great Britain or at int^t upon Governm^t or real securities in England or Wales with power for them or him from time to time to alter &vary the same investm^{ts} for or into others of the like nature with the consent of the s^d Evelyn Hardoff Harcourt Vernon during his life & after his death with the consent of the s^d Jane Catherine St John Mildmay during her life and after the decease of the sur'vor of them of the proper authority of such trees or tree and that they or he the s^d trees or tree should stand poss'ed *{Page 103}* of all & singular the s^d trust monies stocks funds and securities & the int^t dividends & annual proceeds thof

  Upon trust to pay the s^d dividends & annual produce unto the s^d E. H. H. Vernon or his assigns for his life & after his decease unto the s^d Jane Catherine St John Mildmay or her ass^s for her life and after the de'ce of the sur'vor of them the s^d E. H. H. Vernon & Jane Catherine St John Mildmay

  In trust for the children of the s^d marr'e as thin ment^d And if there should be no child who should become entitled to the s^d trust monies stocks funds & securities under the trusts thinbef^e declared subject to any appointm^t as afs^d the s^d trust monies stocks funds and securities & the int^t dividends & ann^l produce thereof resply should if the s^d E. H. H. Vernon should die in the lifetime of the s^d J. C. St John Mildmay then after the decease of the s^d E. H. H. Vernon in the lifetime of the s^d Jane C St John Mildmay & such failure issue as afs^d be

  In trust for the s^d Jane Catherine St John Mildmay her ex'ors adm'ors & ass^s for her & their own absolute use & benefit But if the s^d E. H. H. Vernon should survive the said Jane Catherine St John Mildmay then after the dece of the s^d E. H. H. Vernon so surviving the s^d Jane Catherine St John Mildmay & such failure of issue as afs^d upon & for such trusts pposes as the s^d Jane Catherine St John Mildmay by Deed or Will notwithst^g her coverture as thin ment^d should appoint and in default of such appointm^t & so far as any such should not extend

In trust for the person or persons who under the statutes made for the distribution of the estates of Intestate would at the time of her decease be entitled to the same trust monies & premises as part of the personal estate of the s^d Jane Catherine St John Mildmay in case the s^d J. C. St John Mildmay having survived *{Page 104}* he s^d E. H. H. Vernon had died possessed by the same Intestate.

Covenant by s^d G. E. H. Vernon (with the privity & approb'n of s^d E. H. H. Vernon & Jane Catherine St John Mildmay) with s^d P. P. Bouverie & G. H. Vernon that he his hrs ex's & ad's would on or before 18th april 1850 if s^d marr'e should be duly had and solemnised pay unto s^d E. P. Bouverie £1000 & within 12 months after his death pay unto them £6000 & in case s^d E. H. H. Vernon should & would pay unto s^d E. P. Bouverie & G. H. Vernon during the residue of the natural life of s^d G. H. Vernon an annuity of £300

Decl'on that in all cases whatsoever where any money should be payable by virtue of the Indre now being abstracted to any trees or tree for the time being of the same Indre the receipt or receipts in writing of such trees or tree should be an effectual discharge to the person or persons paying the same for so much money as in such receipt or receipts should be expressed or acknowledged to be received and that such person or persons as afores^d should not afterwds be answerable or accountable for the loss misappli'on or nonappl'on of such money or any part thereof or be obliged or concerned to see to the applon throf or any part throf

Executed by parties of first 4 parts and attested (the execution of s^d E. St John Mildmay attested by 2 witnesses)

As to the interest of Arthur Geo St John Mildmay the son of the s^d Edwd St John Mildmay in his fathers share

10th August 1849

By Indre made between the s^d Edwd St John Mildmay of the 1st part Arthur Geo St John Mildmay & Louisa Latham Mildmay his wife late Louisa Latham Ord Spinster of the 2nd part & John Thomas Ord of Farnham in the County of Suffolk Esquire & Reginald augustus Warren of Great Russell Street Bloomsbury in the County of Midd'x Gent^n of the 3rd part.

Reciting that a marre had been then lately solemnised between the s^d Arthur Geo St John Mildmay & the s^d Louisa *{Page 105}* Latham Mildmay.

And reciting verbatim (mutatis mutandis) as is recited in the last abstracted Indre

And reciting that it had be agreed that the one undivided third part or share of the s^d Arthur Geo St John Mildmay under the s^d Equitable Settlem^t of & in the s^d one undivided 7th part & of all other parts or shares of the s^d Edwd St John Mildmay in the s^d manors & heredits in the counties of Southampton & Midd'x trinbef^e ment^d should be conveyed assigned & assured upon the trusts & for the pposes & in the manors thrinafter expressed & cont^d

And reciting that for strengthening perfect^g & confirming the s^d settlem^t so to be made on the part of the s^d Arthur Geo St John Mildmay as afores^d the s^d Edwd St John Mildmay had agreed to concur in these presents as such heir at law of the s^d Edwd Wheatley St John Mildmay deced & as having such power of appointm^t under the said Indenture of the 21st December 1826 afores^d in manner thinaf^r appearing.

It was witnessed that in pursuance of the s^d agreem^t & for making a provision for the s^d Arthur Geo St John Mildmay & Louisa Latham his wife & for the issue (if any) of the s^d marr'e and also in conson of the sum of 5/ to the s^d Arthur Geo St John Mildmay paid by the s^d John Thomas Ord & Reginald augustus Warren He the s^d Arthur Geo St John Mildmay Did grant bargain sell alien convey & confirm & the s^d Edwd St John Mildmay as such heir at Law of the s^d Edwd Wheatley St John Mildmay deced as afs^d & in respect of all the estate & int^t which vested in the s^d E. W. St John Mildmay deced under the s^d hrinbef^e ment^d equitable settlement Did grant bargain sell alien convey & confirm unto the s^d John Thos Ord & R. a. Warren & their heirs & ass^s

All that one full equal 3rd part or share of & in the one equal undivided 7th part or share and of & in every other the share & shares as well contingent as vested of or to which the s^d Edwd St John Mildmay had thrtofore or should *{Page 106}* thrafr become possessed or entitled under or by virtue of the afores^d lim'ons thrinbef^e recited in favor of the youngest Sons & Daughters of the s^d Sir H^y Paulet St John Mildmay deced & Dame Jane St John Mildmay his wife of & in all those the s^d sev^l manors mess'es lands tenem^{ts} heredits & all & singular other the premises compri^d in & assured by the s^d Indres of the 27th & 28th days of Novr 1789 & 24th aug^t 1804 or expressed or int^d to be thrin comprised or thrby assured and of & in all & every other the manors and heredits whatsoever & wheresoever now subject by any manner or means whatsoever to the uses or lim'ons of the s^d Indres and of & in the hdits rights members & appurt's thrto belong^g or appertain^g and of & in the revon or revons &^{c}

And all the este &^{c}.

To hold the said part or share heredits & all and singular other the premises (subject to the estate for life thrin of the s^d Dame Jane St John Mildmay and subject also to the equitable estates of the s^d Edward St John Mildmay & Marianne Catherine Mildmay resply thrin under the afs^d equitable settlem^t)

To the use of the s^d J. T. Ord & R. a. Warren their heirs & ass^s for ever

Upon the trust thinaf^r cont^d concern^g the same.

And it was thereby declared & agreed that they the s^d J. T. Ord & R. a. Warren their heirs & ass^s should stand possessed of & interested in the s^d parts & shares of the s^d manors heredits & premises thrinbef^e conveyed to them by the s^d Arthur Geo St John Mildmay & Edward St John Mildmay

Upon trust but subject to the life int^{ts} & other estates thrinbef^e ment^d that they the s^d J. T. Ord & R. a. Warren or the survor of them or his heirs or their or his ass^s should as soon as conveniently might be as to the s^d share heredits & premises so conveyed by the s^d Arthur St *{Page 107}* John Mildmay & Edwd St John Mildmay after the dece of the survor of them the s^d Dame Jane St John Mildmay Edwd St John Mildmay & Marianne Catherine Mildmay or in the lifetime of them or of the survor of them with their his or her consent in writing absolutely sell & dispose of all & every the s^d shares heredits & premises & the inhance throf in fee simple either tog^r or in parcels & either at one time or at several times to any person or person whomsoever for such price or prices in money & under & subject to such conditions of sale & generally & in all respects to such manner & under such arrangements as to them the s^d J. Thos Ord & Reginald augustus Warren or the survor of them or the heirs ex'ors or adm'ors of such survor or their or his ass^s should seem reasonable or expedient or owise should join & concur with the person or psons entitled to any other undivided shares or interests in all or any of the manors lands heredits & premises a part or share whof was thrby conveyed in selling & disposing of such premises or any part or share or parts or share throf resply in such manner as should be thought fit and upon further trust that they & he should upon paym^t of the money to arise by sale of the s^d share heredits and premises or any part throf give & sign receipts for the money for which the same should be sold which receipts should be sufficient discharges to the person or persons paying the same resply for the money for which the same should be so given or for so much throf as in such receipts should be resply acknowledged to be received that the person or persons paying the same resply & taking such receipt or receipts for the same resp'ly as aforesaid should not afterwards be answerable or accountable for the loss misappl'on or nonappl'on or be in anywise obliged to see to the application thereof or any part thereof respectively.

Declon that the s^d J. T. Ord & R. a. Warren their hrs ex's ad's & ass^s *{Page 108}* should stand possessed of the monies which should be received by them resply upon or for any sale or sales to be made in pursuance of the trusts and provisions thrinbef^e declared & contained (after thereout discharging all incid^l expenses) upon the trusts & for the purposes thrinaf^r declared & contained of & concerning the same.

And it was thrby fur^r witnessed that for strengthening perfect^g & confirming the settle^t intended to be thrby made of one undivided 3rd part of all & every such share & shares as afores^d & in pursuance of the afores^d agreem^t in that behalf on his part & in conson of the s^d marr'e He the s^d Edwd St John Mildmay in pursuance of the power to him for that purpose given by the s^d recited Ind're of the 21st December 1826 Did by s^d Deed or Instrument in writing by him sealed & delivered in the presence of the two credible persons whose names were thereupon endorsed as witnesses attesting the sealing & delivery thereof irrevocably direct & appoint that the equal undivided third part of the monies arising or to arise by any sale of the two third parts or shares & premises by the s^d Indre of the 21st December 1826 conveyed unto or vested in the s^d Humphrey St John Mildmay & Carew Anthony St John Mildmay their heirs & assigns upon trust for sale as afores^d or expressed or int^d so to be should from and immediately after the decease of the s^d Edwd St John Mildmay go & be paid unto the s^d Arthur Geo St John Mildmay his ex'ors adm'ors & ass^s subject to the paym^t thereout unto the s^d Marianne Catherine Mildmay her ex'ors adm'ors or ass^s of the sum of £1 which was thrby appointed unto her for her absolute benefit

Proviso that nothing thrin cont^d should be deemed or taken to establish or set up the settlem^t made or purported or int^d to be created by the s^d Indre of the 21st Decr 1826 so far as the s^d Equitable Settlem^t made by virtue of the s^d Bond of the 11th June 1818 had legal or equitable precedence or priority to or over the s^d Settled estates or the s^d trusts made or created by the s^d Indre of the 21st Decr 1826 or int^d so to be the intention of the s^d parties thrto being merely to make use of the afores^d power of appointm^t cont^d in the s^d last ment^d Indre so far as the same might be subsisting & capable of being exercised for the purposes of strengthening perfecting & confirming the settlem^t int^d to be thrby made as afs^d.

{Page 109}

Declon that the s^d John Thomas Ord and Reginald augustus Warren their ex'ors adm'ors & ass^s should stand possessed of the monies which should arise by virtue of the sale of all the s^d shares & heredits thrby conveyed under the trusts thrinbef^e cont^d and also of & in the one third share thrinbef^e expressed to be appointed by the s^d

Edwd St John Mildmay in pursuance of the s^d power thrinbefore ment^d (if and so far as such appointm't should or might or could have any effect or be acted upon under the circumstances afores^d) which share the s^d Edwd St John Mildmay did thrby assign unto the s^d John Thomas Ord & Reginald augustus Warren their ex'ors adm'ors & ass^s & did direct the same to be paid and assigned to them upon the trusts & for the purposes & with under & subject to the powers provisos & agreem^{ts} thrinaf^r expressed & contained concerning the same (that is to say) upon trust to lay out & invest the same as thrin ment^d with power to vary the investments with the consent of the s^d Arthur Geo St John Mildmay during his life & after his death with the consent of the s^d Louisa Latham Mildmay during her life & after the decease of the survor of them of the proper authority of such trees or tree & to stand possessed of the s^d trust monies upon trust to pay the interest &^{c} unto the said Arthur Geo St John Mildmay or his assigns for his life and from and immediately after his dece unto the s^d Louisa Latham Mildmay or her assigns for her natural life and from & after the decease of the survivor of the s^d Arthur George St John Mildmay & Louisa Latham his wife In trust for the Children or Child of the marr'e subj^t to the appointm^t of the s^d Arthur George St John Mildmay & Louisa Latham his wife during their joint lives and in default of any such appointm^t to the appointm^t of the sur'vor and in default In trust for all the Children of the marriage in equal shares as tenants in common and if but one such child the whole to be in trust for that one child and if there should be no child in trust for the s^d Arthur George St John Mildmay his ec'ors adm'ors & ass^s.

Maintenance & advancement clauses

Power to appoint new trees

Declaration that in all cases whatsoever where any money should be payable by virtue of the Indenture now being abstracted *{Page 110}* to any trustees or trustee for the time being of the now abstracting Indenture the receipt or receipts in writing of such trustees or trustee should be an effectual discharge to the person or persons paying the same for so much money as in such receipt or receipts should be expressed or acknowledged to be received & that such person or persons as afores^d should not afterwards be answerable or accountable for the loss misapplication or nonapplication of such money or any part thereof or be obliged or concerned to see to the application throf or of any part thereof.

Executed by s^d Edward St John Mildmay Arthur George St John Mildmay & Louisa Latham Mildmay & attested.

Memorandum of acknowledgem^t by said Louisa Latham wife of s^d Arthur George St John Mildmay in margin signed by 2 perpetual commissioners.

As to the share to which the Revd Carew Anthony St John Mildmay became entitled in the above estates

15th & 16th November 1830

By Indentures of Lease & Release the Release between s^d Dame Jane St John Mildmay & the s^d Carew St John Mildmay th'rin described as the Revd Carew Anthony St John Mildmay Rector of Chelmsford Co'y Essex one of the youngest sons of the s^d Sir H^y Paulet St J. Mildmay by the s^d Dame Jane St John Mildmay of the first part Augustus Warren Junr Gent^n of the 2nd part & Reginald Bray Gent^n of the 3rd part.

Reciting that by virtue of the before abstracted Indres of the 27 & 28[th] Nov[r] 1789 the manor & o[r] heredits thrinaf[r] described & granted & rel[e]d stood limited & settled but subj[t] to certain incumbrances in the s[d] Indre of Release ment[d] to the use of H[y] Peters & W[m] Bragge Esq[res] their exors ads & ass[s] for 1000 years upon certain trusts in the s[d] Indre of Release ment[d] & subject thrto to the uses of s[d] Dame Jane St John Mildmay & her ass[s] for her life & after her decease to the use of all the Sons & Daughters *{Page 111}* of the s[d] Dame Jane St John Mildmay by the s[d] Sir H. Paulet St John Mildmay (except the two eldest of such sons) as tenants in common in tail with cross rem[rs] among them with sev[l] rem[rs] over

And recit[g] that there were 13 Children of s[d] Dame J. St J. Mildmay by the s[d] Sir H. Paulet St J. Mildmay (besides the two eldest sons) 3 of which s[d] 13 Children had died & that s[d] C. Anthony St John Mildmay was one of such sur'vors & youngest sons.

And rict[g] that s[d] C. Anthony St J. Mildmay was desirous of suffering a Recovery of his share in the afs[d] h'dits as well present as future expectant eventual or reversionary & of sett[g] & assur[g] such share to the use of them the s[d] C. Anthony St John Mildmay his hrs ass[s] & that in order to enable him to suffer such recovery he had applied to s[d] Dame Jane St John Mildmay to execute such assurance as thrinaf[r] expressed which she had agreed to do.

It is witnessed that in pursuance of s[d] agreem[t] & for docking bearing & extinguishing all e'sts tail of him the s[d] C. Anthony St John Mildmay & all rem[rs] & rev'ons thrupon expectant or depend[g] of & in the manors & o[r] hdits thrinaf[r] described & int[d] to be thrby granted & rel'ed & for convey[g] selling & assur[g] the same to for & upon the uses intents & pposes thrinaf[r] decl[d] & cont[d] of & concern[g] the same and also in cons'on of 10/ to s[d] Dame Jane St J. Mildmay p[d] the rect &[c] She the s[d] Dame J. St J. Mildmay Did grant b'gain sell rel'e & confirm unto s[d] Augustus Warren in his actual posson &[c] & to his ass[s]

All those the manors &[c] by the desc'p[on] in the Rele of 28th Nov[r] 1789

And also all & sing[r] the manors mess'es farms lands tenem[t] & hdits in the s[d] p'hes of Twyford & Owslebury or elsewhere in the s[d] C'oy of Southamp[n] (if any such these were) ment[d] & comp[d] in the afs[d] Indres of the 27th & 28th Nov[r] 1789

And all house &[c] and the rev[on] &[c] and all the este &[c]

Sav[g] & except[g] nevless & always reserv[g] & retain[g] to the s[d] Dame J. St. J. Mildmay her ex's ad's & ass[s] all sums of money to which she was in anywise entitled either in her own right or as extrix of her s[d] deced husband w'ch were charged upon the same premises or any part throf

{Page 112}

To hold the same with their appurt's unto the s[d] Augustus Warren & his heirs.

To the use of him s[d] Augustus Warren & his assigns during the joint lives of him the s[d] Augs Warren & the s'd Dame Jane St John Mildmay to the intent that the s'd Augu Warren might become a perfect tenant of the freehold and inh'ance of the same manors & other heredit's th'rinbef^e granted and released in order that one or more Common Recovery or Recoveries might be thof had & suffered in such manor as was therein ment^d for which purposed.

It was thereby agreed & declared that it should be lawful for the s'd Reg^d Bray before the end of the then present Michas Term or some subsequent term to sue forth one or more writ or writs of entry sur disseigin in le post returnable before the Justices of Common pleas thereby demanding against said Augustus Warren the s'd manors and other heredits thereby granted & released with their appurt's by such descriptions as should be suffic^t to ascertain the same to which said writ or writs the s'd Augustus Warren should appear gratis in person or by attorney & vouch to warranty the s'd Carew Anthony St John Mildmay who should also appear gratis in person or by attorney and enter into warranty to vouch over to warranty the common vouchee who should in like manner appear & imparle and allen imparlance make default to the end that judgement might be thereupon given and such further proceedings had in the premises that one or more good proper common Recovery or Recoveries might be perfected of the premises according to the usual course of common Recoveries for assurance of lands

Declaration that the s'd common recovery or Recoveries when suffered as af'sd and all other recoveries fines conveyances & assur^{ces} theretofore levied sufferd or ex'ted of s'd manors & other heredits thr'inbe granted and released by s'd parties to the Indre now being abst^g or any of them or whereunto they or any of them were or was parties or privies or a party or privy should enure & the Recoveror or recoverors in s^d Recovery or Recoveries names & his or their h'rs sho^d stand & be seized of s'd manors and hered's

To the use of the s'd Dame Jane St John Mildmay & her assigns for life sans waste in corrobtion and *{Page 113}* confirmation of the life estate limited by said abst^d Indenture of 28th November 1789 & of the powers of leasing and the powers to such life estate appended or annexed and after the decease of s'd Dame Jane St John Mildmay.

Then as to for and concerning all and every the then present & immediate and use and every the future expectant eventual and reversionary share or shares right title and interest of the said Carew Anthony St John Mildmay of and in the said manors & other hereditaments thereby granted and released

To the only use and behoof of the s'd Carew Anthony St John Mildmay his hrs & ass for ever.

Executed by s'd Dame Jane St John Mildmay Carew Anthony St John Mildmay Reginald Bray & attested.

Michaelmas Term 1st W^m 4th

Exemplification of Recovery wherein s'd Reginald Bray was Demandant s'd Aug^s Warren tenant & s'd Carew Anthony St John Mildmay vouchee who vouched over the Common Vouchee of

The Manors of Twyford & Marwell otherwise Old Marwell with the appurts & 30 messes 3 dovehouses 1 water corn mill 60 gardens 1500^a of land 300^a of meadow 300^a of pasture 400^a of wood 200 of furze and heath and 40^s/ rent & common pasture for all manner of cattle view of frankpledge courts leet courts barons goods and chattels of felons and felons of themselves fugitives estrays deodands customs franchises liberties and privileges with the appurt's in Shawford Twyford and Marwell otherwise Old Marwell & in the parish of Twyford & Owslebury & also the advowsons of the Churches of Twyford & Owslebury

11th & 13th December 1830

By Indentures of Lease and Release the Rele betw'n said Carew Anthony St John Mildmay of the first part the Honble Eliz[th] Caroline *{Page 114}* Waldegrave Spinster one of the daughters of The Right Hon'able Lord Radstock Baron Radstock deced of the second pt & The Right Honable William Earl of St Germans of the County of Cornwall The Right Honable Granville George Baron Radstock of Castletown Queens's County in Ireland and Paulet St John Mildmay of Haslegrove House Somerset Esquire of the third part.

Reciting inter alia the before abst[d] Ind'res of the 15th and 16th November 1830 and Recovery of Mich'as Term 1st W[m] 4th.

And reciting that a marriage had been agreed upon between the said Carew Anthony St John Mildmay and Eliz[th] Caroline Waldgrave & the agree[t] for a settlement.

It is witnessed that in pursuance of s[d] agreement and in conson of said intended marriage and of 10/ to s[d] Carew Anthony St John Mildmay paid (the rec[t] &[c]) he the s[d] Carew Anthony St John Mildmay with the privity and approbation of the said Elizabeth Caroline Waldegrave (testified &[c]) did grant bargain sell release and confirm unto s[d] Wm Earl of St Germans Granville George Baron Radstock and Paulet St John Mildmay (in their actual possession and their heirs.

All those the said undivided parts or shares of or to which the s[d] Carew Anthony St John Mildmay was seized or entitled in any manner howsever of & in (inter alia All those the manors and heredits comprised in the before abst[d] Indres of 15th & 16th Nov[r] 1830.

And of and all and sing[r] house &[c].

And the rev'on &[c].

And all the estate &[c].

To hold the same with the appurt's but without prejudice to the uses estates and charges which precede the estates and interest of the said Carew Anthony St John Mildmay in the said premises resp'ly unto the said William Earl of St Germans Granville Geo[e] Baron Radstock and Paulet St John Mildmay their heir and ass[s].

To the use of the said Carew Anthony St John Mildmay until the said marriage should be *{Page 115}* solemnised and after the solemnization th'of

To the use if s^d William Earl of St Germans Granville George Baron Radstock and Paulet St John Mildmay their heirs and assigns upon and for the trusts intents and purposes and with and subject to the powers agreements and declarations thereinafter mentioned

Declaration that after the solemnization of said intended marriage said William Earl of Saint Germans Granville George Baron Radstock and Paulet St John Mildmay and the survivors and survivor of them and the heirs and assigns of such survivor should with the consent of the said Carew Anthony St John Mildmay and Elizabeth Caroline Waldegrave during their joint lives and after the decease of either of them then with the consent in writing of the survivor of them during his or her life absolutely sell and dispose of any of the said undivided parts or shares hereditaments and premises thereby respectively granted and released at any time or times after the undivided share or shares to be sold should have vested in possession either together or in parcels and either by public sale or private contract to any person or persons willing to become the purchaser or purchasers thereof for such price or prices sum and sums of money as to the said William Earl of St Germans Granville George Baron Radstock and Paulet St John Mildmay or the survivor or survivors of them and the heirs or assigns of such survivor should seem proper and should for the purposes aforesaid (with such consent as aforesaid) enter into and make and execute all such covenants and agreements conveyances and assurances deeds acts matters or things as the said trustees or the survivors or survivors of them or the heirs or assigns of such survivor should deem reasonable and should buy in the said premises at any sale or sales by auction and resell the same either by public auction or private contract and either enforce or attempt to enforce any contract for sale and take all legal or equitable steps or means for that purpose or to recind or abandon any such contract without being answerable for any loss to be occasioned *{Page 116}* by any of the ways or means afs^d as to the s^d trustees or trustee should seem meet and should insert in any contract or contracts of sale any clauses or stipulations which to the s^d tr'ees or trustee should seem advisable.

Declaration that the receipt or receipts in writing of the s^d trustees or trustee for the time being for the monies so to be raised should effectually discharge the person or persons paying the same his or their ex'ors or adm'ors from seeing to the application th'rof or being answerable for the loss misapplication and nonappl'on of the same.

Declaration that the said trustees or trustee should stand possessed of the money to arise by such sale made in pursuance of the Indre now being abst^d upon and for such trusts intents and p'pses and with under and subject to such powers as well cont^d in an Ind're of even date being the Ind're next abstracted

Covenant by the s^d Carew Anthony St John Mildmay that he had good right to convey for quiet enjoyment free from incumb^s except as appears by the Indre now being abst^d and for further assurance

Proviso that if the said tr'ees in and by the Indenture now being abstracted nominated and appointed or any of them should happen to die or become incapable to act in the trusts or powers thereby in them resp'ly reposed or to them resp'ly given as afs^d before said trusts should be fully ex'ted performed or discharged or should become incapable to act then & in such case it should and might be lawful to and for the s^d Carew Anthony St John Mildmay and Elizabeth Caroline Waldegrave by any Deed or Deeds Instrument or Instruments in writing sealed and delivered by them in the presence and attested by two or more credible witnesses from time to time to nominate substitute or appoint any other pson or p'sons to be a trustee or trustees in the stead or placed of the trustee or trustees so dying desiring to be discharged refusing declining or becoming incapable to act as afs^d and that when any new tr'ee or tr'ees should be nominated and appointed as afs^d all the trust estate monies and prem's if any should then be vested in the tr'ee or tr'ees so desiring to be discharge or refusing declining or becoming incapable to act as aforesaid wither solely or *{Page 117}* jointly with the other tr'ee or trustees of the same resp'ly or in the surviving trustee or tr'ees of the same resp'ly or the heirs ex's or adm'ors of the last surviving trustee of the same respectively should with all convenient speed be conveyed assigned and transferred in such sort and manner and so as that the same should and might be legally and effectually vested in the surviving or continuing tr'ee or tr'ees of the same respectively and such new or other tr'ee or tr'ees upon the same trusts as were thrinbef^e declared or referred to of and concerning the same resp'ly or such of the same trusts as should or might be then subsisting or capable of taking effect

Declaration that the trustee or tr'ees so to be nominated substituted or appointed as afs^d should and might in all things act and assist in the management carrying on and execution of the trusts to which he or they should be so appointed in conjunction with the other then surviving or continuing tr'ee or tr'ees of the same resp'ly as fully and effectually and with all the same power and powers authority and authorities to all intents effects constructions & purposes whatsoever as if he or they had been originally in and by the Ind're now being abstracted nominated a tr'ee or tr'ees for the purposes for which the said new tr'ee or tr'ees resp'ly should be appointed tr'ee or tr'ees and as the tree or tr'ees in the Indenture now being abst^d in or to whose place such new tr'ee or tr'ees should resply come or succeed were or was enabled to do or could or might have done under and by virtue of the Ind're now being abst^d if then living and continuing to act in the trusts th'rby reposed in him or them any thing thrinbefe contained to the contrary th'rof in anywise notwiths'td^g

Executed by all parties & attested

7th July 1848

By Ind're (indorsed upon an Ind're of the 13th Decr 1830 being the Ind're of even date with the lastly abst^d Ind're and referred to thrin as declaring the trust upon which the purchase monies to arise from the sale of the heredit's th'rby assured were to be held and made bet^n the s^d Carew Anthony St John Mildmay and Elizabeth Caroline Waldegrave then his wife of the 1st part the said Granville George Baron Radstock of the 2nd part and Charles George Barnett of no. 3 Lowndes street Belgrave square Midd'x Esq and the Revd John Bramston Clerk Vicar of Witham Essex of the third part

Reciting that s^d Wm Earl of St Germans and Paulet St John *{Page 118}* had died

And reciting that s^d Carew Anthony St John Mildmay and Eliz'th Caroline his wife were desirous of appointing the said Charles George Barnett and John Bramston to be tr'ees in the place and stead of the said William Earl of St Germans and Paulet St John Mildmay and that s^d Charles Geo^e Barnett & John Bramston had consented to become such tr'ee

And reciting that the several estates or undivided shares of estates in the Parishes of Twyford and Owslebury or elsewhere in the County of Southampton had not been sold

It is witnessed that the s^d Carew Anthony St John Mildmay and Elizabeth Caroline his wife by virtue and in ex'on of the power and authority given and reserved to them by the th'rin within written Ind're and of every other power or authority enabling them in that behalf did by the Deed or Instrument in writing now being abstracted sealed and delivered by them in the presence of the two credible persons whose names were thereunder written as witnesses attesting the sealing and delivery of the Indenture now being abst^d by the s^d Carew Anthony St John

Mildmay and Elizabeth Caroline his wife nominate substitute and appoint the s^d Charles George Barnett and John Bramston in the place or stead of the s^d Wm Earl of St Germans and Paulet St John Mildmay to be trustees of the th'rin within written Indenture and of the before abstracted Indenture of even date with the s^d th'rin written Indenture to carry on and execute jointly with the s^d Granville George Baron Radstock or orwise such and so many of the trusts powers and authorities ends and purposes expressed and declared on & by the th'rin within written Indenture or the before abst^d Indenture of even date with the th'rin within written Ind're as were then subsisting undetermined and capable of taking effect

And the s^d Charles George Barnett and John Bramston did th'rby severally declare their acceptance of the s^d trust

It is further witnessed that in conson of the prem's & of 5/- He said Granville Geo^e Baron Radstock did grant rel'e & convey unto s^d Chas George Barnett and John Bramston and their heirs

All and every the messes or tenem^ts lands & hereditaments or parts or shares of messes tenements lands & her'es situate in the Parishes of Twyford & *{Page 119}* Owslebury afs^d which were described in or intended to be conveyed by the before abst^d Ind're of even date with the th'rin within written Ind're or which were ment^d and referred to in the th'rin within written Indenture with their and every of their appurt's

And the revon &^c

And all the estate &^c

To hold the same unto the said Charles George Barnett & John Bramston and their heirs

To the use of the s^d Granville George Baron Radstock Charles George Barnett and John Bramston their heirs and assigns.

Declaration by said Granville Geo^e Baron Radstock Charles Geo^e Barnett and John Bramston that they and the survivors and survivor of them and the heirs of such survivor should stand possessed of the s^d heredit's & prems thrby granted or intended so to be upon trusts and for the intents & p'pses and with and subject to the powers provisos and declarations expressed and declared in and by the before abst^d Ind're of even date with the thrin within written Indre or such & so many of them as were then subsisting undetermined and capable of taking effect & that they and the survivors and survivor of them & the ex's or ad's of such survivor would also stand poss^d of the monies arising from the sale of the s^d her'es & prem's when the same should have been sold and disposed of upon the trusts & for the intents and p'pses & with under & subject to the powers provisos and decl'ons expressed and declared in and by the thrin within written Indre or such and so many of them as were the subsisting undetermined and capable of taking effect.

Executed by all the parties & attested – the ex'ons by the s^d Carew Anthony St John Mildmay & his wife are attested by 2 witnesses

Abstract Number Three: Abstract Relating to the Charges upon the Estates in the County of Southampton Comprised in a Settlement of 28th November 1789

{Front Cover}

No.3

Abstract Relating to the Charges upon the Estates in the County of Southampton Comprised in a Settlement of 28th November 1789

Bradley Castleford

{Page 1}

Abstract Relating to the Charges upon the Estates in the County of Southampton Comprised in a Settlement of 28th November 1789

29th September 1815

By Indenture between John Clerk of Bownham near Minchinhampton Gloucestershire Esqre & George William Ricketts of Twyford Co'y Southampton Esq of the 1st part William Bray of Great Russell Street Bloomsbury Midd'x Esqre of the 2nd part s^d Henry Peters of Betchworth Castle Surrey Esqre and William Bragge of Edward Street Portman Square Midd'x Esqre of the 3rd part Dame Jane St John Mildmay of Dogmersfield Park County of Southampton W^o & Relict of Sir Henry Paulet St John Mildmay Bart dec'ed of the 4th part Sir Henry St John Carew St John Mildmay of Dogmersfield Park afs^d Baronet eldest Son & heir at Law of the s^d Sir Henry Paulet St John Mildmay by s^d Dame Jane of the 5th part Sir Henry Tempest of Thorpe House near Staines Middx Baronet of the 6th part Henry Lloyds Graham a Captain R.N of the 7th part and Henry Elliot Graham of the University of Oxford Esqre of the 8th part.

   Reciting that Henry Mildmay then late of Shawford Southampton Esqre dec'ed by his Will dated 1st November 1704 devised all those his Manors of Marwell o'wise Old Marwell & Twyford both in the County of Southampton with their appurt's & all other his purch^d leasehold & copyhold messuages lands & tenem^{ts} within the s^d Manors of Marwell & Twyford & a certain copyh^d estate in Midd'x unto his kinsman Carew Harvey otherwise Mildmay of Marks near Romford Essex Esqre & his s^d Testators brother Walter Mildmay & their heirs & assigns for ever In trust out of the rents issues & profits of the premises to pay his s^d Testators debts & an annuity of £150 to Mary Mildmay for her life and such legacies as should be given by the said Will & he allowed s^d Carew Mildmay £150 yearly for the mainten^{ce} of his (the Testators) Grand daughter Letitia Mildmay till she should attain her age of 18 years and declared that if his said Grand daughter at her age of 18 years or before or soon after should marry Humphrey or Richard (the younger sons of the said Carew Harvey o'wise Mildmay or if they should die or fail if she should marry Francis the younger brother of the s^d Carew Harvey o'wise Mildmay (neither of them *{Page 2}* being heir to the father or brother then and not o'wise he directed that s^d Carew Harvey o'wise Mildmay & Walter Mildmay & the survivor of them & the heirs of such sur'vor should imm'dly after such marriage stand seized of the s^d Manors of Marwell & Twyford & all other his freehold & copyhold messuages lands tenements & heredit's in the s^d Co'ys of Southampton & Midd'x In trust for the s^d Letitia Mildmay & such of them the said Humphrey Richard or Francis as she should marry for their respective lives and the life of the longest liver of them And after the decease of the survivor of them to the use of the eldest or only son of their bodies for the term of his life & after his decease then to the eldest or only son of his body or grandson of the s^d Letitia for his life and after his decease then to the eldest or only son of his body or grandson of the s^d Letitia Mildmay & his heirs for ever provided that if the said Letitia should have one or more daughters then her son & heir was to stand charged with & pay £1000 a piece as portions for the s^d daughters And s^d testator did by his s^d Will in case s^d Letitia should die with^t issue male give & devise all the premises in Hampshire to the s^d Walter Mildmay for life & after his decease then to the eldest or only son of his body begotten & the heirs male of such son lawfully coming & for default of such issue then to his brother Geo Mildmay his heirs & ass^s for ever provided the s^d Walter Mildmay or those that should claim under him should pay or secure before his entry on the premises £1000 to each daughter of the s^d Letitia Mildmay at the time of her death

And reciting that the s^d Henry Mildmay dies in the year 170 with^t revoking or altering his s^d Will save that he made some dispos^on as to the s^d copyh^d premises in Middx by a codicil thereto And the s^d Letitia Mildmay intermarried with the s^d Humphrey Mildmay by whom she had issue one son named Carew Mildmay & two daughters namely Ann who intermarried with Sir William Mildmay Bart & Katherine who died unmarried.

And reciting that by articles of agreement dated 27th March 1744 & made between the s^d Humphrey Mildmay & Letitia his *{Page 3}* wife & said Carew Mildmay therein ment^d to be the only son & heir apparent of s^d Humphrey & Letitia of the 1st part the Honble John Cotterell Esqre of 2nd part s^d Walter Mildmay of 3rd part s^d Carew Henry Mildmay of 4th part & Edwd Hooker & William Davis Esqre 5th part it was agreed that one or more common recovery or recoveries should be suffered of s^d Manors & premises in co'y of Southampton devised by the s^d Will of the s^d Henry Mildmay wh'rin proper parties were to join & that the recoveror or recoverors in such recovery or recoveries sh^d stand seized of the s^d Manors & premises To the uses & subject to the trusts thereina^r ment^d (i.e.) in the first place by mtg^e or fall of timber to raise the sum of £5,000 to discharge four several mtges (i.e.) one to the Revd Dr Harris for £1,200 to the repre'ves of the Revd Dr Cheney £1,350 to Godman Jenkins Esqre £1,000 to William Davis £500 (being a fine due to the master of St Cross for renewing a lease of the Great tythes parsonage house &^{c} at Twyford afores^d a fine to James Colebrook Esq for admission of s^d Carew Henry Mildmay to copyhold messuages in Middx And after raising s^d £5,000 in trust to raise fur^r sum of £4000 and apply same as therein ment^d & after rais^g s^d sum in trust to keep down the growing interest of s^d sums of £5,000 & £4000 & after paym^t thereof then to permit s^d Humphrey Mildmay to receive an ann'y of £300 for his life to pay a like ann'y to the s^d Letitia for her life for her use & for the maint^{ce} of her daughters & an ann'y of £200 to the s^d Carew Mildmay dur^g the lives of the s^d Humphrey & Letitia & the survivor of them & to pay half of the rent of Shawford to the s^d Humphrey Mildmay at the time his ann'y was made payable & the other moiety to be placed in South Sea Stock for the purposes thrin ment^d & then subject to the several trusts before ment^d & after the determ'on of the sev^l estates thrinbef^e created it was declared that the s^d premises should be settled to the use of the s^d Carew Mildmay his heirs and ass^s for ever & to be subject to such dispos^on as he s^d Carew Mildmay should by deed or will duly attested direct limit & appoint & for want of such apptm^t then to the right heirs *{Page 4}* of the said Carew Mildmay for ever with a proviso that if either the s^d Ann or Katherine should marry in the lifetime of the said Humphrey & Letitia his wife then the s^d trustees should by sale or mortgage or fall of timber or orwise raise out of the premises in Hampshire £1000 as a portion for her that should so marry And in case the s^d Ann and Katherine should marry in the lifetime of the s^d Humphrey or Letitia then £2000 should be raised & in case of those paym^{ts} the before ment^d ann'y to the s^d Letitia was to be reduced & a proviso that if the s^d Ann & Katherine or ei'r of them should survive both the s^d Humphrey & Letitia Mildmay then the trustees should by mtge sale or fall of timber pay unto such of them the s^d Ann & Katherine as should be unmarried at the time of the death of such sur'vor or to such person or persons as he or they should by deed or will appoint £1000 & should pay them an ann'y of £40 each till their marriage & upon such marriage should pay unto her or them so marrying the fur^r sum of £1000 and should pay unto such of them the s^d Ann & Katherine as should be married at the death of the sur'vor of the s^d Humphrey & Letitia £1000 & on paym^t of the s^d sums the s^d ann^s were to cease.

And reciting that by Indres of Lease & Release dated resply 3rd and 4th april 1744 the release between the s^d Humphrey Mildmay Letitia his wife & Carew Mildmay 1st part William Chapman of the 2nd part & the s^d Edward Hooker & William Davis of the 3rd part for barring all estates tail & remainders or reversions depending thereon of & in the Manors & heredit's thrin described & for the consons thrin ment^d the s^d Humphrey Mildmay Letitia his wife and Carew Mildmay did grant release and confirm unto the s^d William Chapman

All those the Manors of Twyford and Marwell o'wise Old Marwell in the s^d Co'y of Southampton and also all those capital messuage or tenement called or known by the name of Shawford situate lying & being in the Parish of Twyford afs^d with *{Page 5}* the stables granary coach house brewhouse dovehouse hop garden hop kiln gardens orchards fish ponds and premises thereunto belong^g with their & every of their appurts as the same was then lately held occupied & enjoyed by the s^d Humphrey Mildmay and also all that the Manorhouse called or known by the name of Twyford Farm situate lying & being in the p'sh of Twyford afores^d with the barns stables dovehouse outhouses garden & orchard & all & singular the arable lands meadows & pasture grounds thereunto belonging contain^g by estimation 351^a (were the same more or less) with their & every of their appurts as the same then were in the tenure or occ'on of Charles Snuggs his undertenant^s or ass^s and also all that mess'e or tenem^t & water corn mill situate & being at Shawford afores^d in the parish of Twyford afs^d with the stables outhouses garden orchard & prem'es thrunto belonging with their & every of their appurt's as the same then was in the tenure or occ'on of William Sturgess his undertent^s or ass^s and also all that messu'e or tenem^t called or known by the name of the Phoenix Inn situate & being in Twyford afores^d with the stables brewhouse g'dens & orchards & two acres of aarable land thrunto belong^g and all & singular the premises with their & every of their appurt's as the same then were in the tenure or occ'on of Thomas Frost his underten'ts or ass^s And also all that tenem^t or farmhold called or known by the name of Golden farm situate & being in Twyford afors^d with the barns stables outhouses garden & orchard & all & singular other the premises thrunto belong^g with their & every of their appurt's as the same then were in the tenure or occ'on of Charles Snuggs his underten'ts or assigns And also all *{Page 6}* that messu'e or tenem^t called or known by the name of the Parsonage situate & being in Twyford afs^d with the barns stables outhouses garden & orchard & three acres of pasture land & prem'es thereunto belong^g with their & every of their appurt's as the same then were in the tenure or occ'on of the Revd Walter Mildmay clerk his underten^{ts} or ass^s and also all that mess'e tenement or cottage situate & being at the Wears in the parish of Twyford afs^d with the garden & orchard & all & singular other the premises thrunto belonging with their & every of their appurt's as the same then were in the tenure or occ'on of Stephen Taylor his undertenants or ass^s and also all that the Manor house of Old Marwell situate & being in the parish of Owslebury in the County of Southampton with the barns stables outhouses gardens & orchards and all & singular the arable lands meadows and pastures thrunto belonging containing by estimation 311^a or th'bts (were the same more or less) with their & every of their appurt's as the same then were or late were in the tenure or occ'on of Thomas Over his underten^{ts} or ass^s and also all that messu'e or tenem^t called or known by the name of Law Hill Farmhouse situate & being in Owslebury afs^d with the barns stables outhouses gardens & orchard & premises thereunto belonging with their & every of their appurt's as the same were then in the tenure or occ'on of the s^d Thomas Over his undertent^s or assigns and also all that messue or tenem^t called or known by the name of Hensting Farmhouse situate & being in Owslebury afores^d with the barns stables outhouses garden & orchard *{Page 7}* & all and singular the arable lands meadows pastures & coppice thrunto belong^g containing by estimation 439^a or thereabouts were the same more or less as the same then were in the tenure or occ'on of William Page his undertent^s or assigns and also all that mess'ue or tenement called or known by the name of Stoudwood Farmhouse situate and being in Owslebury afs^d with the barns stables outhouses garden

& orchard with all & singular the arable lands meadows and pastures thrunto belonging contain^g by estimation 190 acres ot thereabouts (were the same more or less) with their & every of their appurt's as the same were then in the tenure or occ'on of Thomas Lavingston his undertent^s or assigns and also all that messuage or tenem^t called or known by the name of Uphill Farmhouse in Owslebury afores^d with the barns stables granary outhouses garden & orchard & all & singular the arable lands meadow & pastures thrunto belonging contain^g by estimation 200 acres or thereabouts (were the same more or less) with their & every of their appurt's as the same then were in the tenure or occ'on of [blank space] Tice his undertenants or ass^s and also all that messuage or tenem^t called or known by the name of Rough Hay Farmhouse in Owslebury afores^d with the barns stables gardens and orchards and all & singular the lands meadow & pastures thereunto belong^g contain^g by estimation 50 acres or thereabouts (were the same more or less) with their & every of their appurt's as the same then were in the tenure or occ'on of the s^d [blank space] Tice his undertenants or ass^s and also all *{Page 8}* that messue or tenement called or known by the name of the Pond house situate and being on Owslebury afores^d with the garden & premises thereunto belonging with their & every of their appurt's as the same then were in the tenure or occupation of [blank space] Barnett his underten^{ts} or ass^s and also all that piece or parcel of meadow ground containing by estimation 50 acres or thereabouts (were the same more or less) called or known by the name of the Lower Moor situate lying & being in the p'sh of Twyford afores^d with the appurtenances thereunto belong^g as the same then were in the tenure of occ'on of William Sturges & Gilbert Cole their undertent^s or assigns and also all that other piece or parcel of pasture ground contain^g by estimation 4 acres or thereabouts were the same more or less situate lying & being in the s^d parish of Twyford with the appurt's thereunto belonging as the same then were in the tenure or occ'on by the said William Sturges & Gilbert Cole their undertent^s or ass^s and also all that other piece or parcel of pasture ground containg^g by estimation 25 acres or thereabouts (wre the same more or less) called or known by the name of the Barley Field situate lying and being in the s^d p'sh of Twyford with the appurts thrunto belong^g as the same then were in the tenure or occ'on of the said William Sturges and Gilbert Cole their undertent^{ts} or ass^s and also all that other piece or parcel of meadow ground called or known by the name of Hackett Mead containg^g by estimation 10 acres or thereabouts (were the *{Page 9}* same more or less) situate lying & being in the s^d parish of Twyford with the appurts thrunto belonging as the same then werein the tenure or occ'on of Richard Wool his undertent^s or ass^s and also all that piece or parcel of meadow ground called or known by the name of Long Neithen cont^g by estimation 16 acres or thereabouts (were the same more or less) situate lying & being in the s^d parish of Twyford with the appurts thrunto belong^g as the same then or late in the tenure or occupation of Thomas Oades his undertent^s or ass^s And also all that other piece or parcel of pasture ground adjoin^g to the garden of the s^d Humphrey Mildmay situate lying & being in the s^d parish of Twyford contain^g be estim'on 25 acres or thereabouts (were the same more or less) with the appurts thereunto belonging as the same then or late were in the tenure or occ'on of the s^d Humphrey Mildmay his undertenants or ass^s And also all that piece or parcel of woodland called or known by the name of Twyford Park contain^g by estimation 200 acres or th'bts (were the same more or less) situate lying & being in the s^d parish of Twyford with all the trees woods underwoods coppices & shrubs thereon growing as the same then or then late in the tenure or occ'on of said Humphrey Mildmay his undertent^s or ass^s & also all that other piece or parcel of woodland called or known by the name of Rough hay contain^g by estimon 90 acres or thereabouts (were the same more or less) situate lying & being in the parish of *{Page 10}* Owslebury afores^d with all the trees woods underwoods coppices & shrubs thron growing as the same then or then late were in the tenure or occ'on of the s^d Humphrey Mildmay his undertent^s or ass^s and also the advowsons right of patronage & presentation to the Churches of Twyford & Owslebury afores^d and all other the messuages lands tenemt^s & heredits of them s^d Humphrey Mildmay & Letitia his wife & Carew Mildmay or any or either of them situate in Marwell Owslebury or Twyford afores^d or elsewhere in the s^d County of Southampton

To hold to the s^d William Chapman his heirs & ass^s to the intent to make him tenant to the freehold of the s^d premises against whom one or more common recovery or recoveries might be had of the s^d premises in manner thrin ment^d and it was thereby declared that the s^d common recovery or recoveries should enure to the use of s^d

Humphrey Mildmay & Letitia his wife for their lives & the life of the longest liver of them from & after the decease of the survor of them to the use of said Carew Mildmay his heirs & assigns for ever

And reciting that a Common Recovery was accordingly suffered of the the s^d Manors heredits & premises in the s^d County of Southampton in Court of Common Pleas at Westminster as of Trinity 17th & 18th George 2nd in which s^d Edwd Hooker & William Davies were Demandants s^d William Chapman Tenant who vouched the s^d Humphrey Mildmay & Letitia his wife & Carew Mildmay who vouched the common vouchee.

And reciting that by an Indenture dated the 6th Septr 1744 & made between s^d Humphrey Mildmay & Letitia his wife & Carew Mildmay 1st part s^d Walter Mildmay (thrin ment^d to be the surviving trustee of the s^d will of the s^d Henry Mildmay) 2nd part & Edward Hooker & W^m {Page 11} Davies 3rd part Sir John Hartopp of Epsom Surrey Bart & Obadiah Hughes of Aldermanbury London D. D. 4th part & The Hon'ble George Bridges & Ann his wife 5th part

Reciting (among other things) that s^d Edwd Hooker & Wm Davies (at the request of s^d Humphrey Mildmay and Letitia his wife & Carew Mildmay) had borrowed of the s^d Sir John Hartopp & Obadiah Hughes the s^d 2 sums of £5000 & £4000 by the s^d articles of 27th March 1744 directed to be raised which s^d sums the s^d Sir John Hartopp & Obadiah Hughes had lent by the direction of s^d Geo Bridges & Ann his wife. It was witnessed that s^d Humphrey Mildmay Letitia his wife and Carew Mildmay in cons'on of £9000 to s^d Edwd Hooker & William Davies paid by s^d Sir John Hartopp & Obadiah Hughes & for other consons thrin expressed the s^d Humphrey Mildmay Letitia his wife Carew Mildmay Walter Mildmay Edwd Hooker & William Davies did demise grant bargain & sell unto the s^d Sir John Hartopp & Obadiah Hughes All the s^d Manors of Twyford and Marwell o'wise Old Marwell in s^d County of Southampton messuages & premises & all other the Manors mess'es lands tenem^{ts} & heredits in Marwell & Twyford afores^d which were then late the estate of s^d Henry Mildmay deced To hold to s^d John Hartopp & Obadiah Hughes their executors admin's & ass^s from the day next before the day of the date of the Indre then being recited for 1000 years at the rent of one pepper corn without impeachm^t of waste subject nev'less to a proviso for redemption of s^d premises on paym^t by s^d Humphrey Mildmay Letitia his wife & Carew Mildmay or s^d Edwd Hooker & William Davies their heirs & ass^s unto s^d Sir John Hartopp & Obadiah Hughes their ex's ads & ass^s of £11.16.0 on 6th Septr 1750 being the s^d principal sum of £9000 with interest to that time

And it was thereby declared that s^d £9000 was thrby secured for the benefit of s^d Geo Bridges & Ann his wife subject to the trusts expressed concern^g her fortune in {Page 12} certain Indres of Lease & Release thrin referred to & made before the marriage of the s^d Geo Bridges with the s^d Ann then Ann Wolfe Spinster

And reciting that by Indenture dated 30th July 1750 & made between s^d Humphrey Mildmay 1st part s^d Wm Davies 2nd part s^d John Hartopp & Obadiah Hughes 3rd part & s^d Geo Bridges & Ann his wife 4th part Reciting s^d mtge of 6th September 1744 & that s^d Letitia Mildmay Walter Mildmay & Edwd Hooker were dead the s^d several mortged premises were charged with the paym^t to s^d Sir John Hartopp & Obadiah Hughes their exors admors & ass^s of the further sum of £1000 (other part of the trusts monies under the s^d marr'e settlem^t) & int^t for the same.

And reciting that by virtue of certain subsequent acts & assurances in the law & par'larly an Indenture dated 21st May 1773 & made between Francis Lord Le Despencer and Saml Dashwood Esqre 1st part Charles Vere Dashwood Esqre 2nd part Jane Mildmay (Widow & Relict of s^d Carew Mildmay then deced) 3rd part & Carew Hervy Mildmay of Haslegrove C'oy of Somerset Esqre (since deced) 4th part the securities for the s^d sums of £9000 & £1000 & int^t & par'larly the residue of s^d term of 1000 years in s^d freehold premises thrin comprised became vested in s^d Carew Hervey Mildmay for securing to him s^d Carew Hervey Mildmay his ex's ad's & ass^s the paym^t of s^d sums of £9000 & £1000 together £10,000 & Interest.

And reciting that s^d Carew Hervey Mildmay by will dated 14th July 1778 after devising his Manors & heredit's & real estates subject to a term of 99 years thrby limited throf to tr'ees for the purposes thrin ment^d to the use of his daughters Ann (afterw^{ds} called Ann Hervey) Mildmay for her life with rem^r to certain uses th'rin limited and noticing that he was possessed of (among other mortgages) a mortgage of certain heredits in Twyford & Owslebury amount^g to £10,000 (mean^g the s^d securities for the s^d sums of £9000 & £1000 before ment^d) gave the s^d mortg'es & the principal sums thron *{Page 13}* amount^g to £22,700 to James Rivers & H^y Eaton (both since dec'ed) upon trust to invest the same in the purchase of heredit's in England And he directed the same heredits to be settled to the use of his s^d daug^r for her life rem^r to such uses as by that his will were thrinbef^e limited & declared to take effect after the decease of his s^d daug^r Ann of & concern^g his Manor & Estate of East Camell o'rwise Queens Camell Co'y Somerset and he appointed his s^d daug^r & James Rivers exors of his s^d will.

And reciting that s^d Carew Hervey Mildmay dies without reworking or altering his s^d will & that same was proved by s^d Ann Hervey Mildmay in the Prerogative Court of Canterbury in March 1784 and after her decease was proved by s^d John Rivers in same Court.

And reciting that s^d James Rivers (who survivied s^d Henry Eaton) made his last will dated 23rd August 1794 & appointed Dame Martha Rivers Gay Widow ex'trix throf & by a codicil dated 29th Jany 1798 gave all & singular the este & estates term & terms for years lands tenem^{ts} mtges int^t trusts rights titles powers & authorities which were then vested in him as surviv^g tree & exor named in s^d will of s^d Carew Hervey Mildmay dec'ed to s^d John Clerk & Geo Wm Ricketts & the survor of them & the exors & adm'ors of such survor upon the trusts & for the uses intents & purposes & to do perform & execute all & every the acts matters & things named & declared in the s^d will of s^d Carew Hervey Mildmay .

And reciting that s^d James Rivers died in 1806 with^t having revoked s^d will & codicil & that Dame Martha Rivers Gay proved s^d will & codicil in same Court in Augt 1806.

And reciting that upon the decease & failure of issue of s^d A. H. Mildmay (who died without having been married) the s^d Dame Jane St John Mildmay then wife of the s^d Sir Henry Paulet St John Mildmay (under or by virtue of the lim'ons contained in s^d will of s^d C. H. Mildmay) became seized of the s^d Manors & heredits (including the s^d Manor of East Camell otherwise Queen Camell afores^d) with rem^r to the *{Page 14}* said Sir Henry St John Carew St John Mildmay in tail male.

And reciting that by an Order of the Court of Chancery dated 31st May 1808 grounded on the act 39th & 40th of His then Majesty for the relief of persons entitled to entailed estesto be purchased with trust monies It was ordered (among other things) that s^d £10,000 secured on s^d m'tge of the Twyford & Owslebury Estates should be transposed or paid as s^d Henry Paulet St John Mildmay & Dame Jane his wife & Henry St John Carew St John Mildmay then Sir Henry St John Carew St John Mildmay or as the sur'vors or sur'vor of them the s^d Sir Henry Paulet St John Mildmay & Dame Jane his wife & Sir Henry St John Carew St John Mildmay the s^d Sir Henry St John Carew St John Mildmay being one of the survivors or the sole survor should by Deed executed & attested by two or more witnesses appoint and for want of & until such appointm^t should remain subj^t to the trusts which were declared by the s^d will of the said C. H. Mildmay.

And reciting that s^d Sir Henry Paulet St John Mildmay died without having joined in any appointm^t of or concern^g s^d £10,000 or any part thereof leaving s^d Dame Jane St John Mildmay & Sir Henry St John Carew St John Mildmay him surviving

And reciting that by Lease & Release dated resp'ly 11th & 12th Feby 1761 the Release between S^d Carew Mildmay (the s^d Letitia as well as the s^d Humphrey Mildmay being then dead) 1st part Jane Pescod Spinster afterw^ds his wife) 2nd part Sir Villiers Chernock Bart & Paulett St John Esqre 3rd part Charles Pescod Esqre & Chas Lawrence Gent^n 4th part & Nicholas Preston Clerk & Geo Dacre Esqre 5th part (being the settlem^t made in cons'on of the marr'e then intended between s^d Carew Mildmay & Jane Pescod) divers heredits part of the estate of the s^d Carew Mildmay in the C'oy of Southampton were limited & assured after the solemnisation of said marr'e To the use of s^d Carew Mildmay for his life rem^r in strict settlem^t but subject to the yearly rent of £350 *{Page 15}* thrby limited in use to s^d Jane Pescod for her life for her jointure & the remedies of distress & entry thrby given for the recovery throf & to the term of 99 years thrby limited in use to trustees for better securing the same & to the term of 500 years th'rby limited in use to trees In trust for raising portions in an event which did not happen viz there being a Son & one or more other Child or Children of the s^d then intended marr'e To the first & every o^r Son of the s^d then intended marr'e successively accord^g to their priority of birth & the heirs male of their respive bodies & for default of such issue To the use of the s^d Nicholas Preston & Geo Dacre their ex's adm'ors & ass^s for 1000 years Upon the trusts thrin declared concerning the same and in Ind're now being abstracted after ment^d & after the expiration of s^d term To the use of s^d Carew Mildmay his heirs & ass^s for ever And it was thrby declared that s^d term of 1000 years was so limited upon trust in case there should be no Son Carew Mildmay by s^d Jane Pescod or there being such if they should die before their respive ages of 21 years without issue male & there should be issue one or more daugh^r or daugh^rs the Upon trust that s^d Nicolas Preston & Geo Dacre the sur'vor of them his ex'ors adm'ors or ass^s after failure of issue male either in the life time of s^d Carew Mildmay if he should so think fit or else after his decease out of the rents and profits of the heredit's & premises comprised in s^d term of 1000 years or by sale mortgage or other disposit^n thereof raise the sum of £4500 for the portions of the daugh^rs of the s^d then intended marr'e to be equally divided between them if more than one to be paid at her or their respive ages of 21 years or marriage the s^d Carew Mildmay being then dead or if being within 3 months after his de'ce with int^t as therein ment^d unless such portion or portions should be raised & paid in his life time by his dir'on in writing under his hand which might be done if he *{Page 16}* should think fit with such yearly sums by way of maint^ce for such daur until their respive portions should become payable as therein ment^d & it was declared that after the trusts of the s^d term should be satisfied & the trustees charges paid & all arrears maint^ce provided for such daughter or daughters being satisf^ed the s^d term should cease.

And reciting that the s^d Carew Mildmay by his will dated 27th June 1768 after reciting s^d Recovery suffered by him as before ment^d & that a Recovery had also been suffered of certain copyhold heredits in Islington & that he had lately purchased in the name of William Collins a small copyhold estate of one Hall which estate was then let by him with Hensting Farm & that the Great Tythes of the Parish of Twyford were part of the s^d estates in the Parish of Twyford devised his s^d Manors at Twyford & Marwell & the lands tenem^ts & heredits to them severally belonging & within the Parishes of Twyford & Owslebury afores^d & his s^d copyhold estate in the Parish of Islington to the Revd Sir Peter Rivers Bart Sir William Mildmay Bart James Rivers before named & Geo Pescod Esqre Upon trust to permit his the s^d testator's wife s^d Jane Mildmay to receive out of the rents of s^d premises an ann'y of £120 during her life above what she should be entitled to under her jointure nevless she was to apply the same on the education of his s^d daug^rs over & above the interest of s^d sum of £4,500 ment^d in his marr'e settlem^t as a provision for his s^d daugh^rs and in case his s^d wife should be inclined to reside at his House at Shawford then she should hold & enjoy the same with the garden & ground then occupied by him rent free for so long a time as she should reside at Shawford House but in case she should not choose to reside at Shawford House then he desired his s^d trees or the survor of them to let the s^d House gardens & premises then occupied by him for the benefit of his estates in general

& after the decease of him s^d Carew Mildmay & his s^d wife Jane he devised all his afores^d Manors lands tenem^ts & heredits *{Page 17}* in the County of Southampton & his s^d copyhold estate in Islington to his eldest daur the s^d Jane the Dame Jane St John Mildmay & to the heirs male of her body with rem^rs over and in case the s^d Jane should live to be possessed of all his estates & should have issue male then his s^d estates should be charged & chargable with the sum of £6000 to each of her sisters the said testators daughters Ann & Letitia

And reciting that s^d C. Mildmay died without revoking or altering his s^d will & without issue male leaving 3 da'rs viz the s^d Jane then Dame Jane St John Mildmay Anne afterwards the wife of the s^d John Clerk & Letitia afterwards the wife of the s^d G.W. Ricketts his coheirs at Law & s^d will was proved in s^d Court of Canterbury 21st July 1768.

And reciting that s^d Sir William Mildmay died in the life time of s^d Sir Peter Rivers James Rivers & Geo Pescod & that s^d Geo Pescod having been found a lunatic an order of s^d Court of Chancery was obtained for a convey^ce (in pursuance of the Statute for enabling Idiots & Lunatics seized of Estates In Trust or by way of Mortgage to make Convey^ces throf) of the Legal Estate vested in s^d Sir Peter Rivers then Sir Peter Rivers Gay James Rivers & the Revd Thos Salmon Clerk upon the trusts of the said will & such convey^ce was duly made accord'ly

And reciting that by Indres of Lease & Release dated 27 & 28 November 1789 the Release between s^d Sir Peter Rivers Gay James Rivers & Thos Salmon 1st part s^d Jane Mildmay Widow of s^d Carew Mildmay 2nd part s^d Sir Henry Paulet St John Mildmay & Dame Jane then his wife of 3rd part s^d Anne Mildmay & Letitia Mildmay of 4th part Edwd Bray 5th part The Rev^d W^m St John & John Pollen Esqre 6th part & s^d Henry Peters & Wm Bragge 7th part & of a Common Recovery suffered in pursuance of a Covenant contained in same Indre in which s^d William St John & John Pollen were Demandants s^d Edwd Bray Tenant who vouched the s^d Sir Henry Paulet St John Mildmay & Dame Jane his wife who vouched the *{Page 18}* common vouchee all the s^d manors heredits & premises comprised in s^d recited Indres of 3rd & 4th April 1744 were limited & assured to the use & intent in the first place to confirm s^d jointure of £350 to s^d Jane Mildmay & also to corroborate s^d term of 1000 years by s^d settlem^t of 12th Feby 1761 limited in use to s^d Nicolas Preston & Geo Dacre for securing portions for the daugh^rs of s^d Carew Mildmay by s^d Jane his wife so far as respected the portions of £1500 for each of them & so subject to the use of the s^d Henry Peters & Wm Bragg their exors admors & ass^s for the term of 1000 years from the day next before the date of s^d Ind're of 28th Novr 1789 sans waste upon the trusts thrin declared and in the Indre now being abstracted after ment^d with rem^r To the use of s^d Sir Henry Paulet St John Mildmay for his life sans waster rem^r to the use of the s^d Dame Jane St John Mildmay their assigns for her life sans waste with rem^r over in strict settlem^t And it was thrby declared that s^d term of 1000 years was limited to s^d Henry Peters & William Bragg Upon trust to permit s^d Jane Mildmay Widow to reside at Shawford House & to pay the s^d sev^l yearly sums of £120 & £350 for her life & subject as to the lands charged therewith to the s^d portions of £1500 each to which she the s^d Dame Jane St John Mildmay A. Mildmay & L.Mildmay were entitled under the s^d settlem^t of 11th & 12th Feby 1761 & to the trusts for raising same Upon trust by sale or mtge or other disposition of the premises comprised in the s^d term of 1000 years or by & out of the rents & profits of s^d premises to levy & pay £6000 for the portion of the s^d Ann Mildmay with int^t at £4 per cent from the de'ce of the s^d Jane Mildmay the mother & £6000 for the portion of the s^d L. Mildmay with int^t at the s^d rate from the s^d period the s^d sums to become vested in s^d Ann Mildmay & L. Mildmay reply from the days of their attain^g their ages of 21 years & to carry int^t as afores^d till the times of paym^t And it was declared that s^d portions & int^t were to be paid over & above the s^d portions of £1500 each to which the s^d Ann Mildmay & Letitia *{Page 19}* Mildmay were entitled under their fathers marre settlem^t but in lieu & satisfaction of the portions of £6000 a piece provided for them by the s^d will of their s^d father & which s^d portions of £6000 & £6000 secured by s^d Indre of Rele the s^d Ann Mildmay & Letitia Mildmay thrby agreed to accept accordly And by the s^d Indre of 28th Novr 1789 the s^d Parsonage of Twyford & other the leasehold premises held of the Master & Brethren of the Hospital of St Cross were duly conveyed & assured unto & to the use of the s^d Henry Peters & Wm Braggs their heirs & ass^s during the lives thrin ment^d upon trust to raise a competent sum for renewing the then lease & future leases of the same premises & subject to the same trusts for renewal upon trust by the ways & means thrin ment^d to raise & pay such sum & sums of money for and towards the s^d portions of £6000 & £6000 thrinbef^e provided & secured for the s^d Ann Mildmay & Letitia Mildmay as they s^d H^y Peters & Wm Bragge or the survor of them or the heirs or ass^s of such survivor should think requisite to the intent that the s^d parsonage tithes & heredits lastly thrby released might come in & aid of the s^d manors & heredits comprised in s^d term of 1000 years by the now reciting Ind're created for the more speedy raising & paying the s^d portions of £6000 & £6000 & Int^t as secured & directed to be raised under the trusts of the s^d last ment^d term of 1000 years & subject to raising & paying the s^d portions & int^t as afores^d in trust for the s^d Sir Henry Paulet St John Mildmay & his heirs for his life & after his de'ce in trust for s^d Dame Jane St John Mildmay & her ass^s for her life & after her de'ce of the survor of s^d Sir Henry Paulet St John Mildmay & Dame Jane his wife in trust as thrin ment^d

And reciting that s^d Jane Mildmay the widow of said C. Mildmay died in 1799

And reciting that by Indre dated 29th Septr 1806 & made between s^d Sir H^y Paulet St John Mildmay & Dame Jane his wife 1st part s^d John Clerk & Ann his wife *{Page 20}* 2nd part s^d Geo William Ricketts & Letitia his wife 3rd part s^d Wm Bragge Edwd Bray & Edmund Antrobus (the then surviving trustees named in the settlem^t made prevly to the marr'e of the s^d John Clerk & Ann his wife) 4th part Sir Wm Rowly Bart S^d Wm Bragge & Robert Serle (the then surviving trees named in the settlem^t made prev'ly to the marr'e of the s^d Geo Wm Ricketts & Letitia his wife) 5th part s^d Sir Henry Paulet St John Mildmay 6th part s^d Geo Dacre (who had survived the s^d Nicholas Preston his co-tree of the s^d term of 1000 years created by the s^d Indre of the 12th Feby 1761) 7th part Henry Peters & William Bragg (trustees of the s^d term of 1000 years created by the s^d Indre of the 28th November 1789) 8th part & the s^d William Bray of the 9th part. Reciting s^d will of s^d H^y Mildmay the Indres of the 27th March & 3rd & 4th April 1744 & the Recovery And the reciting that Ann Mildmay intermarried with the s^d Sir Wm Mildmay in the life time of s^d Humphrey & after the death of the s^d Letitia Mildmay and thrupon became entitled to £1000 & having survived s^d Humphrey Mildmay she became entitled to the further sum of £1000 and reciting that s^d Katherine Mildmay survived her father & mother & thereby became entitled to £1000 & she died unmarried in 1763 having by her will dated 19th October 1763 given s^d £1000 to Carew Mildmay And reciting that s^d Sir William Mildmay died in the life time of s^d Dame Jane his wife without having received s^d sums of £1000 & £1000 or either of them & without having made any dispos'on throf And reciting that s^d Dame Jane Mildmay made her will dated the 27th October 1794 & thrby appointed s^d Sir Henry Paulet St John Mildmay & John Oxley Parker Esqre ex'ors throf but did not make any specific mention of the s^d £1000 & £1000 so due as afores^d And reciting that the s^d Dame Anne Mildmay by a codicil to her s^d will dated the 12th Decr 1796 (after certain bequests made by her s^d will & codicil) as to all the rest of her personal property which she should be possessed of or entitled to at the time of her decease not otherwise disposed *{Page 21}* of in her will or in her s^d codicil she gave to be equally divided between her s^d 2 nieces Anne Clerk & Letitia Ricketts

And reciting that s^d Dame Anne Mildmay died in the year 1796 & that the s^d Sir Henry Paulet St John Mildmay & John Oxley Parker proved s^d will & codicil in the Prerogative Court of Canterbury by virtue of which s^d codicil s^d Anne Clerk & Letitia Ricketts became beneficially intitled to s^d £2000 in equal shares And reciting s^d Indres of the 11th & 12th Feby 1761 And also reciting (amongst other things) that s^d Sir Henry Paulet St John Mildmay with his own money previously to the year 1794 paid to s^d Anne Mildmay £4,750 in part of s^d £6000 & to s^d Letitia Ricketts then Letitia Mildmay the like sum of £4,750 in part of her £6,000 & to the intent that he might as to the s^d two sums & the interest throf stand in place of the s^d Anne Clerk & Letitia Ricketts & might have an equitable lien for the same on the s^d heredits charged with the paym^t of the s^d sums as afores^d (the repaym^t of which s^d sums the s^d John Clerk & Anne his wife & Geo Wm Ricketts & Letitia his wife did thrby acknowledge) And reciting an Indre dated the 14th November 1794 & made between s^d John Clerk of 1st part s^d Anne Clerk by her then name of Anne Mildmay Spinster 2nd part & William Bragge & Edwd Bray & William Moleson Esqre then since deced & s^d Edwd Antrobus 3rd part whrby s^d Anne Mildmay in conson of the then intended marr'e between her & s^d John Clerk assigned unto s^d Wm Bragge Edwd Bray Wm Molleson & Edwd Antrobus s^d sum of £1500 the 3rd part of s^d sum of £4500 directed to be raised under the trusts of s^d term of 1000 years limited by s^d Indre of 12th Feby 1761 & all int^t in respect throf Upon the trusts thrin declared concern^g the same And whrby the s^d John Clerk covenanted that if during the then intended marr'e s^d Anne Mildmay should become entitled to any further sums of money then as hrinbef^e ment^d (except s^d £1250 the residue of the portion of s^d portion of £6000 after deducting s^d £4750 & a sum of £500 thrin ment^d) the *{Page 22}* s^d John Clerk would assign the same to s^d Wm Bragge Edwd Bray William Molleson & Edwd Antrobus Upon such trusts as were declared concerning s^d sum of £1500 And recit^g that by virtue of the covenant for that purpose contained in the thrin lastly recited Ind're £1000 part of the s^d £1000 & £1000 which by virtue of s^d will of s^d Henry Mildmay & s^d Indres of 27th March 1744 were charged upon the afs^d heredits in favor of s^d Dame Anne Mildmay & to which s^d £1000 s^d Anne Clerk became entitled as part of the residuary personal estate of s^d Dame Anne Mildmay became equitably bound by & subjected to the trusts of the s^d Indre of Settlem^t of 14th November 1794 And reciting that by Indre bearing date [Blank space] & made between s^d Geo William Ricketts 1st part s^d Letitia his wife (by her then name of Letitia Mildmay Spinster 2nd part s^d Sir William Rowley Geo Poyntz Ricketts Esqre (then since deced) s^d Wm Bragge & Robert Serle 3rd part s^d Letitia Ricketts in conson of the then intended marr'e between her & s^d Geo William Ricketts assigned to the s^d Sir William Rowley Geo Poyntz Ricketts Wm Bragge & Robert Serle the s^d sev^l sums of £1500 (being her 3rd of s^d sum of £4,500) & £1250 (being the residue of her s^d portion of £6000 after deduct^g s^d 4750£ & all int^t in respect throf & to grow due for the same Upon the trusts thrinaf^r ment^d And further reciting that s^d Sir Henry Paulet St John Mildmay had with & out of his own monies (by the direction of the s^d John Clerk and Anne his wife) paid unto the s^d Wm Bragge Edwd Bray & Edmund Antrobus (as surviving trustees named in s^d Ind're of the 14th Novr 1794) s^d £1000 to which s^d Anne Clerk became entitled as part of the residuary personal estate of the s^d Dame Anne Mildmay and also s^d £1500 to which she became entitled under s^d settlem^t of 12th Feby 1761 & also with & out of his proper monies had paid to the s^d John Clerk s^d £1250 (being the residue of s^d sum of £6000 to which s^d Anne Clerk became entitled as afs^d & that s^d Sir Henry Paulet *{Page 23}* St John Mildmay had with & out of his own monies by the direction of s^d Geo William Ricketts & Letitia his wife paid unto s^d Sir Wm Rowley William Bragge & Robert Serle (as surviving trees in the settlem^t made previously to s^d marr'e s^d sum of £1500 to which s^d Letitia Ricketts became entitled under s^d Indre of 12th Feby 1761 and also s^d sum of £1250 being the residue of s^d sum of £6000 & had also with & out of his own monies paid to s^d Geo Wm Ricketts £1000 being the remaining part of s^d sums of £1000 & £1000 to which Dame Anne Mildmay dec'ed became entitled as afs^d which s^d several sums of £1000 £1500 £1250 £1500 £1250 & £1000 were so paid by Sir Henry Paulet St John Mildmay as afs^d to the intent that he might as to the same sums resply stand in the place of the several persons beneficially entitled to the several charges in respect of which the same resply were paid & might have an equitable lien for the same & the interest throf upon the heredits subject to such charges resply It was witnessed that in conson of s^d sum of £4750 so paid to s^d Anne Clerk & of s^d sum of £1250 so paid to s^d John Clerk as afores^d & also in cons'on of s^d sums of £1000 & £1500 so paid to s^d William Bragge Edwd Bray & Edmund Antrobus as trees under s^d Indre of 14th Novr 1794 They s^d Wm Bragge Edwd Bray & Edm^d Antrobus by the diron of s^d John Clerk & Anne his wife according to their respive rights shares & proportions did on the nomin^on of s^d Sir Henry Paulet St John Mildmay assign all the s^d sums of £1000 £6000 & £1500 & all interest in respect of s^d sums unto s^d Wm Bray his exs ads & ass^s In trust for s^d Sir Henry Paulet St John Mildmay his exs ads & ass^s And it was further witnessed that in conson of s^d sum of £4750 to s^d Letitia Ricketts & of s^d sum of £1000 to the s^d Geo Wm Ricketts paid as afores^d & also in cons'on of the s^d sums of £1500 & £1250 so paid to the s^d Sir Wm Rowley William Bragge & Robert Serle as afores^d they the s^d Sir Wm Rowley William Bragge & Robert Serle (by the diron of the s^d Geo William Ricketts & Letitia his wife (according to *{Page 24}* their respive rights & proportions) did on the nomin^on of the s^d Sir Henry Paulet St John Mildmay assign all s^d sums of £1000 £6000 & £1500 & all interest in respect of the same to the s^d Wm Bray his ex'ors ads & ass^s in trust for s^d Sir Henry Paulet St John Mildmay his exs ads & ass^s.

And after reciting that s^d Nicholas Preston died leaving said Geo Dacre him surviving It was fur^r witnessed that for the consons thrin ment^d s^d Geo Dacre by the dir'on of said Sir Henry Paulet St John Mildmay & Dame Jane his wife John Clerk & Anne his wife Geo Wm Ricketts & Letitia his wife & also with the consent of s^d William Bragge Edwd Bray & Edm^d Antrobus Sir Wm Rowley & Robert Serle resply did bgain sell & assign unto s^d Wm Bray all & singular the messu'es farms lands tenem^ts & heredits with the appurts comprised in s^d term of 1000 years created by s^d Indre of 12th Feby 1761 & thrby limited to the s^d Nicholas Preston & Geo Dacre as afores^d To hold the same unto s^d Wm Bray his exs ads & ass^s for all the residue of s^d term of 1000 years In trust for the more effectually securing unto s^d Wm Bray his ex'ors adm'ors & ass^s In trust for s^d Sir Henry Paulet St John Mildmay his ex'ors ad's & ass^s paym^t of as well s^d sums of £1500 & £1500 as of s^d sev^l other sums of £6000 £1000 & £1000 & the int^t throf resply & subject to the paym^t of s^d sums & the int^t In trust to permit s^d term to attend the rev'ons & inheritance of s^d heredits And it was thrby declared that s^d H^y Peters & Wm Bragge (at the request & by the diron of s^d Sir Henry Paulet St John Mildmay & Dame Jane his wife John Clerk & Anne his wife Geo Wm Ricketts & Letitia his wife & with the consent of the s^d Edwd Bray Edmund Antrobus Sir William Rowley & Robert Serle should stand possessed of the heredits comprised in the s^d term of 1000 years created by the said Indre of 25th November 1789 Upon trust for better securing unto the s^d William Bray his exs ads & ass^s (Upon trust for the s^d Sir Henry Paulet St John Mildmay his ex'ors adm'ors & ass^s) paym^t of s^d sums of £6000 & £6000 & the interest & for that purpose to be assigned & disposed of as he or they *{Page 25}* should require

And reciting that by a Deed Poll dated 2nd December 1807 endorsed on last recited Indre under the hands & seals of Thomas Dacre Esqre thrin ment^d to be administrator of the goods chattels & credits of Geo Dacre . Recit^g that s^d Geo Dacre died sometime before the date of the last recited Indre but that his death was not then known and that administration of his goods chattels & credits were on the 17th Septr then last granted by the Prerogative Court of Canterbury to the s^d Thos Dacre the eldest son & one of his next of kin It was witnessed that in pursuance of the diron & appointm^t in that behalf & cont^d in the s^d Indre s^d Thos Dacre did bgain sell & assign unto the s^d Wm Bray All and singular the heredits with the appurts comprised in the s^d term of 1000 years created by the s^d Indre of the 12th Feby 1761 To hold unto the s^d Wm Bray his exors ads & ass^s for all the residue of s^d term of 1000 years according to the tenure & effect of the assignm^t intended to have been made by the last recited Ind're & on the same trusts as were by the same Indre expressed to be declared for the benefit of the s^d Sir Henry Paulet St John Mildmay

And reciting that s^d Sir Henry Paulet St John Mildmay by his will dated 6th July 1808 gave all the property of which he should die possessed both real & personal unto his wife said Dame Jane St John Mildmay her heirs & ass^s for ever & appointed her sole extrix of his s^d will

And reciting that the s^d Sir Henry Paulet St John Mildmay died without revoking or altering his s^d will & that s^d Dame Jane St John Mildmay proved same in s^d Court of Canterbury on 13th Feby 1809

And reciting that by Ind're dated 5th Augt 1809 & made between s^d John Clerk & Geo Wm Ricketts of the 1st part s^d Dame Martha Rivers Gay of the 2nd part s^d Dame Jane St John Mildmay of the 3rd part s^d Sir Henry St John Carew St John Mildmay of the 4th part Sir Wm Bray of the 5th part s^d Henry Peters & Wm Bragge of the 6th part The Hon'ble Bartholomew Bouverie & Charlotte Bouverie Spinster his eldest Daughter then an infant of the 7th part Robert Blake Gent^n of the 8th part & The Right *{Page 26}* Hon'ble Archibald John Lord Viscount Primrose then Earl of Rosebury Henry James Bouverie Esqre the s^d John Clerk & Edwd Bray of the 9th part recit^g amongst other things that a marr'e had been agreed upon between s^d Sir Henry St John Carew St John Mildmay & Charlotte Bouverie & that it had been agreed that the sum of £1500 being the original 3rd to which s^d Dame Jane St John Mildmay became entitled of s^d sum of £4500 & the sums of £1000 £1000 £1500 £1500 £6000 & £6000 being the sums which were assigned in manner before ment^d to s^d Wm Bray In trust for s^d Sir Henry Paulet St John Mildmay

& the s^d mtge debt of £10,000 should be assigned to s^d Viscount Primrose Henry James Bouverie John Clerk & Edwd Bray Upon the trusts thrinaf^r expressly or by reference declared concerning the same And that with a view to such agreem^t so far as related to the assignm^t of s^d £10,000 they s^d Dame Jane St John Mildmay & Sir Henry St John Carew St John Mildmay had applied to & requested & by the Indre now being recited did direct & appoint s^d John Clerk & Geo W. Ricketts & also s^d Dame Martha Rivers Gay to assign the afores^d mtge debt of £10,000 in manner thrinaf^r ment^d It was witnessed that in pursuance of said agreem^t so far as related to s^d £10000 & in conson throf & in cons'on of s^d marr'e & other the consons thrin ment^d s^d John Clerk & Geo Wm Ricketts with the assent of s^d Dame Martha Rivers Gay & at the request & by the dir'on of s^d Dame Jane St John Mildmay & St H^y St John Carew St John Mildmay & with the privity of s^d Bartholomew Bouverie & Charlotte Bouverie and also s^d Dame Martha Rivers Gay at the like request & by the diron of s^d Dame Jane St John Mildmay & Sir Henry St John Carew St John Mildmay & with the like privity of s^d Bartholomew Bouverie & Charlotte Bouverie & accord^g to the several & respective rights & interests of s^d John Clerk Geo Wm Ricketts & Dame Martha Rivers Gay to or in said £10000 so far as they resply could or might do at law & in equity & not fur^r or otherwise Did assign & the s^d Jane St John Mildmay & Sir Henry St John Carew St John Mildmay Did confirm unto s^d Robert Blake all the s^d mtge debt or sum of £10,000 assigned to the s^d Carew Henry Mildmay by the s^d Indre of 21st May 1773 & by him s^d Carew H^y Mildmay bequeathed upon such trusts as before ment^d & all int^t in respect of the s^d sum of £10000 To hold {Page 27} unto s^d Robt Blake his exs ads & ass^s Upon trust nev'less immedly after the ex'on of the Indre then being recited to assign the same to s^d Viscount Primrose H^y James Bouverie John Clerk & Edwd Bray their exors ads & assigns to be by them held & applied upon & for such trusts intents & purposes as were or should be declared concern^g the same by an Indre then proposed & intended to bear even date with the same Indre & it was also witnessed that in conson afores^d & in pursuance of s^d agreem^t so far as the same related to the proposed assignment of the securities for s^d mtge debt of £10000 s^d John Clerk & Geo Wm Ricketts with the assent of s^d Dame Martha Rivers Gay & at the request & by the dir'on of s^d Dame Jane St John Mildmay & Sir H^y St John Carew St John Mildmay & with the privity of s^d Bartholomew Bouverie & Charlotte Bouverie & also s^d Dame Martha Rivers Gay at the like request & by the like dir'on of s^d Dame Jane St John Mildmay & Sir H^y St John Carew St John Mildmay & with the like privity of s^d Bartholomew Bouverie & Charlotte Bouverie & accord^g to the sev^l & respective rights & interests of them s^d John Clerk Geo Wm Ricketts & Dame Martha Rivers Gay to or in the manors & heredits thrinaf^r assigned & so far as they resply could or ought to do at law & in equity & not fur^r or otherwise Did b'gain sell & assign unto s^d Robt Blake all the s^d Manors or Lordships messu'es farms lands tenemts & other hdits assigned to s^d Carew Henry Mildmay by the s^d Indre of the 21st May 1773 for all the then residue of the s^d term of 1000 years created by s^d Indre of 6th Sepr 1774 To hold unto s^d Robt Blake his ex'ors ad's & ass^s for all the then residue of s^d term of 1000 years Upon trust nevless to assign or demise the same premises unto s^d Viscount Primrose H^y James Bouverie John Clerk & Edwd Bray for all the then residue of s^d term want^g the last day of the same term (which s^d exception was proposed to be made for the purposes of preventing a merger of s^d term of 1000 years in the heredits comprised in a certain other term of 1000 years thrinaf^r ment^d to be demised to s^d Viscount Primrose Henry James Bouverie John Clerk & Edwd Bray their ex's ad's & ass^s for all the then residue of the s^d last ment^d term wanting the last day throf but subject nevless to the equity of red'on in s^d heredits upon paym^t of s^d sum of £10000 {Page 28} & int^t unto s^d Viscount Primrose Henry James Bouverie John Clerk & Edwd Bray their exs ads & ass^s And by s^d Indre in pursuance of s^d agreem^t & in conson of s^d the unt^d Marr'e & other the consons thrin ment^d the s^d £1500 (being the original 3rd part to which s^d Dame Jane St John Mildmay became entitled of s^d £4500 was assigned by s^d Dame Jane St John Mildmay & s^d sev^l sums of £1000 £1000 £1500 £1500 £6000 & £6000 which were so assigned to s^d Wm Bray in trust for the s^d Sir Henry Paulet St John Mildmay as aforesaid were assigned by the s^d Wm Bray to s^d Viscount Primrose Henry James Bouverie John Clerk & Edwd Bray their exors ads & ass^s upon such trusts as were or should be declared concerning the same by s^d Indre then prepared & int^d to bear even date th'rwith And it was by the s^d Indre fur^r witnessed that s^d Wm Bray by the diron of s^d Dame Jane St John Mildmay & upon the nom'on of s^d Sir Henry St John Carew St John Mildmay Bartholomew Bouverie & Charlotte Bouverie demised to s^d manors & premises assigned to him s^d Wm Bray by s^d Indre of 29th September 1806 for the then residue of s^d term of 1000 years created by s^d Indre of the 12th Feby 1761 unto s^d Viscount Primrose Henry James Bouverie John Clerk & Edwd

Bray their exors ad's & ass^s for the then residue of same term wanting the last day of the s^d term for the purpose of prevent^g a merger of s^d term in the term of 1000 years after assigned upon the trusts thrin^r declared and it was lastly witnessed that for the cons'ons thrin ment^d s^d H^y Peters & Wm Bragge by the dir'on of s^d Dame Jane St John Mildmay & upon the nomination of s^d Sir Henry St John Carew St John Mildmay Bartholomew Bouverie & Catherine Bouverie Did grant sell & assign unto s^d Viscount Primrose Henry James Bouverie John Clerk & Edwd Bray all manors & o^r heredits so limited in use to said H^y Peters & Wm Bragge for s^d term of 1000 years by s^d Indre of 28th Novr 1789 To hold unto s^d Viscount Primrose H^y James Primrose John Clerk & Edwd Bray their exors ads & ass^s for the residue of s^d term of 1000 years upon the trusts thrinaf^r decl^d And it was thrby declared that s^d Viscount Primrose H^y James Bouverie John Clerk & Edwd Bray should stand possessed of the residue of s^d term of 1000 years first thrinbef^e vested in them want^g the last day And also *{Page 29}* of the residue of s^d term of 1000 years thrinbef^e assigned to them as afs^d in trust for secur^g to s^d trees their exs ads & ass^s the paym^t of s^d sev^l sums of money thrinbef^e assigned & int^t & after such paym^t & subject thrto upon trust to permit s^d terms to attend the inhance of the heredits comprised thrin And the s^d H^y Peters & Wm Bragge did thrby cov^t that they & the survor of them & the heirs & ass^s of such survor should stand seized of s^d heredits & Premises held by Lease or Leases for life & conveyed to s^d H^y Peters & Wm Bragge & their heirs by s^d Indre of the 28th Novr 1789 In trust fur^r securing to them the s^d Viscount Primrose H^y James Bouverie & John Clerk & Edwd Bray s^d sev^l sums of £6000 & £6000 & int^t & should for that purpose convey & dispose of the same as s^d Viscount Primrose H^y James Bouverie John Clerk & Edwd Bray or the sur'vors or sur'vor of them or the ex'ors ads or ass^s of such survor should direct but subject & without prejudice to the trusts in s^d Indre of the 28th of Novr 1789 contained concern^g s^d leasehold premises subsequently to the trusts thrby declared for securing s^d sums of £6000 & £6000 thrby directed to be raised under the trusts of s^d term of 1000 years thrby created.

And reciting that by an Indre endorsed on the s^d lastly recited Indre dated 5th aug^t 1809 & made between Robt Blake of the 1st part s^d Dame Jane St John Mildmay 2nd part Sir H^y St John Carew St John Mildmay of 3rd part s^d Bartholomew Bouverie & Charlotte Bouverie of 4th part & s^d Viscount Primrose H^y James Bouverie John Clerk & Edwd Bray of 5th part It was witnessed that in pursuance of the trusts reposed in s^d Robt Blake by the last recited Indre & in conson of 10/ by s^d Viscount Primrose H^y James Bouverie John Clerk & Edwd Bray paid to s^d Robt Blake He s^d Robt Blake by the dir'on of s^d Dame Jane St John Mildmay & Sir H^y St John Carew St John Mildmay & with the appro'n of s^d Bartholomew Bouverie & Charlotte Bouverie did bgain sell & assign unto s^d Viscount Primrose H^y Jame Bouverie John Clerk & Edwd Bray all s^d principal sum of £10,000 assigned or expressed to be assigned to him s^d Robt Blake by the last recited Indre & all int^t in respect of the same To hold unto s^d Viscount Primrose H^y James Bouverie John Clerk & Edwd Bray their exs ads & ass^s Upon such trusts as *{Page 30}* were declared in s^d Indre of settlem^t bearing even date with the Ind're then recited And it was witnessed that in fur^r pursuance of the trusts in s^d Robt Blake reposed & in conson of 10/ paid by s^d Viscount Primrose Henry James Bouverie John Clerk & Edwd Bray to s^d Robt Blake by the like dir'on & with the appro'n did demise unto s^d Viscount Primrose Henry James Bouverie John Clerk & Edwd Bray all s^d messue & other heredits thrin ment^d to be assigned to s^d Robt Blake by s^d last recited Indre to hold unto s^d Viscount Primrose H^y James Bouverie John Clerk & Edwd Bray their exs ads & ass^s for all the residue of s^d term of 1000 years created by the Indre of 6th Septr 1744 want^g the last day being an exception to prevent a merger of the s^d term subject nevless to an equity of red'on on paym^t of s^d £10,000 to s^d Viscount Primrose Henry James Bouverie John Clerk & Edwd Bray their ex's ads & ass^s

And reciting that by Indre also dated 5th aug^t 1809 & made betw^n s^d Dame Jane St John Mildmay of 1st part s^d Sir H^y St John Carew St John Mildmay of 2nd part s^d Bartholomew Bouverie & Charlotte Bouverie of 3rd part & s^d Viscount Primrose H^y James Bouverie John Clerk & Edwd Bray 4th part It was agreed & declared that s^d Viscount Primrose Henry James Bouverie John Clerk & Edwd Bray should stand possed of s^d sev^l sums of £10,000 £1500 £1000 £1000 £1500 £1500 £6000 & £6000 & also a sum of £1500 thrby covenanted to be paid to them by the s^d Dame Jane St John Mildmay & Sir H^y St John Carew St John Mildmay such s^d several sums amounted together to

£30,000 & of the interest throf upon trust after the solemnisation of s^d int^d marre during the joint lives of s^d Sir Henry St John Carew St John Mildmay & Dame Jane St John Mildmay to pay the int^t of same sev^l sums to s^d Dame Jane St John Mildmay & if she should depart this life in his life time after her decease to pay the int^t to the s^d Sir Henry St John Carew St John Mildmay for his life & after his decease whether he should die in her life time or should survive her Upon trust if there should be any child of s^d marr'e except an eldest or only son to stand possessed of s^d monies In trust for such younger children as thrin ment^d And it was thrby fur^r agreed & declared that after the decease of s^d Sir H^Y St John Carew St John Mildmay & such *{Page 31}* failure of issue of s^d marr'e s^d trees should stand possessed of the s^d trust monies Upon trust in the first place to raise £1500 & to pay the same to such of them the s^d Dame Jane St John Mildmay & Sir H^y St John Carew St John Mildmay as should have paid the s^d sum thrinbef^e covenanted to be paid & subject thereto should stand possessed of the surplus or residue of s^d trust monies upon the following trusts i.e. as to 1/3rd throf in trust for s^d Dame Jane St John Mildmay for life and after her decease In trust for s^d Sir H^y St John Carew St John Mildmay his exs ads & ass^s and as to the remaining 2/3rd throf In trust for s^d Dame Jane St John Mildmay her exors ads & ass^s and after reciting that by Indre of covenant then being recited & made between s^d Sir Henry St John Mildmay of 1st part s^d Dame Jane St John Mildmay of 2nd part s^d Bartholomew Bouverie & Charlotte Bouverie of 3rd part & s^d Viscount Primrose & H^y James Bouverie of 4th part He s^d Sir H^y St John Carew St John Mildmay had covenanted with s^d Viscount Primrose & H^y James Bouverie that he would in pursuance of a certain power thrin referred to charged certain estates thrin ment^d with the paym^t of such sums of money for his younger children by s^d Charlotte Bouverie as thrin ment^d It was agreed that if s^d Sir Henry St John Carew St John Mildmay should in pursuance of s^d cov^t charge s^d heredits thrin ment^d with the sums thrin ment^d or if he should during his life settle the sum of £30,000 or property to that value or amount upon or in favor of his Daughters & younger Sons befs^d to Catherine Bouverie & the s^d Viscount Primrose H^y James Bouverie John Clerk & Edwd Bray or the survor of them should by writing under their hands declare themselves satisfied with such charge or settlem^t & that the portions expressed to be secured by such charge were well & effectually secured & made payable accord^g to the intent of the s^d Indre then all the trusts thrinbef^e expressed of s^d sev^l sums should absolutely cease & s^d trees & the sur'vors of them should stand possessed of the s^d trust monies & annual produce thof upon the trusts thrinaf^r declared (that is to say) as to one third throf under & subject to such powers provisos agreem^{ts} & decl'ons & with under & subject to such powers provisos agreem^{ts} & declons under & subject to which s^d mtge debt of £10,000 stood subject or liable to before the exon of the Indre then being recited and should stand possessed of the remaining 2/3rd of s^d monies subject nevless to a declon of £1500 in case s^d Dame Jane St John Mildmay & Sir H^y *{Page 32}* St John Carew St John Mildmay or either of them should previously to such lesser or determination have paid in s^d sum in pursuance of s^d covenant In trust for s^d Dame Jane St John Mildmay her ex's ads &ass^s & should stand possessed of s^d £1500 in case the same should have been so paid in as afores^d In trust for s^d Dame Jane St John Mildmay & their respive exors ads & ass^s to be divided betw^n them accord^g to the shares & proportions in which they should have paid the same £1500 or in case one of them should have paid the whole in trust for such one of them & his or her executors ad^s & ass^s

And reciting that s^d marr'e between s^d Sir Henry St John Carew St John Mildmay & Charlotte Bouverie was duly solemnised soon after the date of s^d Indres of 5th aug^t 1809

And reciting that by Indre bearing date 9th July 1810 & made between s^d H^y St John Carew St John Mildmay of 1st part & s^d Charlotte Bouverie then Dame Charlotte Mildmay of 2nd part s^d Viscount Primrose & H^y James Bouverie 3rd part & Revd Edward Bouverie & s^d John Clerk 4th part s^d Sir Henry St John Carew St John Mildmay duly subjected & charged the h'dits thrin ment^d for the portions of his daughters & younger sons by s^d Dame Charlotte his wife accord^g to the intent of s^d Ind're of cov^t

And reciting that s^d Dame Charlotte Mildmay died leaving an only son & no other issue of s^d marr'e & s^d Edwd Bray (one of the trees named in s^d Indre of settlem^t of 5th aug^t) died in the year 1814

And reciting that by an Indre dated 16th May 1815 & made between sd Archibald John Viscount Primrose then Earl of Rosebery H^y James Bouverie & John Clerk of 1st part s^d Dame Jane St John Mildmay of 2nd part s^d Sir H^y St John Carew St John Mildmay of 3rd part & Wm Bray of 4th part after reciting amongst other things that s^d Archibald John Then Earl of Rosebery Henry James Bouverie & John Clerk (as such surviving trees as afores^d were perfectly satisfied & by the writing then being recited under their respive hands did declare themselves perfectly satisfied with the charge by way of portions so made by the s^d Sir H^y St John Carew St John Mildmay as afores^d & that the portions expressed to be secured *{Page 33}* thrby were effectually secured & made payable according to the intent of the s^d Ind're of 5th aug^t 1809 & that by reason of such charge as afores^d the trusts by s^d Ind're of settlem^t declared of s^d sums of £10,000 £1,500 £1000 £1000 £1500 £1500 £6000 £6000 & £1500 had ceased & determined and reciting that none of s^d sev^l sums had been invested in the funds or on Governm^t or real securities as authorised by s^d Ind're of settlem^t but still contained in their original state of investm^t & that neither s^d Dame Jane St John Mildmay nor Sir H^y St John Carew St John Mildmay had paid s^d sum of £1500 in pursuance of the covenant for that purpose contained in s^d Indre of settlem^t & that s^d trusts of s^d sev^l sums of money having so ceased & determined s^d Sir H^y St John Carew St John Mildmay & Dame Jane St John Mildmay had requested s^d Archibald John Earl of Rosebery Henry James Bouverie & John Clerk as such surviving trees as afs^d to assign the s^d sums resply and to execute such releases in relation thrto as thrinafter contained

It was witnessed that in cons'on of the premises & of 10/ to s^d Archibald John Earl of Rosebery Henry James Bouverie & John Clerk paid by s^d Wm Bray they the s^d Archibald John Earl of Rosebery H^y James Bouverie & John Clerk (upon the nomination & appointm^t of s^d Dame Jane St John Mildmay & Sir Henry St John Carew St John Mildmay Did assign unto s^d William Bray all the s^d mtge debt or sums of £10,000 & the interest then due or thereafter to become due for the same & the securities for the same so assigned to them the s^d Archibald John Earl of Rosebery Henry James Bouverie & John Clerk jointly with the s^d Edward Bray as thrinbef^e ment^d unto the s^d Wm Bray his exs ads & ass^s Upon trust to assign the same unto the s^d John Clerk Geo Wm Ricketts their ex's ad's & ass^s to be by them held and applied upon & for such trusts intents & purposes as were declared by a certain Indre bearing even date thrwith and thrinaf^r recited & did assign unto s^d Dame Jane St John Mildmay all the s^d sums of £1500 £1000 £1000 £1500 £1500 £6000 & £6000 so assigned to the s^d Archibald John Earl of Rosebery H^y James Bouverie John Clerk & Edwd *{Page 34}* Bray as thereinbef^e recited & the interest for the same resply To hold unto s^d Dame Jane St John Mildmay her exs ads & ass^s for her absolute use & benefit & did release the s^d Dame Jane St John Mildmay & Sir H^y St John Carew St John Mildmay resply from the paym^t of s^d £1500 so covenanted to be paid by them as afores^d & from all claims on account of the same

And reciting that by an Indenture bearing date 16th May 1815 endorsed on the last recited Ind're & made between the s^d William Bray 1st part s^d Dame St John Mildmay & Sir Henry St John Carew St John Mildmay 2nd part & s^d John Clerk & Geo Wm Ricketts 3rd part It was witnessed that in pursuance of the trusts reposed in him by s^d last recited Ind're & of 10/ to s^d Wm Bray did assign unto s^d John Clerk & Geo William Ricketts their exors ads & ass^s all s^d mtge debt or sum of £10,000 & interest so assigned to him s^d Wm Bray as afores^d To hold unto s^d John Clerk & Geo Wm Ricketts their exs ads & ass^s nevless upon & for such & the same trusts intents & purposes & with under & subject & the same powers provisos agreem^ts & decl'ons to upon for with under & subject to which s^d John Clerk & Geo William Ricketts held & stood possessed of the same premises at the time of the ex'on of s^d Indre of assignm^t to s^d Robt Blake of 5th aug^t 1809

And reciting that neither s^d John Clerk nor s^d Geo Wm Ricketts ever executed s^d Ind're of 9 parts of s^d 5th aug^t 1809 or any part of s^d Ind're so that the s^d term of 1000 years so limited to or to the use of s^d Sir John Hartopp & Obadiah Hughes by s^d Indre of 6th Septr 1744 as thrinbef^e ment^d in s^d manors & premises thrin comprised & so devised to s^d John Clerk & Geo Wm Ricketts by s^d codicil to the will of Sir James Rivers as afores^d or any part throf did not to the s^d Robt Blake & consequently no legal estate or interest possessed by s^d Indre of 5 parts of even date therewith & endorsed thron to the s^d Viscount Primrose Henry James Bouverie John Clerk and Edwd Bray but the residue of same term of 1000 years in s^d manors & premises thrin comprised (except so much throf as had been sold for redeeming land tax) continued vested in s^d John Clerk & George *{Page 35}* William Ricketts

And reciting that neither s^d Wm Bray Henry Peters or William Bragge ever executed s^d recited Ind're of 9 parts of 5th aug^t 1809 or any part thereof so that no legal estate or interest passed thrby to s^d Viscount Primrose Henry James Bouverie John Clerk & Edwd Bray or any of them but the whole residue of s^d term of 1000 years created by s^d Indre of 12th Feby 1761 in the premises thrin comprised continued vested in s^d William Bray & the residue of s^d term of 1000 years by s^d Indre of 28th Novr 1789 limited in use to s^d Henry Peters & William Bragge in the premises thrin comprised (except so much throf as had been sold for redeeming land tax continued vested in s^d H^y Peters & Wm Bragge

And reciting that s^d Sir Henry St John Carew St John Mildmay for certain pecuniary consons granted or secured to be paid to s^d Sir H^y Tempest the life of s^d Sir Henry St John Carew St John Mildmay certain annual sums or yearly rents charge amount^g together to the yearly sum of £1,300 but that each of them was redeemable on the terms ment^d in the securities for the same resply

And reciting that s^d parties had agreed for the redemption of s^d annuities or other terms than those so ment^d namely s^d Sir H^y Tempest was to have £10,175 secured to him as the price for the redemption or repurchase of s^d annuities with int^t & to have all arrears of s^d annuities discharged & s^d Sir H^y Tempest upon such security being given & payment of s^d arrears agreed to release s^d Sir H^y St John Carew St John Mildmay & his s^d estates from the same & all claims in respect throf

And reciting that s^d Sir H^y St John Carew St John Mildmay has satisfied all arrears of s^d sev^l annuities & had executed a Bond of even date with the Indre now being abstracted unto s^d Sir H^y Tempest in £20,350 with a condition for making same void on payment by s^d Sir H^y St John Carew St John Mildmay his hrs exs or ads unto the s^d Sir H^y Tempest his exors ads or ass^s of £10,175 & int^t at £5 per cent per annum on the days thrin ment^d

And reciting that on the treaty for such red'on of s^d annuities s^d Dame Jane St John Mildmay agreed to join with s^d Sir Henry St John Carew St John Mildmay on assigning s^d £10,000 & the securities for the same unto s^d Sir Henry Tempest by way of mortgage *{Page 36}* for better securing s^d £10,175 & int^t and that it had been agreed between S^d Dame Jane St John Mildmay & Sir Henry St John Carew St John Mildmay that subject to s^d proposed m'tge of s^d £10,000 should be subjected to such trusts as were thereinaf^r mentioned.

And reciting that s^d Dame Jane St John Mildmay in conson of £3,200 lent to her by s^d Sir H^y Tempest had executed a Bond of even date with the abstracting Ind're unto s^d Sir Henry Tempest in £6,400 with a condon for making void the same on payment by the s^d Dame Jane St John Mildmay her hrs ex'ors or administrators unto the s^d Sir H^y Tempest his ex's ad's or assigns of £3,200 with interest at five per cent per annum on the days thrin ment^d

And reciting that s^d Dame Jane St John Mildmay had agreed fur^r to secure the paym^t of s^d £3,200 & int^t by a mtge of said securities for s^d sums amounting to £8500 & fur^r to secure in like manner the paym^t of £175 part of s^d £10,175 & int^t in respect of s^d £175 in manner after ment^d

It is witnessed that in pursuance of s^d agreem^t & in conson of the premises & for fur^r & better securing the paym^t of s^d £10,175 unto said Sir Henry Tempest his ex'ors ads & ass^s with int^t as afores^d and in conson of 5/ of s^d John Clerk Geo Wm Ricketts Dame Jane St John Mildmay & Sir Henry St John Carew St John Mildmay paid by Sir H^y Tempest the s^d John Clerk &Geo Wm Ricketts at the request & by the direction & appointm^t of s^d Dame Jane St John Mildmay & Sir H^y St John Carew St John Mildmay did & each of them did bgain sell & ass^s & s^d Dame Jane St John Mildmay & Sir Henry St John Carew St John Mildmay did & each of them did bgain sell & assign ratify & confirm unto the s^d Sir H^y Tempest his exors admors & assigns

All the s^d principal sum of £10,000 secured by s^d term of 1000 years created by said Indenture of the 6th September 1744 or otherwise & all interest throf and the benefit of all securities for the same or any part throf

And all the right &^c

{Page 37}

To have hold receive & take s^d £10,000 & the int^t throf & by s^d Sir Henry Tempest his ex's ad's & ass^s & for his or their own proper monies but subj^t to the proviso after contained for redemption throf

And it was fur^r witnessed that in cons'on of the premises & for fur^r & better securing the paym^t of s^d £10,175 with int^t as afs^d and also in cons'on of 5/ to s^d John Clerk & Geo Wm Ricketts paid by s^d Sir Henry Tempest the s^d John Clerk & Geo Wm Ricketts (at the request & by the diron & appointm^t of s^d Dame Jane St John Mildmay & Sir Henry St John Carew St John Mildmay did & each of them did bgain sell & assign unto s^d Sir Henry Tempest his ex'ors ad's & ass^s

All the s^d manors heredits & premises comprised in the s^d term of 1000 years by s^d Indre of 6th Septr 1744 granted or created & which by virtue of s^d codicil to the s^d will of s^d Ja^s Rivers or orwise became vested in s^d John Clerk & Geo Wm Ricketts with their rights &^c except such of them as had been sold for redeeming land tax namely certain mess'es & lands in the parish of Owslebury thrin specified thrtofore in the occ'on of the s^d Humphrey Mildmay his undertenants or ass^s

And all the estate &^c

To hold the same (except as before excepted) unto s^d Sir Henry Tempest his ex'ors ad'mors & ass^s thenceforth for & during the residue of same term of 1000 years but subject to such equity of red'on as the same were subject to & to the proviso for redon thrinaf^r cont^d

Several covenants from s^d John Clerk & Geo Ricketts with s^d Sir Henry Tempest that they had done no act to incumber

Proviso & Declon & agreem^t between s^d Sir H^y Tempest & said Dame Jane St John Mildmay & Sir H^y St John Carew St John Mildmay that if s^d Dame Jane St John Mildmay & Sir Henry St John Carew St John Mildmay or either of them their or either of their respive heirs &^c should pay unto s^d Sir Henry Tempest his ex'ors *{Page 38}* ads or ass^s at the request & costs of the person or persons paying the same reassign s^d monies & premises unto s^d Wm Bray his exs ads and ass^s nevless upon the trusts thrinaf^r declared viz

In trust to pay unto or empower the s^d Dame Jane St John Mildmay & her ass^s to receive the int^t throf during her life & after her decease then as touching the s^d principal money & the future interest throf & the s^d securities for the same In trust for s^d Sir Henry St John Carew St John Mildmay his exs ads & ass^s

Covenants from said Sir Henry St John Carew St John Mildmay with s^d Sir Henry Tempest for paym^t of s^d £10,175 & int^t & for fur^r assurance after default in paym^t

And it was fur^r witnessed that in fur^r pursuance of s^d agreement & in cons'on of the premises & of 5/ to s^d Dame Jane St John Mildmay paid by s^d Sir H^y Tempest the s^d Dame Jane St John Mildmay did bgain sell & ass^d unto s^d Sir Henry Tempest

All the s^d sums of £1500 £1000 £1000 £1500 £1500 £6000 & £6000 (making £18,000) secured as before ment^d & the int^t throf & the benefit of all securities for the same

And all the right &^{c}

To have hold receive & take the same unto & by the s^d Sir Henry Tempest his ex'ors ads & ass^s But subject to the proviso for redemption hinaf^r conf^d

And it was fur^r witnessed that in fur^r pursuance of s^d agreem^t & in cons'on of the premises & of 5/ to said Wm Bray paid by s^d Henry Lloyds Graham The s^d Wm Bray (at the request & by the diron of the s^d Dame Jane St John Mildmay & Sir Henry St John Carew St John Mildmay did bgain sell and assign unto s^d H^y Lloyds Graham his exs ads & ass^s

All the messues lands tenements heredits & premises by s^d Indre of the 12th Feby 1761 limited to said Nicholas Preston & Geo Dacre (both since deceased) their exors &^{c} for s^d term of 1000 years

And by s^d Deed Poll of 2nd Decr 1807 assigned by *{Page 39}* s^d Thos Dacre (administrator of s^d Geo Dacre who survivied s^d Nicholas Preston) to s^d Wm Bray with the appurts (except so much as had been sold for redeem^g land tax as afores^d

And all the estate &^{c}

To hold the same (except as afores^d) unto s^d Henry Lloyds Graham his ex'ors ad's & assigns for the residue of the last ment^d term of 1000 years subject nevless to such equity of redemption as same premises were liable to & also subkect to the proviso for redemption thrinaf^r cont^d

Covenant from s^d Wm Bray with s^d Henry Lloyds Graham that he had done no act to incumber (except as appeared in the abstracting Ind're

And it was fur^r witnessed that in fur^r pursuance of s^d agreem^t & in conson of the premises & of 5/ to s^d Henry Peters & Wm Bragge paid by s^d H^y Ellis Graham The s^d H^y Peters & Wm Bragge at the request & by the diron and appointment of s^d Dame Jane St John Mildmay & Sir H^y St John Carew St John Mildmay (did & each of them did bgain sell & assign unto s^d H^y Elliot Graham his exs ads & ass^s

All the s^d manors heredits & premises by s^d Indre of 28th November 1789 limited in use to s^d Henry Peters & Wm Bragge their exs &^c for the thrin ment^d term of 1000 years with the rights &^c (except so much throf as had been sold for redeeming land tax & was & were thrinbef^e excepted

And all the estate &^c

To hold the same (except as afores^d) unto s^d H^y Elliot Graham his exs ads & ass^s for the residue of s^d last ment^d term of 1000 years but subject to such equity of red'on as was subsist^g concern^g the same and also subject to the proviso thereinbef^e contained for redemption

Several covenant from s^d Henry Peters & Wm Bragge with s^d Henry Elliot Graham that they had done no act to incumber

Proviso & Declaration between the parties that if s^d Dame Jane St John Mildmay her hrs exors or adm'ors should pay unto s^d Sir H^y Tempest his ex'ors ads or ass^s the sum of £3,200 with int^t at £5 per cent per ann on the days thrin ment^d and also in case s^d Sir H^y St John Carew *{Page 40}* St John Mildmay his h'rs &^c should make default in paying to s^d Sir Henry Tempest his ex'ors &^c said £10,175 or any part throf or any int^t for the same Then if said Dame Jane St John Mildmay her ex'ors &^c should pay unto s^d Sir H^y Tempest his ex'ors &^c £175 with int^t at £5 per cent per ann towards the discharge of s^d £10,175 & int^t or so much of said £175 & int^t as should be required to make up the deficiency (if any) of s^d paym^t by said Sir H^y St John Carew St John Mildmay his h'rs &^c Then s^d Sir Henry Tempest Henry Lloyds Graham & Henry Elliot Graham their respive ex'ors &^c should at the request &^c of s^d Dame Jane St John Mildmay her exors &^c assign s^d sums making tog^r £18,500 and s^d securities for the same resply unto s^d Dame Jane St John Mildmay her ex's ad's & ass^s but subject to such equity of red'on as was subsisting concerning the same

Covenants from s^d Dame Jane St John Mildmay with s^d Sir Henry Tempest for paym^t of s^d £3200 & int^t And for further assurance after default

Executed by all parties except s^d H^y Lloyds Graham and Henry Elliot Graham & attested

23rd May 1821

By Indenture endorsed upon the before abstracted Indenture of 29th September 1815 & made between s^d Dame Jane St John Mildmay of the 1st part Sarah Graham of Manchester St Manchester Square Co'y Midd'x Widow (the executrix acting under & by virtue of the will of s^d Henry Tempest (then deceased) of the 2nd part s^d Mary Anne Catherine Bray of G^t Russell Square Bloomsbury C'oy Midd'x Widow of the 3rd part s^d H^y Elliot Graham of the 4th part Sir Chas Morgan Bart Tudgar Co'y Monmouth Richd Clark Chamberland of the City of London of the City of

London Richard Frewin Esqre of Montague Square Russell Sq Midd'x Sir John Silvester Bart Russden of London & Robt Ray one of the Prothonotaries of the Common Pleas of the 5th part & H^y Dealtry Esqre of the Temple of 6th part

Reciting that by Indre dated 27th July 1820 between s^d Dame Jane St John Mildmay of the one part & Mary Anne Catherine Bray of the other part after reciting partly to the effect recited by the thrin within written Indre and also reciting that by an Indre dated 26th July 1820 ment^d to be endorsed in the thrin within written Indre s^d Dame Jane St John Mildmay did *{Page 41}* charge s^d several sums amount^g to £18,500 & the int^t respl^y & other the premises assigned by the thrin within written Indres with the paym^t unto the personal respive for the time being of s^d Sir H^y Tempest of the principal sum of £1000 & int^t at £5 P cent per ann and also reciting that by a Bond under the hand & seal of s^d Dame Jane St John Mildmay dated 29th Sepr 1816 she became bound unto s^d Wm Bray in £3,660 with a condition for making the same void the same on paym^t by s^d Dame Jane St John Mildmay her hrs ex's or adm'ors unto s^d Wm Bray his ex's ads or assigns of £1834.15.5 with int^t at £5 per cent per annum on 29 Sepr then next and also reciting that by another Bond under the hand & seal of s^d Dame Jane St John Mildmay dated 2nd Octr 1816 she became bound unto s^d Mary Anne Catherine Bray in £13000 with a condition for making void the same on payment by s^d Dame Jane St John Mildmay her heirs ex's or ad's unto s^d Mary Anne Catherine Bray her ex's ad's or ass^s of £5977.16.9 with int^t at £5 p cent per ann on the 2nd Octr then next & of the fur^r sum of £500 but without int^t thron during the life of Dame Jane St John Mildmay and also reciting that by an Indre dated the [Blank space] Feby 1820 made betw^n s^d Wm Bray of the one part & s^d Mary Anne Catherine Bray of the other part for the consons thrin expressed s^d Wm Bray did assign unto s^d Mary Anne Cather^e Bray her exs ads & ass^s s^d £1834.15.3 secured by the first ment^d Bond & all int^t for the same and also reciting that s^d Mary Anne Cath^e Bray had requested s^d Dame Jane St John Mildmay to chg^e £5812 part of s^d sums of £1834.15.3 £5977.16.9 & £500 & int^t on the afores^d sev^l sums of money amount^g to £18,500 & the int^t throf respl^y which she had agreed to do & also reciting that the adval duty paid by virtue of the act of parliament in force at the time of ececuting s^d Bonds was duly paid & stamps for such duty duly affixed to such Bonds It is witnessed that in conson of the premises & of 10/ to s^d Dame Jane St John Mildmay paid by s^d Mary Anne Cathe^e Bray the s^d Dame Jane St John Mildmay for fur^r & better securing the repaym^t of s^d £5812.12 with interest as afores^d unto s^d Mary Anne Cathe^e Bray her ex's ads & ass^s did thrby charge the sev^l sums secured as thrin ment^d *{Page 42}* amounting to £18,500 & the int^t throf respl^y & other the premises by thrin within written Indre assigned with the paym^t unto s^d Mary Anne Catherine Bray her exors adm'ors or ass^s of £5612.12.0 with the int^t then due & thraf^r to become due thereon as expressed by s^d two sev^l Bonds on the 27th day of Jany then next & s^d Dame Jane St John Mildmay did thrby cov^t with s^d Mary Anne Catherine Bray to pay to s^d Mary Anne Catherine Bray s^d £5812.12 & int^t that after default it should be l'ful for s^d Mary Anne Catherine Bray her ex'ors &^c to hold s^d sums amounting to £18500 & int^t (subject & without prejudice in the first place to the paym^t of s^d £3200 & £1000 for her & their own use and it was thrby declared & agreed that the [illegible text] of s^d term of 1000 years created by the thrin within recited Ind're of 6th Sepr 1744 & assigned to s^d Sir H^y Tempest by the thrin within written Indre Edwd Lloyds Graham by the thrin within written Indre called H^y Lloyds Graham (in whom s^d term of 1000 years limited by s^d Indre of 12th Feby 1761 was then vested) but who was then dead his exors &^c the within named H^y Elliot Graham in whom the term of 1000 years limited by the thrin within recited Indre of 28th (in the s^d Indre then being recited mentioned by mistake to be dated the 12) Novr 1789 was then vested should thereafter during the residue of the sev^l terms stand seized of the s^d manors & premises In trust subject to the payment of s^d £3200 & £1000 & the int^t & without prejudice thrto for securing the said Mary Anne Catherine Bray her exors &^c said £5812.12 & int^t And that s^d mortgaged premises should not be redeemed till paym^t of s^d £5812.12 & int^t as afores^d

And reciting that the s^d Sir H^y Tempest died in the year 1819 having first made his will dated 10th Feby 1815 with^t having made any special bequest of s^d £10,175 & £3,200 & appointed the s^d Sarah Graham tog^r with Wm Glover Carter Esqre in the said will called Wm Carter & Edwd Lloyds Graham executrix & exors throf which will with 5 codicils were on 27th Feby 1819 proved by s^d Edwd Lloyd Graham in the Prerogative Court of Canterbury power being reserved to the s^d Sarah Graham to prove same s^d W. G. Carter the other ex'or having first renounced probate *{Page 43}* And that s^d Edwd Lloyd Graham having soon afterw'ds died & will & codicils were on 11th aug^t 1820 proved by s^d Sarah Graham in s^d Court whereby she became the legal personal rep'ive of s^d Sir H^y Tempest & entitled as such extrix to s^d principal sums of £10,175 £3200 & £1000 & the interest throf resply

And reciting that the sum of £1000 ment^d in the s^d recited Indre of 26th July 1820 & intended to have been secured was actually paid & advanced to s^d Dame Jane St John Mildmay by s^d Sarah Graham out of the personal estate of the s^d Sir H^y Tempest but no such Deed of 26th July 1820 was ever indorsed made or executed for securing the same or any part throf

And reciting that all interest on s^d principal sums of £10,175 £3,200 & £1000 had been paid to s^d Sarah Graham & that all interest on s^d £5812.12.0 had been paid to s^d M. A. C. Bray up to the date of the abstracting Indre

And reciting that s^d Dame Jane St John Mildmay had applied to & requested s^d Sir Chas Morgan, Richard Clark Richd Frewin Sir John Silvester & Robt Bray to advance & lend to her the sum of £22,700 upon security of a transfer of the thrin within ment^d sum of £10,000 & of the thrin within ment^d other sums amount^g to £18,500 & of the sev^l securities for the same & throut to pay the s^d sev^l sums of £10,175 £3,200 & £1000 making together £14,375 to s^d Sarah Graham as extrix as aforesaid & s^d sum of £5812.12 to s^d M.A.C. Bray as afores^d which they had agreed to do

And reciting that s^d Dame Jane St John Mildmay in cons'on of £22,700 then lent to her by the s^d Sir Chas Morgan Richd Clark Richd Frewin Sir John Silvester & Robt Ray had executed to them a Bond of even date in £45,400 conditioned to be void on paym^t of £22,700 with int^t in manner thrin ment^d

It is witnessed that in pursuance of s^d agreem^t and also in cons'on of the sum of £14,375 to s^d Sarah Graham as such extrix as afs^d and also of the sum of £5812.12 to said M.A.C. Bray at the request & by the diron of s^d Dame Jane St John Mildmay paid by s^d Sir Charles Morgan Richd Clark Richd Frewin Sir John Silvester & Robt Bray the receipt of which s^d sum of £14,375 the said S. Graham *{Page 44}* & the receipt of which s^d sum of £5812.12 the said Mary Anne Catherine Bray did acknowledge & also in cons'on of the sum of £2512.8.0 to the s^d Dame Jane St John Mildmay paid by the s^d Sir Chas Morgan Richard Clark Richard Frewin Sir John Silvester & Robt Bray the receipt of which s^d sum of £2512.8.0 & Dame Jane St John Mildmay did thrby acknowledge & from same & from s^d sums of £14,375 & £5,812.12 making together the s^d sum of £22,700 did release s^d mtges said Sarah Graham and M.A.C. Bray (at the request & by the diron of s^d Dame Jane St John Mildmay & according to their respive rights & interests & so far as they respectively lawfully could or might) Did bargain sell assign & s^d Dame Jane St John Mildmay did bgain sell assign ratify & confirm unto s^d Sir Chas Morgan Richard Clark Richd Frewin Sir J Silvester & Robt Ray their ex'ors adm'ors & ass^s

The therein within ment^d principal sum of £10,000 and also the thrin mentioned several principal sums amounting to £18,500 (making together £28,500) & all interest throf & the benefit of all securities for same & every of them & every part throf

And all the right &^c

To hold receive & take s^d monies & premises unto & by s^d Sir Chas Morgan Richd Clark Richd Frewin Sir John Silvester & Robt Ray their exs ads ass^s but subject to the proviso for red'on thrin cont^d

And it was fur^r witnessed that in fur^r pursuance of s^d agreem^t & for the cons'on afs^d and also in conson of 5/ to s^d Sarah Graham paid by s^d mtgees s^d Sarah Graham (at the like request & by the like dir'on of s^d Dame Jane St John Mildmay & Mary Anne Catherine Bray) did bgain sell & ass unto s^d Sir Chas Morgan Richd Clark Richd Frewin Sir John Silvester & Robt Ray their ex's ads & ass^s

All the manors messues lands tenements advowsons heredits & premises comprised in *{Page 45}* s^d term of 1000 years by s^d thrin within ment^d Indre of 6th September 1744 granted & by the thrin within Indre assigned to s^d Sir Henry Tempest with their rights members &^{c} (except as thrin within excepted

And all the estate &^{c}

To hold the same except as before excepted unto s^d Sir Chas Morgan Richd Clark Richd Frewin Sir John Silvester Robt Ray their exors ads & ass^s thenceforth for the residue of s^d term of 1000 years (but subject nevless to such equity of redemption as the person or persons in whom for the time being the remainder or reversions expectant on the determination throf was or might be vested should upon the decease of s^d Dame Jane St John Mildmay be entitled to & subject to the proviso for redemption thrinaf^r cont^d

Several covenant from s^d Sarah Graham & M.A.C. Bray that they had not incumbered

And it was thrby provided agreed & declared by & between s^d mtgees & s^d Dame Jane St John Mildmay that if she her heirs ex'ors or administrators should pay unto s^d mtgees their exs ads or ass^s the sum of £22,700 with int^t for same at the rate of £5 per cent per annum on the 23rd May 1822 without deductions s^d mtges their exs ads or ass^s would at the request & costs of s^d Dame Jane St John Mildmay her exs &^{c} reassign s^d monies heredits & premises unto her or them as she or they should direct or appoint free from all incumbrances by the mtgees in the meantime

And it was fur^r witnessed that in fur^r pursuance of s^d agreem^t & for the cons'on afores^d and also in conson of 5/ to s^d H^y Elliot Graham paid by s^d H^y Dealty s^d H^y E. Graham (at the request & by the diron of s^d Sarah Graham M.A.C. Bray Dame Jane St John Mildmay and also at the request & by the diron & upon the nomin'on & appointment of s^d mtgees) did bgain sell & ass unto s^d H^y Dealtry his executors adm'ons & assigns

The manors & premises by the thrin within written Indenture assigned to s^d H^y Elliot *{Page 46}* Graham for the residue of the term of 1000 years created by s^d thrin within recited Indenture of 28th November 1789 with their rights &^{c} (except as thrin within ment^d

And all the estate &^{c}

To hold same (except as last afores^d) unto s^d H^y Dealtry his exors ads & ass^s for all the residue of the last ment^d term of 1000 years thrin but nevless In trust for said Sir Charles Morgan Richd Clark Richd Frewin Sir J. Silvester & Robt Ray their exors admin's & ass^s and subject to such equity of redemption as same manors &

heredits or any part thereof might be subject or liable to for the benefit of the person or persons who upon or after the decease of s^d Dame Jane St John Mildmay should for the time being be entitled to the rem^r or reversions of same manors & premises or any part throf expectant upon the determination of same term and also subject to redemption by s^d Dame Jane St John Mildmay her exs ads & ass^s on paym^t of s^d sum of £22,700 & interest at the times & in manner in the proviso for redemption thereinbefore contained & appointed for payment thof

Covenant from s^d H^y Elliot Graham that he had not incumbered

Covenant from s^d Dame Jane St John Mildmay for paymen^t of s^d £22,700 & int^t in manner afores^d To procure the legal personal repr'tives of s^d Edwd Lloyd Graham deced to assign the residue of the term of 1000 years created by s^d thrin within recited Ind're of 28th November 1789 in the manors & heredits thrin comprised & by thrin within Indenture assigned to him (except as in that Ind're excepted) unto such person or persons as the mortgagees their ex'ors &^{c} should nominate or appoint In trust for thrin but subject to such redemption as afores^d And s^d Dame Jane St John Mildmay did thrby declare & direct that such repre'tives of s^d E. L. Graham should in the meantime stand & be possessed of the residue of s^d term in s^d heredits (except as afs^d) In trust for s^d mtgees their exors &^{c} subject to such redemption as afs^d & for fur^r assurance after default in payment &^{c}

Proviso & Declons subject & without prejudice to s^d securities made to *{Page 47}* mortgees that as between s^d Dame Jane St John Mildmay & the person or persons who for the time being was or were or might be entitled to the remainder or reversion expectant on her decease to s^d heredits comprised in s^d terms of 1000 years & 1000 years or any part thereof s^d Dame Jane St John Mildmay her hrs exs or ad's ahould not be liable to bear said principal sum of £22,700 thrby secured or any part throf

Executed by s^d Dame Jane St John Mildmay J. Graham M.A.C. Bray & H.C. Graham & attested

Receipt for £14,375 signed by s^d Mary Ann Catherine Bray & £2512 & signed by s^d Dame Jane St John Mildmay indorsed

3rd December 1823

By Indenture (also indorsed upon s^d before abstracted Indenture of 29th Sepr 1815) & made between s^d Dame Jane St John Mildmay of the one part & s^d Sir Chas Morgan Richd Clark & Robt Bray parties to the last abstracted Indre of the other part

Reciting that s^d Richd Frewin & Sir John Silvester had died since the date & exon of the last abstracted Indre

And reciting that s^d sum of £22700 remained due to the above ment^d mtgees by virtue of the afores^d securities together with some interest for same

And reciting that s^d Dame Jane St John Mildmay having occasion for the fur^r sum of £3,300 had applied to & requested said Sir Charles Morgan Richd Clark & Robt Ray to lend her the same which they had agreed to do upon the repaym^t throf secured with interest in the meantime in manner thrinaf^r ment^d

It is witnessed that in conson of the sum of £3,300 to s^d Dame Jane St John Mildmay paid by s^d Sir Chas Morgan Richd Clark & Robt Ray (the receipt whof was thrby acknowledged) & for securing the repaym^t of s^d sum with interest in the meantime s^d Dame Jane St John Mildmay did thrby for herself her hrs exs & ads cov^t with s^d Sir Chas Morgan Richd Clark & Robt Ray that the afores^d sum of £10,000 & several principal sums amount^g to £18,500 (making tog^r £28,500 & all int^t throf respy & the securities for same sev^l principal sums should from thenceforth stand charged & chargable with & be subject & liable to & *{Page 48}* should remain continue & be vested in Sir Chas Morgan Richd Clark & Robt Ray their ex's ads & ass^s for the purpose of securing s^d sums of £3,300 with int^t for same after the rate of £5 per cent per ann on the 3rd day of June then next without any dedon whatsoever

Covenants from s^d Dame Jane St John Mildmay for paym^t of s^d £3,300 & int^t at the time thrinbef^e appointed (which s^d £3,300 & int^t due on the same as ment^d in & in part secured by a Bond in £6,600 of even date given by her to s^d mtgees That s^d principal sum of £10,000 & the afores^d principal sums amount^g to £18,500 making tog^r £28,500) & the int^t throf respy should not be redeemable till as well s^d £3,300 & int^t as £22,700 & int^t should be paid & that she had not incumbered (except as appeared by the s^d indorsed Ind're of 23rd May 1821

And s^d Dame Jane St John Mildmay did thrby direct & declare that all & every person & persons in whom the sev^l thrin within ment^d terms for years in the s^d manors & heredits was or were vested In trust as in the last abstracted Indre expressed should stand & be possessed of same terms (except as afores^d) Upon trust for better securing to s^d Sir Chas Morgan Richd Clark & Robt Ray their exors &^c s^d sum of £3300 then lent as well as the afores^d sum of £22,700 & the int^t throf respy

Covenant by s^d Dame Jane St John Mildmay for fur^r assurance

Proviso that (subject to s^d securities) as between s^d Dame Jane St John Mildmay & the person or persons for the time being entitled to the remainder or reversions expectant on her decease to manors & heredits comprised in s^d terms of 1000 years & 1000 years or any part throf s^d Dame Jane St John Mildmay her hrs exors or admors should not be liable to bear s^d principal sum of £3,300 or any part throf

Executed by s^d Dame Jane St John Mildmay & attested

Receipt for £3,300 underwritten signed and witnessed

18th September 1824

By Indenture (also endorsed upon the before abstracted Indenture of 29th September 1815) & made between the s^d Dame Jane St John Mildmay of the one part & the s^d Sir Chas Morgan Richd Clark & Robt Ray of the other part

Reciting that the s^d principal sum of £22,700 & £3,300 with some int^t *{Page 49}* then remaining due

And Reciting that s{^d} Dame Jane St John Mildmay having occasion for the loan of £6000 had applied to & requested the s{^d} Sir Cha{^s} Morgan Rich{^d} Clark & Rob{^t} Ray to lend the same to her which they agreed to do upon having the repaym{^t} secured with interest in the meantime in manner after ment{^d}

It is witnessed that in cons'on of £6000 to s{^d} Dame Jane St John Mildmay paid by s{^d} Sir Cha{^s} Morgan Rich{^d} Clark & Rob{^t} Ray the rec{^t} &{^c} the s{^d} Dame Jane St John Mildmay did for herself her heirs exors & admors covenant with s{^d} Sir Cha{^s} Morgan Rich{^d} Clark & Rob{^t} Ray their exs ad's & ass{^s} that

The principal sum of £10,000 & sev{^l} principal sums amounting to £18,500 (making tog{^r} £28,500 by s{^d} Indre of 23rd May 1821) assigned to s{^d} Sir Cha{^s} Morgan Rich{^d} Clark Robert Ray & all int{^t} throf resply and the securities for the same sums & interest or for any of them or any part thereof respive

Should be thenceforth stand charged & chargeable with and subject & liable to & should remain & be vested in the said Sir Cha{^s} Morgan Rich{^d} Clark & Rob{^t} Ray their ex's ad's & assigns for the purpose of securing to them the payment as well of £2,500 (part of the said sum of £6000 then lent) with int{^t} at 5 per cent as of s{^d} sums of £22,700 & £3,300 thrtofore lent to aforesaid & the int{^t} due & to grow due for the same & should not be redeemed or redeemable until as well the s{^d} sum of £2,500 & int{^t} as the s{^d} sums of £22,700 & £3300 & int{^t} should be fully paid to the s{^d} Sir Cha{^s} Morgan Rich{^d} Clark & Robert Ray their ex'ors adm'ors and ass{^s}

Covenant by s{^d} Dame Jane St John Mildmay for paym{^t} of s{^d} £6000 & int{^t} as thrin ment{^d} on the 18th March then next (which £6000 was the same sum as was ment{^d} in the cons'on of a Bond of even date with the Ind're now being abstracted whby the s{^d} Dame Jane St John Mildmay was bound to s{^d} Sir Cha{^s} Morgan Rich{^d} Clark & Rob{^t} Ray in £12000 & which is in part fur{^r} secured by a certain Indre bearing even date with the Indre now being abstracted whby £3,500 part of s{^d} £6000 had been *{Page 50}* secured with interest by way of mortgage of certain heredits in Midd'x

And s{^d} Dame Jane St John Mildmay did declare direct & appoint that all & every persons & person in whom the s{^d} sev{^l} terms of years ment{^d} in the s{^d} Indre of 29th Sept{^r} 1815 of & in the sev{^l} heredits ment{^d} in the same Indre & comprised in s{^d} terms (except such of them as had been sold for redeeming land tax as afores{^d}) were was or should or might be or become vested in trust as in the s{^d} Indre of 29th September 1815 ment{^d} should be possessed of s{^d} terms as to for & concerning all & every the s{^d} heredits & premises (except as afores{^d}) upon trust for fur{^r} & better securing the paym{^t} to s{^d} Sir Cha{^s} Morgan Rich{^d} Clark & Robert Ray their exors admors & ass{^s} of s{^d} £2500 with int{^t} as afores{^d} as of s{^d} sums of £22,700 & £3,300 & int{^t} due & to grow due for the same

Covenants by s{^d} Dame Jane St John Mildmay that she had good right to charge s{^d} sums amount{^g} together to £28,500 and for fur{^r} assurance

Proviso that subject to s{^d} securities as between s{^d} Dame Jane St John Mildmay on one hand & the person or persons for the time being entitled to the remainder or reversions expectant on her decease in the s{^d} heredits & premises comprised in s{^d} terms or any part throf the s{^d} Dame Jane St John Mildmay her heirs executors or adminrs should not be laible to bear the s{^d} principal sum of £2500 or any part throf

Executed by s{^d} Dame Jane St John Mildmay and attested

Receipt for £6000 signed & witnessed

6th July 1831

By Indenture (also indorsed upon the before abstracted Indenture of the 29th September 1815 & made between said Sir Chas Morgan and Robt Ray which s^d Sir Chas Morgan & Robt Ray had survived their co mortagees Richd Frewin & Sir John Silvester the parties to the said before abstracted Ind're of the 23rd May 1821 and also Richd Clark the party to such Ind're and also to the Indres of the 3rd December 1823 and the 18th September 1824 of the 1st part Arthur Morgan of Bridge Street Blackfriars London Esqre of the 2nd part & the s^d Sir Chas Morgan and Robert Ray Miles Stringer of Effingham place in the County of Surrey Esq Newman Knowlys Esqre Recorder of the City of London & Richard Twining of the Strand in the County of Middx Banker of the 3rd part

Reciting that the security made by the s^d Indre of the 23rd *{Page 51}* May 1821 for the sum of £22,700 & also the security made by the said Indre of the 3rd December 1823 for the sum of £3,300 & also the security made by the s^d Ind're of the 18th Sepr 1824 for the sum of £2,500 were resply made to them the s^d Sir Chas Morgan Richd Clark R Frewin Sir John Silvester & Robt Ray resp'ly jointly on a joint account & the s^d sev^l sums of £22,700 £3,300 & £2,500 making tog^r £28,500 then remained due upon the s^d securities with some int^t for the same

And reciting that s^d Richd Clark R. Frewin & Sir J. Silvester having severally departed this life the s^d sev^l principal sums amount^g together to £28,500 & the securities for the same became vested in the s^d Sir Chas Morgan & Robt Ray by survivor ship & the same principal monies & interest & the securities for the same then belonged to the s^d Miles Stringer Newman Knowlys and Richard Twining jointly with the s^d Sir Charles Morgan & Robert Ray upon a joint account as the s^d Charles Morgan & Robt Ray did thereby acknowledge

And reciting that the said Miles Stringer Newman Knowlys & Richard Twining had requested the said Sir Chas Morgan & Robt Ray to assign the s^d principal monies interest & securities so that the same might become vested in the s^d Sir Chas Morgan Robert Ray Miles Stringer Newman Knowlys & Richd Twining jointly

It is witnessed that in cons'on of the premises & 5/ they the said Sir Charles Morgan & Robert Ray (with the privity & consent of the s^d Miles Stringer Newman Knowlys & Richd Twining testified &^c Did & each of them Did bgain sell assign transfer & set over unto the s^d Arthur Morgan his exors admors & ass^s

All the therein within ment^d principal sum of £10,000

And also the thrin within mentioned several principal sums amounting to £18500 making together the sum of £28,500 & which by the said Indenture of the 23rd May 1821 were assigned to the s^d Sir Chas Morgan Richd Clark Richd Frewin Sir John Silvester & Robt Ray for securing to *{Page 52}* them the said £22,700 & interest & by the s^d sev^l Indres of the 3rd December 1823 & the 18th Day of Septr 1824 were charged with the payment of the s^d sums of £3,300 & £2500 & int^t resply to the s^d Sir Chas Morgan Richd Clark & Robert Ray & all int^t due for the same resply tog^r with the benefit of all securities for the s^d principal monies & interest

And all the right &^c

To hold receive & take the said monies & premises thrinbef^e assigned unto s^d Arthur Morgan his ex'ors ad's & ass^s upon trust nev'less that he the s^d Arthur Morgan sh'd forthwith assign the same unto the s^d Sir Chas Morgan Robert Ray Miles Stringer Newman Knowlys and Richard Twining their ex'ors ad's & assigns

It is fur^r witnessed that for the cons'ons thrinbef^e expressed They the s^d Sir Chas Morgan & Robt Ray did & each of them Did b'gain sell & assign unto the s^d Arthur Morgan his exs ads & ass^s

All & singular the manors heredits & premises comprised in the term of 1000 years by the s^d Indenture of the 26th day of September 1744 granted or created & by the s^d Indre of the 23rd day of May 1821 assigned to the s^d Sir Charles Morgan Richard Clark Richard Frewin Sir John Silvester & Robert Ray for the residue of the s^d term with their & every of their appurt's (except as in the said Indenture of 29th day of Septr 1815 excepted)

And all the estate &^{c}

To hold the s^d manors heredits & premises before lastly assigned with their & every of their appurts unto the s^d Arthur Morgan his ex's ad's & assigns from thenceforth for the residue of the s^d term of 1000 years then unexpired but subject nev'less to such equity of redemption as the s^d heredits were or might be liable on payment to the s^d Sir Chas Morgan Robert *{Page 53}* Ray Miles Stringer Newman Knowlys & Richd Twining their executors admors or ass^s of the s^d several sums of £22,700 £3,300 & £2,500 resply & the interest due & to grow due for the same

In trust that he the said Arthur Morgan should assign all the s^d heredits & premises unto the said Sir Chas Morgan Robert Ray Miles Stringer Newman Knowlys & Richd Twining their ex'ors adm'ors & ass^s for all the residue of the s^d term then expired subject as aforesaid

Several covenants by s^d Sir Chas Morgan & Robt Ray that they resply had not incumbered

Executed by s^d Sir Chas Morgan Robert Ray & Miles Stringer & attested

7th July 1831

By Indenture also endorsed upon the before abstracted Indre of the 29th September 1815 & made between Arthur Morgan of the one part & s^d Sir Chas Morgan Robt Ray Miles Stringer Newman Knowlys & Richd Twining of the other part

It is witnessed that in pursuance of the trusts reposed in the said Arthur Morgan by the lastly abstracted Indenture & in cons'on of 5/ He the s^d Arthur Morgan Did bargain sell & assign unto the s^d Sir Chas Morgan Robert Ray Miles Stringer Newman Knowlys & Richard Twining their exors adm'ors & ass^s

All the principal sums of £10,000 & also the sev^l principal sums amounting to £18,500 making together the sum of £28,500 by the said lastly abstracted Indenture assigned to the s^d Arthur Morgan his ex's ads & ass^s

And all interest due & to become due for the same tog^r with the benefit of all securities for the same

To hold receive & take the s^d monies & premises unto the said Sir Charles Morgan Robert Ray Miles Shingler Newman Knowleys & Richard Twining their ex'ors admors & ass^s

{Page 54}

And it is fur^r witnessed that in fur^r pursuance of the trusts reposed in the s^d Arthur Morgan by the s^d lastly abstracted Indre & for the consons before expressed He the s^d Arthur Morgan did bgain sell & assign unto the s^d Sir Charles Morgan Robert Ray Miles Stringer Newman Knowlys & Richd Twining

All & singular the manors heredits & premises comprised in the term of 1000 years by the lastly abstracted Indre assigned to the s^d Arthur Morgan his exors admors & ass^s for the residue of the s^d term of 1000 years with their & evry of their appurts (except as in the same Indenture is excepted)

And all the estate &^{c}

To hold the said manors messu's lands tenements advowsons heredits & premises with their & every of their appurts unto the s^d Sir Chas Morgan Robert Ray Miles Stringer Newman Knowlys & Richard Twining their exors admors & ass^s for & during all the residue & remainders of the s^d term of 1000 years then unexpired but subject nevless to such equity of redemption as the s^d heredits were or might be liable to on payment of the several principal sums of £22,700 £3,300 & £2500 (making together the sum of £28,500) & int^t due to the s^d Sir Charles Morgan Robt Ray Miles Stringer Newman Knowlys & Richard Twining their exors admors or ass^s

Executed by said Arthur Morgan & attested

14th December 1842

By Deed Poll (also endorsed upon the before abstracted Indre of the 29th Sepr 1815) under the hands & seals of s^d Sir Chas Morgan R Twining & Dame Jane St John Mildmay

Reciting that since the date of the last abstracted Indenture Robert Ray Miles Stringer & Newman Knowlys parties thrto jointly with the s^d Sir C. Morgan & Richard Twining had died

And reciting that by an order of the Court of Chancery dated the 25th Feby 1842 made by his Honor the Vice Chancellor of England on the petition of the s^d Dame St John Mildmay in *{Page 55}* the of an act of Parliament of the 42 year of the Reign of King Geo 3rd relating to the redemption & sale of the land tax & in the Deed Poll now being abstracted more parlary described it was referred to the master to enquire whether there was any debt affecting the heredits the land tax whrof had been redeemed as in the said petition ment^d in discharge wh'of or of any part whrof so much of the money to arise from the sale of the Bank annuities in the petition ment^d might be properly applied & to whom such debts (if any) was payable

And reciting that in pursuance of the s^d order Mr Wingfield the master to whom the s^d order was referred made his report dated the 11th July 1842 whrby after referring to the before abstracted Indre of the 29th September 1815 & the several Indres & other instruments thrin recited & the several Indres & referring to a state of facts & charge & an amended state of facts & charge resply laid before him supported by the affidavits thrin referred to he found that the s^d Robt Ray Miles Stringer & Newman Knowlys had died leaving the said Sir Charles Morgan & Richard Twining them surviving & that the sev^l sums amounting together to £28,500 so assigned & assured to he said Sir Chas Morgan Robert Ray Miles Stringer Newman Knowlys & Richard Twining as in the before abstracted Ind're of the 7th July 1831 ment^d then remained due to the s^d Sir Chas Morgan & Richd Twining upon the said thrinbefore stated securities together with some interest for the same and he found that in or about 1808 Sir Henry Paulet St John Mildmay Bart in the s^d hrinbef^e abstracted Indre of the 29th Sepr 1815 named (the late husband of the s^d Dame Jane St John Mildmay then being tenant for life in possession of the estates comprised in the s^d Indres of the 27th & 28th Novr 1789 under the s^d Ind'res & Common Recovery suffered in pursuance throf sold under the powers of the s^d act of Parliament passed in the 42nd Geo the 3rd intitled "an act for consolidating the provisions of the sev^l acts passed for the redem'on & sale of the land tax into one act & for making fur^r provisions for the red'on & sale throf & for removing doubts respecting the rights of persons claiming to vote at elections for Knights of the Shire & other members to serve in Parliament in respect of mess'es lands or tenem^ts the land tax which shall have been redeemed or purchased *{Page 56}* part of the estates situate in the Parishes of Twyford & Owslebury comprised in the s^d Indres of the 27th & 28th Novr 1789 for the purpose of redeeming the land tax charged on the estates & that the monies arising from such sale according to the dirons of the said act were paid into the Bank of England & invested in Bank annuities and that it was alleged that after reserving so much of the said Bank ann^s as was agreed to be transferred as the conson for the redemption of the land tax charged upon the s^d estates comprised in the s^d Indres of the 27th & 28th Novr 1789 other estates in the County of Middx which stood settled to the like uses there remained £1121.16.3 3 percent Reduced ann^s & £256.13.4 3 per cent Consolidated ann^s (being the Bank ann^s referred to in the s^d order) and which Bank ann^s resply were then standing to the sev^l acct^s after ment^d (that is to say) the said £1121.16.3 3 per cent reduced ann^s to the account of Sir H^y Paulet St John Mildmay Bart on acct of Twyford estate in account with the comm^rs for the redon of the national debt on acc^t of the sale of the land tax & the s^d £256.13.4 3 per cent consolidated Bank ann^s to the acc^t of Dame Jane St John Mildmay Widow on acc^t of Twyford est^e in acc^t with the comm^rs for the redon of the national debt on acc^t of the sale of the land tax and he found that the div^ds of the Bank ann^s from the time of the transfer thereof to the acct thof afs^d had been received by the s^d Dame Jane St John Mildmay and he found that the manors mess'es lands tenem^ts & heredits comprised in the s^d Indres of the 27th & 28th Novr 1789 the land tax charged thon had been so redeemed as afs^d (except such part throf as had been sold for the ppose of such red'on as afs^d) then remained limited to & were in the posson of the s^d Dame Jane St John Mildmay as te'nt for life thof under & by virtue of the s^d Indre of the 28th Novr 1789 & that the same were subject (amongst o^r charges) to the sum of £6000 princ^l m'oy by the s^d last ment^d Ind're provided for the portion of Ann Clark (thrbef^e Ann Mildmay) & int^t thon & the same sum of £6000 & the int^t throf thinbef^e stated were then payable to the s^d Sir Chas Morgan & Richd Twining And he found that the s^d Dame Jane St John Mildmay by the s^d amended state of facts & charges after stat^g to the effect thrinbef^e ment^d submitted to him that the produce of the s^d surplus stock or Bank ann^s aris^g from sale of part of the s^d settled estate for the ppose of redeem^g the s^d land tax then as thrinbef^e ment^d after dischar^g the costs of the appl'on thof might properly be applied so far as the same would extend in the discharge of such sum and *{Page 57}* he certified that upon cons'on of the sev^l matters afs^d he found that the s^d debt of £6000 (being the portion of the s^d Indre of the 28th Novr 1789 for the s^d Ann Mildmay with the in^t thon was a debt affecting the lands & heredits the land tax wh'on had been redeemed as thinbef^e in disc'ge of part whof so much mo'y to arise from the sale of the s^d Bank ann^s as sh^d remain after paym^t th'out of the costs charges & expensces in the s^d petition & order ment^d might be properly applied and he found that such debt was then payable to the s^d Sir C. Morgan & R. Twining

And reciting that by another order of the s^d Court made by the s^d Vice Chancellor of England in the matter of the s^d Act & of the s^d Dame St John Mildmay dated the 15th July 1842 It was ordered that the s^d masters s^d Report be confirmed and it was ordered that the Secretary or Deputy Sect^y or accountant Genl for the time being of the Governor & Comp^y of the Bank of England or his Deputy should be at liberty to transfer into the name & with the privity of the accountant gen^l of the s^d court In trust to an account entitled "Exparte Dame Jane St John Mildmay W^o on account of Twyford Estate as to surplus stock arisen from sale of settled estate for red'on of land tax" the sev^l sums of £1121.16.3 3 per cent reduced ann^s & £256.13.4 3 per cent Bank ann^s and it was ordered that the s^d £1121.16.3 reduced ann^s & £256.13.4 Bank ann^s when so transfer^d as afs^d should be sold & the money to arise by such sale was to be paid into the Bank with the privity of the s^d accountant gen^l to be there placed to the credit of the like account And it was ordered that it be referred to the s^d master to settle & approve of a proper discharge to be given by the said Sir Chas Morgan & Richd Twining upon so much of the mo'y to arise by the said sale of the s^d Bank ann^s as should remain after providing for the paym^t of the costs & expenses thereafter directed to be paid thereout being applied in discharge of part of the debt of £6000 in the said Report ment^d to be payable to them & it was ordered that upon such discharge being signed or o'wise duly executed as the said master direct by the said Sir Chas Morgan & Richd Twining (such signature or execution to be certified by the said master) so much as aforesaid of the said money to arise by the said sale (the amount to be certified by the said master) be paid to the said Sir Charles Morgan & Richard Twining *{Page 58}* And it was ordered that the s^d master should tax and settle the costs charges & exp'^{ces} of the pet^r of obtaining the s^d order dated the 25th July 1842 & of the now rect^g application & conseq^t throf respect^y And it was ordered that such costs charges and expenses when so taxed and settled as afs^d be paid out of the cash to arise by the said sale of the s^d Bank annuities and reduced annuities to Mr George Harding the solicitor of the pet^r Dame Jane St John Mildmay

And reciting that in pur^{ce} of the s^d last ment^d order the s^d sums of £1121.16.3 3 per cent reduced Bank annuities & £256.13.4 3 per cent consolidated Bank annut's were transferred & sold according to the dir'ons contained in the same order & the money that arose by s^d sale & which amounted to the sum of £1285.19.1 was paid into the Bank with the privity of the Accountant Gentleman of the s^d Court to an acc^t "Exparte Dame Jane St John Mildmay W^o on acc't of Twyford Est^e as to surplus stock arisen by the sale of settled estates for redempt^n of land tax

And reciting that after deducting the expences directed to be paid out of the s^d money there remained the sum of £1144 to be paid to the said Sir Charles Morgan & Richard Twining in part satisf'on of the s^d sum of £6000 as appeared by the Report of the s^d master dated 13th Decr 1842

And reciting that the s^d sum of £1144 is intended to be paid to the s^d Sir Chas Morgan & Richd Twining in part satisf'on of the s^d sum of £6000 and that the s^d master had approved of the said Deed Poll now being abstracted as a proper rel'e and disch'ge to be executed by the s^d Sir Chas Morgan and Richd Twining as appeared by his s^d Report dated the 13th Decr 1842 & by his signing his name to the s^d allowance written in the s^d margin of the engrossm^t of the s^d Deed Poll

It is witnessed that in consideration of the sum of £1144 to be paid by the said Accountant General to the said Sir Charles Morgan & Richard Twining after the execution of the Deed Poll now being abstracted and a receipt for which said sum was intended to be indorsed on or written at the foot of such Deed Poll and signed by them

They the said Sir Charles Morgan and Richard Twining did and each of them did remise release and for ever quit

{Page 59}

All and sig^r the Manors and other heredit's then charged with or liable to the payment of the said sum of £6000 so provided for the portion of the s^d Ann Mildmay Spinster as aforesaid and then vested in the said Sir Chas Morgan and Richd Twining by way of security as aforesaid

And also the said Dame Jane St John Mildmay her heirs executors and administrators and all and every other person and persons ent^d and to become entitled to the s^d Manors & other hereditaments so charged as afs^d for any estate or interest whatsoever of & from the s^d sum of £1144 so to be paid to the s^d Sir Charles Morgan and Richard Twining as afs^d & all interest due and to grow due for the same sum and all claims and demands in respect thereof

Declaration that the s^d £1144 so to be paid as afs^d should be accepted by the s^d Sir Charles Morgan and Richard Twining in part satisf'on of the afs^d sum of £6000 but subject and without prejudice to the pay^t of the residue of the said sum of £6000 or the int^t th'rof or any remedies claims and demands for or in respect throf And that the s^d sum of £1144 should also be taken and accepted in part satisf'on of the said sum of £28500 so assigned and secured to the s^d Sir Chas Morgan Bar't Robert Ray Miles Stringer Newman Knowlys & Richard Twining and then due to the s^d Sir Chas Morgan and Richard Twining as afs^d but subject without prejudice to the payment of the residue of the said sum of £28500 or the int^t th'rof or any remedies claims or demands for or in respect th'rof

Executed by s^d Sir Charles Morgan & Richd Twining & attested

Receipts dated 25th January 1843 for £1144 underwritten signed and witnessed

Master Wingfields approval in the margin

15th September 1847 (Number One)

By Indenture (endorsed upon the bef'e abstracted Ind're) of 29th Septr 1815 and made between Richd Twining of the 1st pat Sir Charles Morgan *{Page 60}* Robinson Morgan of Tudegar in the County of Monmouth Bar't the said R^d Twining Ralph Price of William Street Blackfriars in the City of London Esq Henry Kemble of Grove Hill Camberwell in the County of Surrey Esquire and Wm Saml Jones of the Crown Office Temple in the City of London Esq of the 2nd part and Arthur Morgan of the third part

Reciting the several before abstracted Ind'res of 23rd May 1821 3rd December 1823 18th Sepr 1824 6th July 1831 and Deed Poll of the 14th Decr 1842

And reciting that by the payment of the s^d £1144 the said sum of £28,500 was reduced to £27,356 which was then due upon the said sec^s with some int^t for the same

And reciting that the said Sir Charles Morgan died on the 5th December 1846 and thrupon the said £27356 & all int^t due th'ron tog^r with the sec's for the same became and were then vested in the said Richd Twining alone by survivorship

And reciting that the s^d Richd Twining was desirous to transfer the said principal money interest and securities so that the same might vest in himself and the said Chas Morgan R Morgan R Price H Kemble & W^m S Jones their exs ads and ass^s according to the nature and tenure thereof as joint tenants and to be held by them as property on a joint account

It is witnessed that in cons'on of 10/ to the s^d Richard Twining p^d by the s^d Arthur Morgan the rect &^{c} He the said Richard Twining Did bargain sell and assign unto the said Arthur Morgan his ex'ors adm'ors and assigns

All those the principal monies or sums making tog^r the sum of £27,356 residue of said principal sums amounting together to the sum of £28,500 and which by the before abstracted Indentures of the 6th and 7th July 1831 were assigned to the said Sir Charles Morgan R Ray M Stringer N Knowlys and Richd Twining for securing to them the said sums of £22,700 £3,300 and £2500 and interest and the interest due and to become due for the same and all and every the securities for the same

{Page 61}

And all & sing^r the manors mess'es lands tenements advowsons heredits & premises comprised in the s'd term of 1000 years & by the before abstracted Indres of the 6th & 7th July 1831 or one of them assigned to the s'd Sir Charles Morgan Robt Ray Miles Stringer N. Knowlys & R^d Twining for the then residue of the s'd term & their appurts

And all the estate &^{c}

To hold rec & take the s'd p'pal monies or sums amot^g tog^r to the sum of £27356 int^t & sec^s thereby assigned unto the sd Arthur Morgan his exors ad'mors & assigns with full power & authourity to recover & rec'e the same & give a disch'ge or disch'ges for the same when paid in the name or names of him the s'd R^d Twining his ex'ors &^{c} when & if the same sh^d be necessary

And to have and to hold the sd manors messes lans tenements advowsons heredits & pre's hereby assigned & every part thereof with their appurts unto the s'd Arthur Morgan his ex'ors adm'ors & assigns & from thenceforth for the residue then unexpired of the s'd term of 1000 years sub^t nev'less to such equity of redemption as the s'd prem's were then liable on paym^t of the s'd sum of £27356 & int^t with the except^n nev^s that the s^d sum of £27356 & int^t thof should be paid to the s'd Sir Charles Morgan R Morgan R^d Twining Ralph Price H^y Kemble W S Jones or the survivors or survivor of them or the ex'ors or adm'ors of such survivor or their or his assigns & not otherwise but upon trust nev'less that he the s'd Arthur Morgan his ex'ors or admors sh'd by an Indenture which was then prepared & endorsed also upon the before abstracted Indre of the 29th Sepr 1815 & intended to bear even date with but to be ex'ted immed'ly after the exec'on of the Indre now being abstracted reassign the same ppal monies int^t sec^s heredits & prems & transfer the sev^l powers and authorities assigned & given *{Page 62}* to him the s'd Arthur Morgan under the s'd Sir Charles Morgan R Morgan Richd Twining R Price H^y Kemble & Wm Saml Jones their ex'ors adm'ors & ass as joint tenants & for their joint benefit & disposal

Covenant by s'd Rd Twining that he had not incumbered &^{c}

Executed by s'd R Twining & attested

15th September 1847 (Number Two)

By Indre (also endorsed upon the before abstracted Indre of 29th Septr 1815) & made betw'n Arthur Morgan of the one part & sd Sir Chas Morgan Robinson Morgan R^d Twining Ralph Price H^y Kemble & Wm Saml Jones of the other part

It is witn'ed that in pursuance of the trusts reposed in the s'd Arthur Morgan by the lastly abst^d Indre & in cons'on of 10/ to the s'd Arthur Morgan paid (the rect &^{c}) He the s'd Arthur Morgan Did bargain sell & assign unto the sd Sir Charles Morgan Robinson Morgan Richd Twining Ralph Price H^y Kemble & W^m S Jones

All those the p'pal monies or sums making tog^r the sum of £27336 & the interest thereof & all & every the sec^s for the same

And also all & sing^r the Manors mess'es lands tenemt^s advowsons heredits & prems which were resp'ly assigned & given to the s'd Arthur Morgan by the s'd lastly abstracted Indenture

And all the estate &ᶜ

To hold rec & take the s'd ppal monies intᵗ secˢ & prem's thereby assigned or intended so to be unto & by the sᵈ Sir Charles Morgan R Morgan Rᵈ Twining Ralph Price Hʸ Kemble Wᵐ S Jones their exors admors & ass as joint & for their joint benefit & disposal

And to hold the s'd manors messes lands tentˢ advowsons heredits & prems unto the sd S C Morgan R Morgan Rᵈ Twining R Price Hʸ Kemble & Wᵐ S Jones their executors adm'ors & ass for the residue then unexpired of the s'd term of 1000 years subject nev'ss to such equity of redemption as the s'd prems were then liable to with the exceptⁿ *{Page 63}* in the s'd lastly abstracted Indenture

Declon & agreement by the s'd Sir Charles Morgan Robinson Morgan Rᵈ Twining Ralph Price Henry & Wᵐ S Jones that in case any one or more of them shoᵈ die in the lifetime of any one or more of the other or others of them & during the contᶜᵉ of the sᵈ sum of £27376 or any part thereof upon the s'd secˢ the whole of the p'pal money & intᵗ then due & the secˢ for the same should belong & be paid to the survivor or survivors for the time being of the s'd Sir Charles Morgan R Morgan R Twining R Price Hʸ Kemble & Wᵐ S Jones or the exors or adm'ors of such survivor or their or his assˢ who alone should be competent to give a discharge & discharges for all or any part of the principal moˢ & intᵗ without the concurᶜᵉ of the ex'ors or ad's of such one or more of them the s'd Sir Chas Morgan R Morgan Rᵈ Twining R Price Hʸ Kemble & Wᵐ S Jones as shoᵈ have died prevˡʸ to such paymᵗ being made any law or useage to the contrary notwithstanding

Covenant by sᵈ Arthur Morgan that he had not incumbered

Executed by sᵈ A Morgan & Rᵈ Twining & attested

30ᵗʰ June 1848

By Deed Poll (also endorsed upon the before abstracted Indres of the 29ᵗʰ Septʳ 1815 under the hands & seals of the s'd Sir Charles M R Morgan Rᵈ Twining P Price Hʸ Kemble Wᵐ Samˡ Jones & Dame Jane St John Mildmay

Reciting by an order of the High Court of Chancery dated 14ᵗʰ Apˡ 1848 made by his Honor the Vice Chancellor of England on the petⁿ of the sd Dame Jane St John Mildmay exparte Dame Jane St John Mildmay Wo & In the matter of an act of parlᵐᵗ of the 7ᵗʰ & 8ᵗʰ King Geo 4ᵗʰ intitled "an act to authorise the grantᵍ of buildᵍ cases of the settled estˢ of Dame Jane St John Mildmay in the parish of St Mary Islington in the county of Middlesex & for other purposes It was referred to the master to enquire whether there was any & if any what p'pal of sum charged upon the estᵉ in the parish of Islington or any of the other estᵉ comprised in the settlemᵗ of the 28ᵗʰ Novʳ 1789 in the s'd act of parliamᵗ mentᵈ & referred to & before abstractᵈ in paymᵗ whof or of part whof the Exchequer Bills & Cash in the 3ʳᵈ petⁿ mentᵈ or part thof might be properly applied & to whom such sum or sums of moy if any were payable

{Page 64}

And reciting that in pursuance of the said order Sir Wᵐ Home the master to whom the said matter was referred made his Report dated the 1ˢᵗ June 1848 whereby after referring to a state of facts & proposal laid before him on the part of the said Dame Jane St John Mildmay supported by Affˢ as therein mentioned and referring to or stating the said act of Parliament in the sd order mentioned and the sd Indenture of settlemᵗ of the 28ᵗʰ Novʳ & referring to the before abstracted Ind're of the 29ᵗʰ Septʳ 1815 & the sevˡ Indres and Instruments indorsed thereon together with divers other Indentures & Instrumᵗˢ & tracing and deducting the title of the hereditaments comprised in the same Indentures He certified that he found that under the dir'ons in the said act contained for that purpose divers sums of money had been paid into the Bank of England & that the same sum & also the interest arisen th' had been invested in Exchequer Bills & that there was then remaining in the Bank under the title "Exparte the tr'ees applied by the s'd act" in Exchequer Bills £6,700 in cash £97.17.1 (being the Exchequer Bills & cash in the s'd pet^n & order mentioned) and he found that the sum of £1144 ment^d in the before abstracted Deed Poll of the 14th Decr 1842 being deducted from s'd sum of £6,000 there remained £4856 & that the sev^l princ'l sums by the 2 sev^l h'rinbfe abst^d Ind'res of the 15th day of Septr 1847 resp'ly assigned secured by the s'd Sir Charles M R Morgan R^d Twining Ralph Price H^y Kemble & Wm Saml Jones then remained due to them and he further found that the s^d sum of £4856 part of the sum of £6000 was a principal sum of money charged upon the estate comp^d in the s'd Ind're of the 28th Novr 1789 other than the s'd estate in the s'd parish of St Mary Islington in the s'd order mentioned in the payments & discharge if part whof he was of opinion that the sum of £2500 part of the s'd exchequer Bills & cash might be properly applied and the s'd master also found that a sum of £3,500 was then charged upon the s'd estates in the parish of Islington in discharge whereof further part of the said exchequer Bills & cash might be properly applied and he found *{Page 65}* that both the s'd sums were payable to the s'd Sir Charles M R Morgan Richd Twining Ralph Price H^y Kemble & Wm Saml Jones

And reciting by another order of the s'd Court made by the Vice Chancellor of England exparte the sd Dame Jane St John Mildmay & in the matter of the s'd act on the pet'ion of the said Dame Jane St John Mildmay dated the 9th June 1848 amongst other things ordered that the s'd master's Report should be confirmed & it was referred to the sd master to settle and approve of a proper discharge or proper discharges to be given by the said Sir Chas M. R. Morgan R Twining Ralph Price H^y Kemble & Wm Samuel Jones upon payment to them of £3500 in discharge of the principal sums of that amont charged on the estates in the parish of Islington in the s'd Report ment^d and upn paym^t to them of £2500 in discharge of part of s'd principal sum of £4,856 payable to them and charged upon the other settled estates in the s'd Report ment^d and such discharge or discharges resply being signed or owise duly executed by such person or persons as the s'd master should direct such signature or ex'on to be certified by the s'd master It was endored that so many of the s'd exchequer Bills then remaining in the Bank to the credit of exparte the trustees appointed by the said act or so much of any exchequer Bills for which the same might be exchanged or which might at the time of the sale thereby directed be in the Bank to the credit af'sd as with the sum of £97.17.1 cash then in the Bank to the credit afsd or any other sum of cash which might be in the Bank to credit afsd would be sufficient to raise the amount of £3500 and £2500 making together the sum of £6000 should be sold with the privity of the Accountant General of the sd Court and out of the moy to arise by the sd sale and the s'd cash It was ordered that the sum of £6000 should be paid to the said Sir Charles M R Morgan Richard Twining Ralph Price Henry Kemble & Wm Saml Jones and reciting that s'd sum of £2500 part of the sd sum of £6000 was intended to be paid to the s'd Sir Charles *{Page 66}* Morgan R Morgan Richard Twining Ralph Price H^y Kemble and Wm Saml Jones under the directions in the sd last ment^d order cont^d for that purpose in part satisf'on of the said sum of £4856 immed'ly before the exon of the Deed Poll now being abstracted and that the s^d master had approved of the Deed Poll now being abstracted as a proper release & discharge to be executed by the sd Sir Charles Morgan R Jones as appeared by his Report dated the 29th June 1848 and by his signing his name in the allowance written in the margin of the now abstracting Deed Poll

And reciting that a release in respect of s'd £3500 had been prepared to bear even date to be executed with abst^d Deed Poll as a proper Release in respect of s'd £3500

It is witnessed that in cons'on of £2500 to be paid by the s'd account^t general to the s'd Sir Charles M. R. Morgan Richard Twining R Price H^y Kemble & Wm Samuel Jones after the exon of the Deed Poll now being abstracted and receipt for which was intended to be written at the foot of such Deed Poll and signed by them they the said Sir Chas Morgan R Morgan Richard Twining Ralph Price H^y Kemble and W^m S Jones did and each of them did release & for ever quit claim and discharge all & sing^r the manors and other heredits then discharged with or liable to the payment to the paym^t of the s'd sum of £4856 the remaining part of the sd sum of £6000 so provided for the s'd Ann Mildmay Spinster as afsd & which s'd sum of £4856 was then vested in the s'd Sir Charles M R

Morgan Richard Twining Ralph Price H{{y}} Kemble & W{{m}} Sam{{l}} Jones by way of security as aforesaid and also the said Dame Jane St John Mildmay her ex'ors admors & ass and all and every other person & persons entitled to become entitled to the s'd manors and other heredits so charged as af'sd for any estate or interest whats{{r}} of & from the s'd sum of £2500 so to be paid to the sd Sir C.M.R. Morgan Richard Twining R.Price H{{y}} Kemble & W{{m}} S Jones as af'sd and all int{{t}} due and to grow due for the same sum and all claims & demands in respect thereof

Declaration that s'd £2500 so to be paid af'sd sh'd be taken and accepted by the sd C.M.R. Morgan R{{d}} Twining *{Page 67}* R Price Henry Kimble & W{{m}} Samuel Jones in part satison of the sd sum of £4856 so remaining of the residue of the sd sum of £4856 & int{{t}} further that s'd sum of £2,500 should also be taken and accepted in part satsfon of the principal sums of money by the s'd 2 several Indres of the 15{{th}} Sept{{r}} 1847 respectively assigned & secured & then due and owing to the sd Sir Chas M R Morgan Richard Twining R Price H{{y}} Kemble & W{{m}} Samuel Jones as aforesaid but subject and without prejudice to the paymt of the residue of the s'd princl sums and the interest thereof or any residues claims or demands for or in respect thereof

Executed by s'd Sir C.M.R. Morgan Richard Twining R Price H{{y}} Kemble W{{m}} Samuel Jones & Dame Jane St John Mildmay & attested Receipt for £2500 underwritten signed & witned Master Homes approval in the margin

9{{th}} February 1849

By Deed Poll also indorsed on the before abstracted Indre of the 29{{th}} day of Sept{{r}} 1815 under the hands & seals of the s'd Sir C. M. R. Morgan Richard Twining R Price H{{y}} Kemble W{{m}} S Jones & (Dame Jane St John Mildmay)

Reciting that by an Order of the High Court of Chancery dated the 21{{st}} July 1848 made by his manor the Vice Chancellor of England on the petition of the s'd Dame St John Mildmay & exparte the sd Dame Jane St John Mildmay & in the matter of an act of parliament of the 9{{th}} & 10{{th}} of Her present Majesty intit{{d}} "an act for making a Railway from the East & West India Docks to join the London and Birmingham Railway at the Camden Town Station to be called the East & West India Docks & Birmingham Junct{{n}} Railway" It was referred to Sir W{{m}} Home one of the masters of the sd Court to enquire whether there was any & if any what debt affect{{g}} the land in respect of w'ch the sum of £4500 in the petition ment{{d}} had been paid or affect{{g}} other lands settled therewith to the same or the like uses trusts *{Page 68}* or purposes in discharge whereof or of any part whereof the sd sum might be properly applied & to whom the same if any was payable

And reciting that in pursuance of the s'd order the s'd Sir W{{m}} Home made his report dated 13{{th}} November 1848 whereby after referring to a state of fact & proposals laid before him on the part of the said Dame Jane St John Mildmay supported by afl{{s}} as in the said report ment{{d}} & referred to or stating the s'd Ind're of the 28{{th}} November 1789 & the sd Indre of 29{{th}} Sept{{r}} 1815 & the sev{{l}} Indentures and instruments th'in endorsed & the s'd act of parliament in the title of the s'd petitioner mentioned together with divers other Indentures & instruments He certified that he found that under the circ'es powers & prov'ons of the said act & of the Land clauses consolidation act 1845 The East & West India Docks & Birmingham Junction Railway comp{{y}} had purchased certain pieces of land containing about 3a 2r 32p distinghuished in the map or plan & Book of reference of the said Railway Company deposited with the Clerk of the peace for the sd Coy of Middlesex by the N{{o}} 17 in the parish of St Mary Islington being part of the lands comprised in the s'd Indre of the 28{{th}} November 1789 at the price of £4500 & that the s'd sum had been paid by the s'd company into the Bank of England in the name & with the privity of the account{{t}} general of the s'd court to the credit there exparte the East & West India Docks & Birmingham Junction Railway Comp{{y}} in the matter of the East & West India Docks & Birmingham Junction Railway act 1846 & was the sum of £4500 ment{{d}} or referred to in the sd order & he further found that the sum of £24856 part of the sum of £27356 assigned by the two sev{{l}} before abst{{d}} Indres of 15{{th}} Sept{{r}} 1847 to Sir Charles M. R. Morgan R{{d}} Twining R Price H{{y}} Kemble & W{{m}} S{{l}} Jones in the s'd & sev{{l}} Indres ment{{d}} then rem{{d}} due & owing to them upon the security of the sd bef'e abst'd Indre of 29th Sep'r 1815 & the sev'l Indres endorsed thron and that s'd sum of £24856 included the sum of £6000 provided by the s'd Ind're of the 28th Nov'r 1789 for the portion of Letitia Ricketts formally Letitia Mildmay spinster & thereby made *{Page 69}* a charge upon part of the lands comprised in & put in settlem't by the same Indre other that the sd lands in the parish of St Mary Islington and the sd master found that the s'd sum of £6000 provided for the portion of sd Letitia Mildmay spinster was a debt or incumb'e affecting other lands settled with the land in respect of which the s'd sum of £4500 had been paid to the same or the like uses trusts or purposes in discharge of part hereof the sd sum of £4500 might be properly applied & that the same was pay to the s'd Sir C M R Morgan R^d Twining Ralph Price H^y Kemble & Wm Saml Jones

And reciting that by another order of the s'd court made by the Vice Chancellor of England on petition of the sd Dame Jane St John Mildmay & in the matter of the s'd act It was amongst other things ordered that sd masters s'd Report should be confirmed & it was referred to the sd masters to settle & approve of a proper discharge to be given by the s'd Sir Charles M R Morgan Richard Twining R^d Price H^y Kemble & Wm Jones upon paym't to them of £4500 in discharge of part of the s'd principal sum of £6000 & that upon such dischge being signed or owise duly exted by such p'son or psons as he sd master shod direct such signature or exec'on to be certified by the sd master the sum of £4500 paid into the Bank as afsd & being part of the cash then stand^g in the Bank to the credit of the account^t general of the s'd court exp'e the East & West India Docks & Birmingham Junction Railway Comp^y in the matter of the East & West India Docks & Birmingham Junction Railway act 1846 should be paid to the s'd Sir Charles M. R. Morgan Richard Twining Ralph Price H^y Kemble & Wm Saml Jones

And reciting that the s'd master had approved of the Deed *{Page 70}* Poll now being abstracted as a proper release & discharge to be executed by the sd Sir Chas Morgan Robinson Morgan Richard Twining Ralph Price Henry Kemble & William Samuel Jones & that the s'd sum of £4500 was intended to be paid to them in pursuance of the direction in the s'd last mentioned order contained for that purpose in part satisfaction of the sd sum of £6,000 immediately after the exc'on of these presents

And reciting that the sd Dame Jane St John Mildmay was then tenant for life in posson of the manors & other heredits comprised in & settled by the said Ind're of the 28th Nov'r 1789 under & by virtue of the same Indre

It is witnessed that in cons'on of £4500 to be paid by the s'd account^t general to the s'd Sir Charles Morgan Robinson Morgan Richard Twining Ralph Price Henry Kemble & Wm Samuel Jones after the execution of the Deeds Poll now being abstracted * a receipt for which was to be written at the foot of the s'd Deed Poll & signed by them They the said Sir Charles Morgan Robinson Morgan Richard Twining Ralph Price Henry Kemble & Wm Samuel Jones did & each of them did by these presents remise release & for ever quit claim & disch'ge

All and singular the manors and other her'es then charged with or liable to the payment of the s'd sum of £6000 so provided for the portion of the s'd Letitia Mildmay as afsd & which sd sum of £6000 was then vested in the sd Sir Charles Morgan Robinson Morgan Richard Twining Ralph Price Henry Kemble & Wm Saml Jones by way of security as af'sd and also the s'd Dame Jane St John Mildmay her heirs ex'ors & adm'ors & all and every other p'son or persons entitled to and to become entitled to the s'd manors & other heredit's so charged as af'sd for any estate or interst whatsoever of & from the s'd sum of £4500 so to be paid to the s'd Sir Charles Morgan Robinson Morgan Richard Twining Ralph Price Henry Kemble & Wm Saml Jones

{Page 71}

Declaration that the s'd sum of £4500 so to be paid as af'sd should be taken by the s'd Sir Charles Morgan Robinson Morgan R^d Twining Ralph Price Henry Kemble & Wm Saml Jones in part satisf'on of the s'd £6000 provided for the portion of the sd Letitia Mildmay & so then due & owing to them as aforesaid but subject to the payment of the residue of the s'd sum of £6000 & the interest throf or any remedies claims or demands for or in respect thereof and further that the sum of £4500 should also be taken & excepted in part satisfon of the s^d principal sum of £24,856 so remaining due & owing to the sd Sir Charles Morgan Robinson Morgan R Twining Ralph Price Henry Kemble & Wm Samuel Jones upon the security of the s'd Indre of 29th Septr 1815 & of the several Indres endorsed thereon as afsd but subject & without prejudice to the payment of the residue of the s'd principal sum of £24856 & the interest thereof or any remedies claims or demands for or in respect throf

Executed by s'd Sir Charles Morgan Robinson Morgan R^d Twining Ralph Price Henry Kemble & William Samuel Jones & attested

Receipt for £4500 underwritten signed and witnessed

Master Home's approval in the margin

26th May 1858

By Deed Poll endorsed upon the before abstracted Indre of the 29th September 1815 under the hands & seals of the s'd Sir Charles Morgan Robinson Morgan Ralph Price Wm Samuel Jones & The Revd Carew Anthony St John Mildmay

Reciting that immediately after the execution of the before abstracted Deed Poll of 30th June 1848 the sum of £2500 th'in mentioned was paid by the accountant general of the High Court of Chancery to the s'd Sir Charles Morgan Robinson Morgan R^d Twining Ralph Price Henry Kemble & Wm Saml Jones in part discharge of the s'd sum of £4856

(11)   And reciting that the s'd Henry Kemble died about 18th May 1857 & the s'd Richard Twining died about the 14th October 1857 and reciting that the sum of £2356 the balance of the s'd sum of £4856 then remained charged upon the same *{Page 72}* estates and was payable to the said Sir Charles Morgan Robinson Morgan Ralph Price and Wm Samuel Jones as survivors of the sd Richard Twining & Henry Kemble

(12)   And reciting that the s^d Dame Jane St John Mildmay died 1st May 1857

(13)   And reciting that by an order of the High Court of Chancery dated the 13th day of March 1858 made upon the petition of the s'd Carew Anthony St John Mildmay In the matter of the 3rd act of parliament of the 7th & 8th Geo the 4 & the said Carew Anthony St John Mildmay being then the sole trustee of the sd act as survivor of Humphrey St John Mildmay who was named in the s'd act as a tree jointly with the s'd C. A. St John Mildmay after the decease of the s'd Dame Jane St John Mildmay the sd Humphrey St John Mildmay having died in the lifetime of the sd Dame Jane St John Mildmay It was ordered that the exchequer Bills for £900 then remaining in the Bank to the credit of exparte the trustees appointed by the s'd act or any other exchequer Bills for which the same might be exch^d should be sold with the privity of the s'd accountant general and it was ordered that upon the s'd Sir Chas Morgan Robinson Morgan Ralph Price & Wm Samuel Jones executing a proper discharge for the money to arise by the s^d sale of s'd excehequer Bills and the cash in the Banks and Interest to be paid to them as thrinaft^r ment^d in part discharge of the s'd principal sum of £2356 (such discharge to be settled & verified as thrin mentioned) the money to arise by the s'd sale and the sum of £117.14.9 cash then in the Bank on the credit of the sd matter and any interest to accrue in the s'd exchequer Bills oreviously to the s'd sale should be respectively paid to the Sir Charles Morgan R Morgan Ralph Price & Wm Saml Jones

And reciting that the s'd exchequer Bills had been sold in pursuance of the s'd order and produced £925.9.5 & the sum of £22.0.9 was received for interest on the s'd exchequer Bills previously to such sale making together with the s'd £1117.14.9 cash the sum of £2065.4.11 and reciting that the Deed Poll now being abstracted had *{Page 73}* been agreed upon between the s'd Sir Charles Morgan Robinson Morgan Ralph Price and Willm Saml Jones and the s'd Carew Anthony St John Mildmay as a proper discharge for the s'd sum of £2065.4.11 to be executed by the s'd Sir Charles Morgan Robinson Morgan Ralph Price & Wm Saml Jones

It is witnessed that in consideration of £2065.4.11 to be paid by the s'd accountant general to the s'd Sir Charles Morgan Robinson Morgan Ralph Price & Wm Saml Jones and receipt for which was intended to be indorsed on or written at the foot of the Deed Poll now being abstracted & signed by them They the s'd Sir Chas Morgan Robinson Ralph Price & Wm Saml Jones Did and each and every of them Did release & for ever quit claim & discharge

All and singular the manors & other heredit's then charged with or liable to the paym^t of s'd sum of £2356 the remaining part of the s'd sum of £4856 & which s'd sum of £2356 was then vested in s'd Sir Chas Morgan Robinson Morgan Ralph Price & Wm Saml Jones and all the heirs ex'ors & ad's of the s'd Dame Jane St John Mildmay dec'ed & all & every person & persons entitled and to become entitled to the sd manors & other heredits so charged as aforesaid for any estate or interest whats^r of & from sd sum of £2065.4.11 so to be paid to the s'd Sir Charles Morgan Robinson Morgan Ralph Price & Wm Saml Jones as afsd & all interest due & to grow due for the same & all claims & demands in respect thereof

Declaration & agreement that the sd sum of £2065.4.11 accepted by the s'd Sir Charles Morgan Robinson Morgan Ralph Price and Wm Saml Jones in part satifon of the sd sum of £2356 the balance of the sd sum of £4856 so remaining due as aforesaid subject & without prejudice to the payment of the residue of the s'd sum of £2356 and the interest thereof or any remedies claims or demands for or in respect throf and further that the s'd sum of £2065 *{Page 74}* 4.11 should also be taken and accepted in part satisfon of the principal sums then due to the sd Sir Charles Morgan Robinson Ralph Price and Wm Saml Jones for securing it which the s'd sum of £4856 was assigned together with various other sums charged upon the same heredits & amounting together £27356 to the s'd Sir Charles Morgan R Morgan Richd Twining Ralph Price H^y Kemble & William Saml Jones by the 2 several before abstracted Indres of the 15th Septr 1847 but subject & without prejudice to the paym^t of the residue of the princ^l sums & the interest thof or any remedies claims or demands for or in respect thof

Executed and attested

Receipt for £2065.4.11 in^d & wit^d

23rd June 1858

By Deed Poll indorsed upon the before abstracted Indre 29th Septr 1815 under the hand & seals of the s'd Sir Chas Morgan Robinson Morgan Ralph Price Wm Saml Jones: also of Edm^d St John Mildmay of Shawford Lodge Wimbledon Park in the County of Surrey Esqre & of the s'd Edward St John Mildmay & Reginald Augustus Warren

(14)   Reciting that the s'd Sir Henry St John Carew St John Mildmay died on the 7th Janry 1848 & admon of his goods chattels & credits was on the 6th June 1848 granted by the preroge^e court of Canterbury to s'd Edmund H^y St John Mildmay

(15)   And reciting that the sd Dame Jane St John Mildmay died on the 16th May 1857 having by a cod^l dated 21st November 1853 to her Will dated 13th June 1837 appointed the s^d Edwd St John Mildmay & Reg^d A Warren exors throf who on or about the 22nd Septr 1857 proved the same will & codicil in s'd Prerogative Court of Canterbury

(16)   And reciting that immed'ly after the execution of the bef'e abstracted Deed Poll dated the 26th May 1858 the s'd sum of £2065.4.11 was paid by the account[t] general of the High Court of Chancery to the sd Sir Charles Morgan Robinson Morgan Ralph Price and W[m] Samuel Jones in part discharge of s'd sum of £2356

And reciting that the sum of £18290.15.1 (the residue of the said principal sum of £27356 by the two several *{Page 75}* before abstracted Indentures of the 15th Sept[r] 1847 assigned to the s'd Sir Charles Morgan Robinson Morgan Richard Twining the s'd Ralph Price Henry Kemble & the s'd W[m] Sam[l] Jones for their joint benefit & which was in fact the residue then unpaid of the principal sums of £22700 £3300 & £2500 secured by the before abst'ed Indentures of the 23rd May 1821 the 3rd December 1823 and 18th September 1824 had together with all interest due in respect of the s'd sum of £18290.15.1 been duly paid and satisfied as the s'd Sir Charles Morgan Robinson Morgan Ralph Price & W[m] S[l] Jones did thereby admit

And reciting that by the payment of the s'd sum of £18290.15.1 as aforesd the sum of £1500 the residue of the within ment[d] sum of £6000 originally provided for the portion of the s'd Letitia Mildmay and the sum of £290.15.1 the residue of the s[d] sum of £6000 originally provided for the portion of the s'd Ann Mildmay & the whole of the s'd sum of £10000 £1500 £1000 £1500 & £1500 by the before abst'ed Ind're of the 29th September 1815 resp'ly assigned by the within named Sir Henry Tempest had been paid and satisfied as the s[d] Edmund H[y] St John Mildmay & Edw[d] St John & Reginald Augustus Warren resp'ly did thrby admit

And reciting that all interest due in respect of the s'd sums of £10,000 £1500 £1000 £1000 £1500 £1500 £1500 & £290.15.1 resp'ly had also been paid & satisfied as the same persons resp'ly did admit

It was witned that the s'd Sir Charles Morgan Robinson Morgan Ralph Price & William Samuel Jones Did & every of them Did remise & for ever quit claim and discharge

All & singular the manors and other heredits then charged with or liable to the paym[t] of the s'd sum of £18290.15.1 & also all & every person & persons entitled or to become entitled to the s'd manors & other heredits so charged or laible as aforesaid for any estate or interest whatsoever of and from the s'd sum of £18290.15.1 & all interest due & to grow due for the same & all claims *{Page 76}* & demands in respect thereof To the intent that the same manors & heredits thenceforth be held and enjoyed freed and discharged from the s'd sums of £22,700 £3300 £2500 and every part thereof resply & all interest due & to grow due for the same & all claims & demands in respect thereof

And it was further witnessed that the s'd Edm[d] Hy St John Mildmay & the s'd Edw[d] St John Mildmay & Reginald Augustus Warren Did & every of them Did remise release & for ever quit claim & discharge

All & singular the manors & other her's charged with or liable to the paymtof the s'd sums of £10,000 £1500 £1500 £10,000 £1000 £1500 £1500 £1500 & £290.15.1 or any of them and also all & every person & person entitled or to become intit[d] to the s'd manors & other heredits so charged or liable as afs'd for any estate or int[t] whatsoever of & from same int[s] resp'ly and all claims and demands in respect throf

To the intent that the same manors and other heredits might thenceforth be held & enjoyed freed and discharged from the s'd sums of £10,000 £1500 £1000 £1000 £1500 £1500 £6000 & £6000 resply & every part thereof respively & all interest due & to grow due for the same resply & all claims & demands in respect throf

Executed & attested

Requisitions, Observations etc on Title to Manor of Marwell, County of Southampton and Answers

{Front Cover}

Mildmay Estates

Copy

Requisitions on Title and Answers

Bradley, Castleford

Copy

Requisitions, Observations &c on Title to Manor of Marwell, County of Southampton and Answers

Abstract N° 2

Lady Methuen's Share

Page of abtract	No of requisition	
9	1	Certificate of Burial of Lord Methuen to be produced
		1 Lord Methuen was buried at Wraxhall N^r Chippenham
	2	Certificate of Burial to be produced
		2 query, Lady Methuen buried at the same place
	(3) (4)	Certificates of Burial of Sir Henry St John
		3 Sir H. Mildmay at Dogmersfield Hants
		4 Mr Bouverie buried at Hanwell Middlesex
	(5) (6)	C St J Mildmay, of the Honble B Bouverie and J Clerk showing George Lord Boston to be sur'vor to be produced & certificate of Burial of George Boston to be pro'd
		5 Mr Clerk died 31st Octr 1842 and was buried at all St Southampton
		6 Lord Boston buried at Wiston near Northampton
	7	Lord Boston under the powers of the settlem^t of 30th July 1810 has powers to give Receipts the purchasers is not concerned to see what the trusts of the moy are
10	7	The Deed of appoint^{mt} of 12th augst 1837 in pursuance of the power of the settlem^t of 30th July 1810 could only operate on what was compris^d in such last deed viz 1/13th & inasmuch as by the deed of 1810 an eldest son of the marr'e was specially except^d from being an object of the power in favor of Fred Henry Paul Methuen of 1/16th of 1/13th was inoperable & such 1/16th would th'rfe devolve as in default of appointm't The trusts th'rfe in default (see abstract no 2 p9 x) should be set out as affecting the s'd 1/16th of 1/13th

11	8	I presume 1/17th is a clerical error for 1/17th 8 yes of the shares therefore of Lady Methuen as well original as accruing equivalent to 1/7th of the whole; 1/13th or 7/91 are in the trustees of the settlement of July 30th 1810 and the remaining 6/91 (ie 13/91-1/7) are in Fred^r Henry P Lord Methuen (by his mrtgage The Revd James Bliss for securing £6250 & interest) who must disentail the s'd 6/91 Lord Methuen disentailed this share by the Deed of 23rd July 1857 page 14 of the abstract

Lady Bolingbroke's Share

24	(9) (10)	Certificates of Burial of Thomas Salmon
		9 Thomas Salmon was buried at Odiham Hants
		10 John Clerk, see n° 5
	(11) (12)	John Clerk & Phillip Williams showing Fred^k St John to be surviving trustee should be produced also that of Fred^k St John
		11 Philip Williams was buried at Wooly Green near Hornsey Hants
		12 Mr St John at St Andrews Chapel Waterloo Street Brighton
	(13) &	Probate of Fred^k St John to show acceptance of trusts
25	(14)	By mess^{rs} Beauclere & Merriman to be produced, also the 2 codicils to be examined to see no revocation either of the trusts devise or of app'tment of the s'd ex'ors
		13 & 14 The probate is we believe with Mr Merriman of Marlb' the surviving trustee
	(15)	Certificate of Burial to be produced
		15 query Mr Beauclerk
25	(16)	Certificate of Burial to be produced
		16 query Lady Bolingbroke – She was buried at Lydidrd Treoze Wilts
	(17)	Certificate of Burial of Lorde Bolingbroke to be produced
		17 Lord Bolingbroke was buried at the same place
26	(18)	The addition of the name "Mildmay" after St John is a clerical error
		18 probably
	19	Certificate of Burial of Lady Bolingbroke to be produced and proving of Heirship of Henry St John as her eldest son and therefore entitled cross limit'ons of settlement of 1789 to be furnished
		19 see n° 16 a copy of a Declaration to prove Lord Bolingbrokes heirship can be furnished at the purchasers expense
	(20)	Certificate of Burial of Lady Jane St John (of 1789) to be produced
		Did Lady Mildmay (of 1789) make a will? If so probate to be produced to show her intestacy as to trust estates. Proof of Sir Henry B Paulet St John being her heir should be produced
		20 Lady Mildmay was buried at Dogmersfield Hants
		She made a will but we do not see what the object of this requisition is the heredit's which were vested in her as trustee were not in Hants
	(21)	Does the Deed of 24th August 1804 comprise any and what of the several allotments of 1819^A. 0^r.31^p subject matter of this purchase. This Deed should be produced for purchaser to satisfy himself on this point. 21 This Deed does not relate to the Hants property at all. It can be seen here.
26	(22)	Certificate of Baptism of Henry St John Visc^t Bolingbroke to be produced
		22 We are not aware where this is to be obtained but will ascertain if the purchaser considers it requisite. It shall be at his expence

The shares therefore of Lady Bolingbroke as well original as accruing equivalent to 1/7 of the whole; 1/13 or 7/91 are in the trustees of her marriage settlement of 2nd & 3rd June 1812 or their representative viz J. B. Merriman and the remaining 6/91 are in Henry St John Visc^t Bolingbroke in tail & who must bar the entail in these 6/91

He has barred the entail, see abstract page 26

Lady Radnor's Share

28	(23)	Anne Judith &^{c} should "Judith Anne"
		23 no
31	(24)	"Anne Jane" &^{c} should be "Judith Anne"
		24 Anne Jane should be Anne Judith
36	(25)	Certificate of Burial of Sir Ph. Hales to be produced
		25 His death certificate is mentioned in a Deed upwards of 20 years old
37	(26)	Certificate of Burial of Jacob Earl of Radnor and his Countess should be produced
		26 We are not aware where these are to be obtained but will ascertain if the purchaser considers it requisite. It will be at his expence.
38	(27)	Certificate of Burial of Judith Anne Countess of Radnor to be produced "1751" is a clerical error for "1851"
		27 see last answer
	(28)	Certificate of Burial of Earl Shaftsbury should be produced
		28 see last answer

The marriage settlement of William Earl of Radnor & his wife embracing as well the vested as also " the future expectant eventual or reversionary" shares of the Countess the 1/3 1/13th & 1/7th of 6/13 or 13/97 = 1/7 of the whole are in equity vested in the trustees of her settlement of 1810 viz Ph. P. Bouverie & Robert Marsham but inas much as the the time of suffering recovery (54 Geo 3 anno 1814) Judith Anne St John Mildmay (Lady Radnor) was tenant in tail subject to the life estate th'rin of her mother Ladt Mildmay (of 1789) of 1/3 only, and as a tenant to the precipe can only be made of lands whereof at the time there was actual seizin (for which purpose the Lady Mildmay (of 1789) the tenant for life in poss'on joined) & upon which alone the Recovery can operate, it follows that the recovery operated only on the 1/13th and thereupon in the events which have subsequently happened viz the deaths &^{c} of the other 6 children (whereupon as they respectively died the cross remainders in tail in favor of the sur'vors took effect so that Lady Radnor became ultimately entitled to 1/7th of the whole) and the death of Lady Radnor the 1/7th of the accrued shares viz 1/7th of 6/13th or 6/91^{ths} became and are now vested in law in the heir in tail of Lady Radnor under the settlement of 1789 as trustee for the trustees of Lady Radnor's marriage settlement subject to the life easte therein of the Earl of Radnor in right of his Countess as tenant by the courtesy, such heir at law therefore the present Viscount Folkestone must join in the conveyance for the purpose of barring the entail in these 6/91^{ths} as also Earl of Radnor as to his life estate. Lady Mildmay was tenant for life in poss'on of the whole estate and as she joined in making the tenant to the precipe the recovery operated upon the shares which afterwards accrued to Lady Radnor as well as the 1/13th to which she was entitled in remainder at the time the recovery was suffered the legal estate by the conveyance of 16th Decr 1857 in the entire 1/7th share is vested in messrs Bouverie & Marsham.

George William St John Mildmay's Share

51	(29)	Did this mortge Deed (23 & 24 Novr 1832 p.49) include property in a Register County? or why was it registered
		29 yes
	30	Geo W St John covenants free from incumb^{ces} (except family charges £32000) by which it would appear the Deed of 30th august 1830 creating an ann'y of £128 was surpressed but as the anny was afterwards redeemed (past abstract p.54) it is not material
	(31)	What is the date of the memorandum
		31 – 4th December 1849
55	(32)	Lewis Mildmay of the 2nd part is a clerical error for "Lewis Vulliamy"?
		32 yes
56	(33)	Why was this Deed registered? Did it comprise other property in Middlesex
		33 yes
	(34 & 35)	George Ward was assignee of term of 99 years created for securing repaym^t to L Vulliamy of the £3000 & interest & on Wards death intestate, letters of adm'ors to his bro^r Henry Ward, but as this m'ge is paid off the term has become satisfied & therefore under 8 & 9 Vic cap 112 determ^d the certificate therefore of Burial of Geo Ward & pr'on of letters of adm'on are unnecessary
56	(36)	Letters of adm'on with will annexed of Geo W St John Mildmay to be produced to see that this mtge sum of £3000 empowered to be raised by the marr'e settlem^t not excepted from the residuary gift to his wife
		36 This can be see here
	(37)	Certificate of Burial of Geo W^m St John Mildmay should be produced & proof of heirship of Herbert Alex St J. Mildmay to be furnished – 37 Mr George Mildmay was buried at Dogmersfield Hants a copy of Declaration to prove Mr Herbert Mildmay heirship can be furnished at the purchasers expense
	(38)	What is the date of this Deed?
		38 22nd June 1858
	(39)	Certificate of Burial of Humphrey St John Mildmay & Lady Mildmay (of 1789) should be produced
		39 Mr Humphrey Mildmay was buried at Shoreham Kent see answer 20
	(40)	Is this the same £1000 paid off as is alluded to in the memorandum see p.51 (31)?
		40 yes
57	(41) & (42)	By the Deed of 23rd June 1858 & the [Blank space] day of [Blank space] certain portions of the heredits comprised in the m'tge to Mr Vulliamy were sold. These Deeds should be abstracted in chief to show that no part of the heredits contracted to be sold, viz the Marwell manor were comprised in these sales
		41. These Deeds can be produced to show that they do not include the manors of Marwell but the purchaser is not entitled to an abstract of them
	(43)	£300 clerical error for £3000
58	(44)	By whom is this Deed executed. It is most essential that it should have been executed by Vulliamy to Mrs Mildmay the widow adm'x & resid^y legatee. Is the conson or receipt of these sums indorsed or signed by them resp'ly
		44 – By Mr Vulliamy and Mrs Mildmay. Receipts are signed by them.
60	(45) & (46)	Certificate of Baptism of Herbert (Alexander) St J. Mildmay should be produced and proof given of this being heir in tail and heir at law of George W St John Mildmay
		45 & 46 – Certificate can be produced
		See answer 37
61	(47)	The Deed makes the conveying party as Humphrey (the Uncle of instead of Herbert) St John Mildmay an error but as the only party to the Deed except Mr

Warren is Herbert – it is too clearly a clerical error to be material but if this Deed be recited in conveyance it should be noticed & set right

Of the share of George William St John Mildmay as werr original as accruing equivalent to 1/7 of the whole 1/10 is in the surviving trustee of his marriage settlement James E Baillie and his mortgagee (for £3000) and the remaining 3/7th of 1/10 = 3/70 in Herbert Alexander St Mildmay in tail who must disentail such 3/70 he being in equity a trustee for the trustees of the 26th and 27th april 1832

Mr Herbert Mildmay has disentailed his share by the Deed of 23rd July 1857

He is entitled to the 3/70th in his own right

Humphrey St J. Mildmay and Edward St Mildmay Shares

65	(48)	Through his Deed leading the uses deals with the share of each Brother as well present & immediate as future expectant eventual & reversion^y (p 64 5) at this time each brother was entitled to 1/11th only & the Recovery in accordance with this very properly deals only with 2/11 (i.e 1/11 of each Brother) This results as in Lady Radnors case (ante r) in vesting the sahares subsequently accrued viz 1/7th of 4/11th which would not be affected by the Deeds of recovery in the tenant in tail Humphrey Francis St John Mildmay as to his fathers share to 1/7th of 4/11^{ths} in s'd Edward William St Mildmay as tenant in tail as to his share 48 – see our remark as to Lady Radnors share. The deed leading to the uses dealing with the whole property the mistake in the recovery will be remedied by the Fines and recoveries act 3 & 4 William 4th c.74
	(49) & (50)	Office copy will & codicil to be produced & examined to see that the ultimate limitation in favor of his heir & ass in the Deeds of 4th Novr 1824 was not defeated 50 We have not an office copy it can be obtained at the purchasers expence
66	(51)	Certificate of Burial of Humphrey St John Mildmay to be prod^d & proof given of Humphrey Francis St Jno Mildmay being his eldest son and heir in tail to be furnished 51. See answer 39 facts of Humphrey Francis Mildmay being the eldest son is immaterial
71	(52)	Copy of act by Queens Printer should be produced 52 This can probably be obtained at the purchasers expense
	54	Probate to be produced and it should be seen that the "residue" includes the mortgage by way of annuity 54 We have not this probate
77	(55)	Probate of will of Thomas Harrison to be produced 55 We have not his probate
	(56)	Did L. C. Smyth {illegible} by Deed if so it should be produced 56 We presume so
	(57)	It should be seen that codicil did not affect the residuary gifts nor appointment of ex'ors 57 See answer 54
	(58)	Letters of administration to be produced 58 We do not have these letters
	59	Certificate of Burial of Thomas Chadwick to be produced 59 – Mr Chadwick was buried at St George in the East

79	(60)	What is the date of this Deed – 60. 11th September 1856
82	(61)	Certificate of marriage to be produced
		61 The marriage took place in India
83	(62)	Certificates of Baptism of the 4 children of the burial of the one Deceased and a declaration that they were the only childrenof the marriage and had attained 21 (ie vested interest) to be furnished.
		62. The children wre all born in India – a copy of the Declaration can be furnished at the purchasers expence.
88	(63)	Certificate of marriage to be produced
		63. This can be obtained at the purchasers expence
90	(64)	See requisition n^o (62)
96	(65)	Certificate of Marriage to be produced
		65. This can be obtained at the purchasers expence

as the shares of Humphrey St John Mildmay and Edward St J Mildmay are taken together in the abstract (p62) I will follow the same order.

The Deed of 4th Novr 1824 which embraces the 2/11 of which the 2 Brothers were entitled to 1/11 each, and the recovery suffered in pursuance thereof only operates upon the 2/11th (see opinion on share of Lady Radnor ant^e p) and therefore

As to share of Humphrey St J Mildmay (equivalent to 1/7th of the whole) the eldest son Humphrey St John Francis Mildmay is entitled to 1/11th as Devisees in fee under his father's will and to 1/7 of 4/11th or 4/77 as heir in tail under the cross limitations of the settlement of 1789 and must disentail these 4/77th

Mr Humphrey Francis Mildmay takes 1/7th as devisee under his father's will

As to the share of Edward St John Mildmay (also equivalent to 1/7th of the whole) He is entitled to 1/11th (subject as after mentioned) for life and to 4/77 in tail under the cross remainders of 1789. The ninth condition precludes the purchaser from opening the questions on the effects on each other of the Bonds of 1818 and the settlements of 1826, 1847 & 1849.

But one thing is certain that in as much as Ew^d St J Mildmay is tenant in tail of the 4/77^{ths} he must bar the entail therein; and his position is that as regards these 4/77 not included in the Deed of 4 Novr 1824he is (subject to his own life estate) trustee as to 1/3rd of the 4/77 for each of his three children & their trustees each of which child^n are entitled (subject as aforesaid) as follows. Mr Edward Mildmay is as stated in the table at page 3 entitled for his life to 1/7th Mrs D Orville (formally his wife) is entitled for her life to the same share couting enty on her surviving Mr Mildmay and the trustees of the settlemt of the 3 children are entitled in thirds to the fee of the same subject to the previous life interests –   Mrs Barnett   1/3 of 1/11 x 1/3 of 4/77 = 11/221 = 1/21

Mrs Vernon   1/3 of 1/11 x 1/3 of 4/77 = 11/221 = 1/21

Arthur St John Mildmay   1/3 of 1/11 x 1/3 of 4/77 = 11/221 = 1/21

n.b all this is however subject to the 2 = of –

(66) Who is Mrs D'Orville? (see abstract 2. 83) and what interest does she take?

Share of the Revd Carew Anthony St J Mildmay

101	(67)	As the date of Deed of 15 & 16 Novr 1830 and the Recovery in pursuance thereof there being 3 of the 13 younger children dead he was entitled to 1/10 of the whole and therefore this Recovery operated only on such 1/10 see observations on Lady Radnor's share
		67 The Recovery operated upon the shares to which he afterwards became entitled
107	(69)	Certificates of Burial of Earl St German and Paulet St John Mildmay to be produced
		69. Earl St German was buried at
		Mr Paulet Mildmay was buried at Dogmersfield, Hants
104	(68)	Certificate of marriage to be produced
		68 This can be obtained at the purchasers expence

The rev^d C. A. Mildmay in addition to the 1/10 which is vested in the trustee of his settlement is entitled under the cross limitations of 1789 as tenant in tail to 1/7 of 3/10 = 3/70 of which he is trustee for the trustees for messrs Barnet & Bramston the trustees of the settlement of Decr 13th 1830. He must therefore bar the entail in these 3/70^{ths}

    See above

	(70)	What is the extent of the manor over which manorial Rights exist a schedule of such lands should be furnished together with the nature of the Rights poss'ed by the present vendors the general words in the Deed of Settlement of 1789 should be set out fully.
		70 What manorial rights are here referred to, a schedule of the copyhold is given the particulars and a plan of the lands believed to be the copyholds has been furnished to the purchasers solicitor but the vendors are not to be bound by such plan.
	(71)	Are there any rights of tr'ee warren over the lands contracted to be sold or any other & what rights & in whom vested
		71. It is believed that there are no rights of tree warren
	(72)	When was the last Court for the Manor of Marwell held?
		72. on the 14th instant.
	(73)	Are there any & what special customs of the manor? Proof sh^d be given that the fines are arbitrary (see particulars p2)
		73 The purchaser must satisfy himself by inspection of the rolls upon these points.
	(74)	The vendors on completion of the purchase should hand over the resignation by the steward of the manor of this office.

Abstract N° 3

Page	N^o	
47	(1)	Certificates of Burial of Robert Ray Miles Stringer & Knowlys to be produced
		1. Robert Ray was buried in the Temple Church 2nd Jan'y 1838 Miles Stringer at

		Effingham Surrey 14th Janry 1840 Newman Knowlys in the Temple Church 13th Janry 1836
	(2)	Office Copy Masters Report of 11 July 1842 & order of 15 July 1842 confirming same to be produced
		2 These can be produced here
49	(3)	Certificate of Redemption of Land tax commissioners to be produced
		3 The like
51	(4)	Masters Report (office copy) of 13 Decr 1842 to be produced was this report confirmed? If so order to be produced
		4. The like
52	(5)	Certificate of the Burial of Sir Chas Morgan to be produced
		5 Sir Charles Morgan was buried at Bassalleg Monmouthshire December 1846
55	(6)	Office copy of 14 april 1848 to be produced
		6th This can be produced here
56	(7)	Office copy Master's Report of 1st June 1848 to be produced The office copy order confirming master's report to be produced
		7 the like
	(8)	Office copy order of 9th June 1848 to be produced 8. The like
59	(9)	Office copy masters report of 13 novr 1848 to be produced The office copy order confirming masters report to be produced (9&10) the like
60	& (10)	
62	(11) &	Certificates of Burial of Henry Kemble & Richard Twining to be produced and also Lady Mildmay of 1789
	(12)	11 & 12 Henry Kemble was buried at Bray Berks 27th May 1857 and Richard Twining at Kensal Green Cemetery 20th Octr 1857 see answers 20
	(13)	Office copy of 13th March 1858 to be produced
		13 This can be produced here
64	(14)	Certificate of Burial to be produced 14 What certificate is this?
	(15)	Letters of admon of Sir Henry St John Mildmay to be produced
		15 These can be produced here
	(16)	Probate of Lady Mildmay (of 1789) will to be produced
		16 the like

All the requisitions to be complied with at the vendors expense except where otherwise provided in the conditions as stated in the answers

Is the purchaser of the manor entitled to Deeds abstracted as the largest purchaser if not who will covenant for their production?

No. a list of the persons to covenant for the deeds to be retained is given the estate not being all sold the deeds to be ultimately delivered to the largest purchaser cannot at present be covenanted to be produced (see list on mortgage)

Geo Bradley, Purchasers Solicitor

15th December 1858

Bray & Co

22nd Decr 1858

George Ives	7th July 1810	James Evan Baillie	26 & 27 April 1832
Lord Boston	Trinity George 3rd		Easter Term 2 Wm 4

	25 & 30 July 1810		23 & 24 Novr 1832
Fred^k Hy P. Lord Methuen	20 July 1850 1 June 1854 3 March 1855 3 July 1857	Herbert A St J Mildmay	23 July 1857
Thos Bavistock Merriman	11 May 1812 Easter Term 52 Geo 3 2 & 3 June 1812	Humphrey F St J Mildmay	4 Novr 1824 Mich'as Term 5 Geo 4
H. M. Viscount Bolingbroke	6 March 1858	Henry D'Orville	11 June 1818
William Earl of Radnor	20 May 1814 Easter Term 54 Geo 3 23 & 24 May 1814 22 & 23 August 1825 24 & 25 August 1825 16 Decr 1857 16 Decr 1857 17th Decr 1857	Edward St J Mildmay	20 & 21 Decr 1826
		H Barnett & E. P. Bouverie	16 April 1847
		E.P Bouverie & G. E. H. Vernon	18 April 1849
		Thos Ord & R. A. Warren	10 August 1849
		Chas Geo Barnett & John Bramston	15 & 16 Novr 1830 Michas Term 1 W^m 4 11 & 13 Dec 1830 13 Decr 1830 7 July 1848

Mildmay Title, Manor of Marwell, Answers to Purchasers Requisitions and Replies thereto

{Front Cover}

Mildmay Estate

Copy

Answers to Purchasers Requisitions and Replies thereto

Bradley, Castleford

Mildmay Title –

Manor of Marwell

Answers to Purchasers Requisitions

Lady Methuen's Share

Page of Abstract	No of Requisition		p	n°	Replies
9	1	Lord Methuen was buried at North Wraxham near Chippenham	9	(1)	Sufficient Have not the vendors the certificate in their poss'on?
	2	Query Lady Methuen buried at the same place		(2)	Sufficient The like
	3	Sir H Mildmay at Dogmersfield Hants		(3)	Sufficient The like
	4	Mr Bouverie buried at Hanwell Middlesex		(4)	Sufficient Do
	5	Mr Clark died 31st October 1842 and was buried at all saints Southampton		(5)	Sufficient Do
	6	Lord Boston buried at Wiston near Northampton		(6)	The abstract states that Lord Boston survived his 3 co trustees but does not state when he died The 1/13 to which Lady Methuen was entitled was conveyed by her

10	(6) 7	Lord Boston under the powers of the 30 July 1810 has power to give receipts, the purchaser is not concerned to see what the trusts of the money are		(6)	Marriage settlement to 4 tr'ees upon trusts for sale & this trust is now purported to be exercised by the heir as law of the surviving tree the present Lord Boston and altho' the present purchasers have no concern to see what becomes of the purchase mo'y the vendors must show that the person purporting to sell the power, viz Lord Boston, is the proper person as heir at law of the last tr'ee The certificate therefore of the burial of the late Lord must be produced – Where was he buried?
			10	(7)	This requisition must be answered so that it may be ascertained in whom the 1/16th of 1/13 now is : the appoint^t of it by the Deed of 12 augst 1837 in favor of the eldest son being inoperative
11	8	Lord Methuen disentailed this share by the Deed of 3rd July 1857 p.14 of Abstract	10	8	Sufficient Subject to the above 1/16 of 1/13 sufficient

Lady Bolingbrokes Share

24	9	Thos Salmon was buried at Odiham	24	(9)	Sufficient Have the vendors the certificate of Burial in their poss'on
	10	John Clerk see n° 5			Sufficient The like
	11	Phillip Williams was buried at Wolly Green near Romsey Hants			Do
	12	Mr St John at St Andrews Chapel Waterloo St Brighton			Sufficient The like

25	13 & 14	The probate is we believe with Mr Merriman of Marlbro' the surviving tr'ee		13 & 14	To be attended to & probate seen
	15	Query Mr Beauclerk			Yes (see abst[d]) Where was he buried? Certificate to be produced
	16	Query Lady Bolingbroke She was buried at Lydiard Treoze, Wilts			Sufficient – Have the vendors the certificate in their poss'on
	17	Lord Bolingbroke was buried at the same place	25	(17)	Sufficient The like
26	18	Probably	26	(18)	Sufficient
	19	See no 16 A copy of a Declarat[n] to prove Lord Bolingbroke heirship can be furnished at the purchasers expence		(19)	Sufficient
	20	Lady Mildmay was buried at Dogmersfield Hants. She made a will, but we do not see what the object of this requisition is. The Heredit's which were vested in her as trustee were not in Hants		(20)	Sufficient The like
	21	This deed does not relate to the Hants Estate at all It can be seen here		(21)	Sufficient
26	22	We are not aware where this is to be obtained but will ascertain if the purchaser considers it requisite. It will be at his expence		(22)	Sufficient
		He has barred this entail see abstract p.26			Sufficient

Lady Radnor's Share

28	23	No	28	(23)	Sufficient. No doubt of it being the same person viz late Countess of Radnor
31	24	Anne Jane should be Anne Judith		(24)	Sufficient. No doubt of it being the same

36	25	His death is mentioned in a Deed upwards of 20 years old	36	(25)	person viz late Countess of Radnor Sufficient. Have the vendors the Certificate of Burial in their poss'on
37	26	We are not aware where these are to be obtained but will ascertain if the purchaser considers requisite. It will be at gis expence.	37	(26)	Sufficient
38	27	See last answer		(27)	Sufficient
	28	See Last answer Lady Mildmay was tenant for life in posson of the whole estate and as she joined in making the tenant to the precipe the recovery operated upon the shares which afterward accrued to Lady Radnor as well as the 1/13th to which she was entitled in remainder at the time the Recovery was suffered. The Legal Estate by the conveyance of 16 Decr 1857 in the entire 1/7 part share is vested in Messrs Bouverie & Marsham		(28)	Sufficient It is submitted this is not so; altho' Lady Mildmay (of 1789) was tenant for life of the entirety at the time of the Recovery being suffered her Daughter afterwards Lady Radnor was entitled only to 1/13 & the recovery operated only on that, viz the 1/13, this therefore must be remedied.

Geo: William St John Mildmay's Share

51	29	Yes	51	(29)	Sufficient
	31	4th Decr 1849		(31)	Sufficient
55	32	Yes	55	(32)	Sufficient
56	33	Yes	56	(33)	Sufficient
	36	This can be seen here		(36)	It should be seen
	37	Mr George Mildmay was buried at Dogmersfield Hants A copy of Declaration to prove Mr Herbert Mildmay's heirship can be furnished at the purchasers expence		37	Sufficient Have the vendor the cert^e in their poss'on
	38	22nd June 1858		(38)	Sufficient
	39	Mr Humphrey		(29)	Sufficient (the like)

		Mildmay was buried at Shoreham Kent, see answer 20			
	40	Yes	56	40	Sufficient
57	41	These deed can be produced to show that they do not include the manor of Marwell but the purchaser is not entitled to an abstract of them.	57	(41)	To be seen & examined
			57	(43)	When this Deeds is examined see if £300 be error for £3000
58	44	By Mr Vulliamy & Mrs Mildmay Receipts are signed by them.	58	(44)	Sufficient
60	45 & 46	Certificate can be produced see (answer 37)	60	45 & 46	Where & when was Mr Herbert Alex^r St John Mildmay baptised?
61	47	Mr Herbert Mildmay has dis-entailed his share by the Deeds of 23 July 1857 He is entitled to the 3/70^{ths} in his own right			Sufficient

Humphrey St J Mildmay and Edward St Mildmay Shares

65	(48)	See our remark as to Lady Radnor's share - The Deed leading to the uses dealing with the whole property the mistake in the recovery will be remedied by the Fines & Recoveries Oct 3 & 4 W^m 4th c74	65	(48)	See reply thereto and pst p.8
	50	We have not an office copy it can be obtained at the purchasers expence		(51)	Sufficient
	51	See answer 39 The fact of Humphrey Francis Mildmay being the elderst son is immaterial	66	(51)	Is Humphrey Fras St John Mildmay the eldest son of Humphrey St John Mildmay
71	52	This can probably be obtained at the purchasers expence		(52)	Sufficient
			77	(53)	Where was Harriet Roscoe & Thos

					Harrison buried
	54	We have not this probate			
77	55	We have not his probate	78	54 & 55	
	56	We presume so		(56)	If so is it in vendors posson? Or where
	57	See answer 54			Sufficient
	58	We have not these letters			Sufficient
	59	Mr Chadwick was buried at St Georges in the East			Sufficient
79	60	11th Septr 1856	79	(60)	Sufficient
82	61	The marriage took place in India	82	(62)	In what part of India did this marr'e take place? & when?
83	62	The children were all born in India a copy of the Declaration can be furnished at the purchasers expence	83	(62)	Sufficient
88	63	This can be obtained at the purchasers expence	88	(63)	Where was the marr'e solemnised
96	65		96	(65)	Where was the marriage solemnised It is submitted this is not so that the recovery only operated on the 1/11 to which Mr H F Mildmay is entitled in fee & that he is tenant in tail of the 1/7 of 4/11 of 4/77 which he must bar see reply as to Lady Radnor's share
		Mr Humphrey Francis Mildmay takes 1/7th as devisee under his fathers will			
		Mr Edward Mildmay is as stated in the table on page 3 entitled for his life to 1/7th. Mrs D'Orville (formally his wife) is entitled for her life to the same share couting ently on her surviving Mr Mildmay and the trustees of the settlement of the 3 children are entitled in thirds to the fee of the same share subject to the previous life interests			It is submitted that Mr E S Mildmay is not so entitled (see reply above as to Mr H F Mildmay's share & Lady Radnor's share) that the recovery did not operate on more that the 11th & that he is now tenant on tail of the 4/77 since accrued & which are comprised in his marriage settlement & that the entail in such 4/77 must be barred
				(66)	When was W^m D'Orville married? & where? Evidence of her being the person

divorced from Mr Edw Mildmay should be given? Has she by the act of parliament (Divorce act) or by any other means forfeited her life estate under her marriage settlement

Share of the Reverend Carew Anthony St John Mildmay

101	67	The recovery operated upon shares to which he afterwards became entitled		67	It is submitted that is not so and that his estate tail in the 3/76th must be barred see ante
107	69	Earl St Germans was buried at	107	(69)	Where was Earl St Germans buried? The certificate should be produced
		Mr Paulet Mildmay was buried at Dogmersfield Hants			Sufficient Have the vendors the cert'e in their poss'on
104	68	This can be obtained at the purchasers expence See above		(68)	Sufficient
					See resply to "above" as to the interest of Mr Edwd Mildmay and original requisitions
	70	What manorial rights are referred to : a schedule of the copyholds is given in the particulars and a plan of the land believed to be the copy^{hds} has been furnished to the purchasers sol^r but the vendors are not to be bound by such plan		70	By manorial rights is meant the ordinary rights vested in the Lord & incident to a manor by common law or custom special or otherwise. Are these any o^r lands within the manor (except Lady Mildmays) other than those stated in "par'lars" and have the usual manorial rights hitherto been & are they now exercised over the lands mentioned in "parlars" & over any o^r lands
	71	It is believed that there are no rights of free warren		71	It is not stated if there are "any other & what rights & in whom vested" To be done
	72	On the 14th instant		72	

	73	The purchaser must satisfy himself by inspection of the Rolls upon these points	73		Are the vendors aware of any special customs?
			(74)		The 74th requisition is not answered this should be done

Abstract Nº 3

Page	Nº				
47	1	Robert Ray was buried in the Temple church 2nd Jan'ry 1838. Miles Stringer at Effingham Surrey 14th Janry 1840 – Newman Knowlys in the Temple church 13 Janry 1836	47	1	Sufficient. Have the vendors the cert'e of Burial in their posson?
	2	These can be produced here		(2)	Sufficient to be examined
49	3	The like		(3)	Sufficient – Dº
51	(4)	The like		(4)	Do – Do
52	5	Sir Charles Morgan was buried at Baselleg Monmouthe Decr 1846		(5)	Do Have the vendors the certe of Burial in their poss'on
55	6			(6)	Do to be examined
56	7	The like		(7)	Do – Do
	8	The like		(8)	Do – Do
59 60	9 & 10	The like		(9 & 10)	Do – Do
62	11 & 12	Henry Kemble was buried at Bray Berks 27 May 1857 & Rd Twining at Kensal Green cemetery 20th Oct 1857 see answer 20		11 & 12	Sufficient – Have the vendors the certe of Burial in their posson
	13	This can be produced here		(13)	Sufficient to be examined
	14	What cer'te is this		14	That of Burial of Sir H St J Mildmay but prod'on of probate sufficient
	15	These can be produced here		(15)	Sufficient to be examined
	16	The like		(16)	Sufficient Do
		Except where o'rwise provided in the conditions or stated in these answers			Fras: Webb 26 Chancery Lane Decr 29 / 58

	No. a list of the persons to covenant for the deeds to be retained is given the estate not being all sold the deeds to be ultimately delivered to the largest purchaser cannot at present be covenanted to be produced		The purchaser submits the insufficiency of all the above answers to his requisitions (except those which are hereby admitted to be sufficient) & insists thereon pursuant to the 3rd condition of sale
George Ives Lord Boston	7th July 1810 Trinity George 3rd 25 & 30 July 1810	James Evan Baillie	26 & 27 April 1832 Easter Term 2 W^m 4 23 & 24 Novr 1832
Fred^k Hy P. Lord Methuen	20 July 1850 1 June 1854 3 March 1855 3 July 1857	Herbert A St J Mildmay	23 July 1857
Thos Bavistock Merriman	11 May 1812 Easter Term 52 Geo 3 2 & 3 June 1812	Humphrey F St J Mildmay	4 Novr 1824 Mich'as Term 5 Geo 4
H. M. Viscount Bolingbroke	6 March 1858	Henry D'Orville	11 June 1818
William Earl of Radnor	20 May 1814 Easter Term 54 Geo 3 23 & 24 May 1814 22 & 23 Aug'st 1825 24 & 25 Augst 1825 16 Decr 1857 16 Decr 1857 17th Decr 1857	Edward St J Mildmay	20 & 21 Decr 1826
		H Barnett & E. P. Bouverie	16 April 1847
		E.P Bouverie & G. E. H. Vernon	18 April 1849
		Thos Ord & R. A. Warren	10 August 1849
		Chas Geo Barnett & John Bramston	15 & 16 Novr 1830 Mich'as Term 1 W^m 4 11 & 13 Dec 1830 13 Decr 1830 7 July 1848

Mildmay Title, Manor of Marwell: Replies to Answers to Purchasers Requisitions & Further Answers

{Front Cover}

Mildmay Estates

Copy

Replies to Answers to Purchasers Requisitions and further Answers

Bradley, Castleford

Mildmay Title

Manor of Marwell

Replies to Answers to Purchasers Requisit^{ns} & Further Answers

Lady Methuen's Share

Page	Number		
9	1	Sufficient. Have not the vendors the certificate in their possession	We have no certificates except those we have already offered to produce. This answer applies throughout
	6	The abstract states that Lord Boston survived his 3 children but does not state when he died – The 1/13th which Lady Methuen was entitled to was conveyed by her marriage settlement to 4 trustees upon trusts for sale and this trust is now purported to be exercised by the heir at law of the surviving trustee the present Lord Boston and at the present purchaser has no concern to see what becomes of purchase money, the vendors must show that the person purporting to sell under the power viz Lord Boston is the proper person as heir at law of the last trustee. The certificate therefore of the Burial of the late Lord Boston must be produced – Where was he Buried?	See former answers to this Requisition which has already given this information
	7	This requisition must be answered so that it may be ascertained in whom the 1/11 of 1/13th now is the appointment of it by the Deed of 12th august 1837 in favouring the eldest son being inoperative	The legal estate of the whole of this 1/13th is in Lord Boston The purchaser has admitted in his last requisition that he is not concerned to see what becomes of the purchase money

Subject to the above 1/11th of 1/13th See answer to n° 7
Sufficient

Lady Bolingbroke's Share

Yes – (see abstract) Where was he buried, Certificate to be produced?

Lady Radnor's Share

It is submitted this is not so altho' Lady Mildmay (of 1789) was tenant for life of the entirety at the time of the Recovery being suffered her daughter (afterwards Ladt Radnor was entitled only to 1/13th and the Recovery operated only on that, viz the 1/13th This therefore must be remedied

The former requisition was made upon the ground that a tenant to the precipe could only be made by a person having the actual seizin of the whole estate to which the answer was that Lady Mildmay the tenant for life had such swizin – This having been disposed of we do not understand upon what grounds the Requisition is insisted on. It will not be complied with. This answer applies to the other cases where this requisition is made

George W^m St John Mildmay's Share

45 & 46		Where and when was Mr H alexan^r St John Mildmay Baptised	On the 24th September 1836 at Cadiz

Humphrey St John Mildmay and Edward St John Mildmay's Shares

66	57	Is Humphrey Francis St John Mildmay the eldest son of Humphrey St John Mildmay?	Yes
77	53	Where are Harriett Roscoe and Thomas Harrison buried	We are not aware, but can ascertain at the purchasers expence
	56	If so is it in vendors possession or where?	It is not in the vendors possession we do not know where it is
82	61	In what part of India did this marriage take place and when?	At Palmanavice on the 11th June 1818
83	62	Sufficient	We find on further enquiries that three of the children were born in England. Mrs Vernon was baptised at St Mary's Southampton 5th Sept^r

			1821, Edward Wheatley at West Coker n{r} Yeovil 21 October 1822 buried at St Peters Pimlico July 1840 Arthur George baptised at West Coker 28th February 1824
88	63	Where was the marriage solemnised?	We are not aware
86	65	Where was the marriage solemnised?	We are not aware
	66	When was Mrs D'Orville married? And where	At Berne on the 9th October 1853
		Evidence of her being the person divorced from Mr Edwd Mildmay should be given?	What evidence is required? It will be obtained at the purchasers expence
		Has she by the act of Parliament (Divorce act) or by any other means forfeited her life estate under her marriage settlement?	Not that we are aware of

The Revd Carew Anthony St John Mildmay's Share

107	69	Where was Earl St Germans buried? The certificate should be produced	We believe at Port Eliot Cornwall
	70	By manorial rights is meant the ordinary rights vested in the Lord and incident to a manor by Common Law or custom special or otherwise, are there any other lands within the manor (except Lady Mildmays) other than those stated in par'lars and have the usual manorial rights hitherto been and are they now exercised over the land specified in particulars or over any other lands?	We have already stated that a plan of all the lands believed to be copyhold has been furnished There are no rights (so far as we can understand what is meant) exercised over any of the lands
	71	It is not stated if there are "any other and what rights and in whom vested" to be done	See the last answer. The rights not vested in the Lord must be in the copyholders
	73	Are the vendors aware of any special customs?	Every manor has its own customs – There are no customs in this manor which are not, we believe common in Hampshire
	74	The 74th requisition is not answered this should be done	We do not understand this requisition The steward does not hold his office by patent Bray H{o} 57 G{t} Russell St 14th January 1859

Mildmay Title, Manor of Marwell, Third Set of Requisitions and Answers

{Front Cover}

Twyford Estate

Manor of Marwell

Copy

Third Set of Requisit[ns] and Answers

Bradley, Castleford

Mildmay Title

Manor of Marwell

Third Set of Requisitions and Answers

		Abstract Requisitions	Answers
9	6	The vendors have never stated when Lord Boston who in the abstract page 9 is said to have "survived his 3 cotrustees and died on the [Blank Space] without having made &c " died and this information the purch[r] still requires – that he may satisfy himself that Lord Boston was the survivor	Lord Boston died 12th March 1856 we were not aware the date was blank in the abstract Sufficient F.W
25	15	Where was Mr Beauclerk buried? This original Requisition has not been answered	At Cowfold Sussex on the 31st December 1845 Sufficient F.W
		A statutory Declaration by Mr Edward Mildmay or some member of his family in proof of the identity of Mrs D'Orville married at Berne on the 9th October 1833 with with Mr Edward Mildmay married in 1818 is required	Neither Mr Edward Mildmay nor any one of the family can make this Declaration but Mrs D'Orville's solicitor can do so This Declaration must be obtained F.W
	74	The particulars state "that the purchaser will have the power of appointing the steward of the manor If therefore the present steward was appointed as is usual by a written authority the vendors should give a written revocation of such authority, or obtain from him a written resignation of such office	The present steward was not appointed by a written authority he will deliver up the Court Rolls and papers and we do not see what more is wanted Sufficient F.W

Bray H[o]
57 Great Russell Street
7th February 1859

I am of opinion that the above answers to 3rd set of Requisitions are, subject above as to Mrs D'Orville, sufficient, and that the conveyance may be taken, under the conditions of sale

Francis Webb

26 Chancery Lane

Feb: 8 1859

CPSIA information can be obtained
at www.ICGtesting.com
Printed in the USA
LVOW09s1946120218
566256LV00027B/403/P

9 781478 150916